Understanding Children's Play

UNDERSTANDING CHILDREN'S PLAY

By
Ruth E. Hartley
Lawrence K. Frank
Robert M. Goldenson

Columbia University Press
NEW YORK

Clothbound editions of Columbia University Press books are Smyth-sewn and printed on permanent and durable acid-free paper.

International Standard Book Number: 0-231-01899-1
Printed in the United States of America
20 19 18 17

PREFATORY NOTE

THE DEVELOPMENT of a healthy personality has its beginnings with the beginning of life itself and it is generally recognized today that the groundwork for a lifetime of mental health is laid during the early years.

Parents, teachers, and others who deal with young children have an important role to play in these years. In the promotion of good mental health, it is essential that we help them to acquire insight into the child's emotional needs and the exigencies of his adjustment to life as he learns to understand himself and find his way in the world.

By presenting the play experiences of children within the framework of their living problems, this volume and its companion booklets will give to these adults who help shape their lives a fuller understanding of the significance of children's play, and offer them valuable aids in fostering the development of productive, well-integrated human beings.

NEWTON BIGELOW, M.D.
MENTAL HEALTH AUTHORITY OF
THE STATE OF NEW YORK

FOREWORD

In 1947, under a two-year grant from the National Institute of Mental Health, the Caroline Zachry Institute sponsored and provided facilities for an exploratory study of play in fostering healthy personality development of young children. The undersigned organized and supervised the project which was directed and conducted by Dr. Ruth E. Hartley, Psychological Consultant, with the assistance of Mrs. Ellen Schindel.

A grant from the New York State Mental Health Authority provided the means and opportunity to discuss and evaluate the findings of this study with groups of teachers and directors of nursery schools and child centers. What in Dr. Hartley's report was found by them to be most valuable and especially pertinent for directors, teachers and other staff members of centers for young children, as well as for parents, has been compressed into this volume and two supplementary booklets entitled *Growing Through Play** and *New Play Experiences for Children.†* Preparation and publication of this volume and the booklets were made possible by another grant from the New York State Mental Health Authority.

Dr. Hartley's original manuscript has been condensed, revised, and adapted for maximum usefulness by Dr. Robert M. Goldenson, Assistant Professor of Psychology, Hunter College. He was generously assisted by the valuable criticism and counsel of Dr. Ruth Andrus of the Bureau of Child Study

* Ruth E. Hartley. Columbia University Press, 1952.

† Ruth E. Hartley, Lawrence K. Frank, and Robert M. Goldenson. Columbia University Press, 1952.

and Parent Education, New York State Department of Education and by Dr. Luther E. Woodward of the Mental Health Commission of the State of New York.

It is hoped that the book will (1) be useful in the training of nursery, play, and elementary school teachers and kindergartners; (2) enable directors and teachers to develop the full potentialities of toys, games, creative materials, and play activities for fostering the growth of children into healthy personalities; and (3) interest and help parents in providing suitable play materials for their children, and especially for children who, because of some handicap or chronic illness, might otherwise be deprived of the play experiences they need for emotional expression and maturation.

Practical use of the book should result in a wider and freer utilization of play materials and expressive activities, as well as in further investigation of their value for young children. Amid the array of records and comments offered, one impression will stand out: to read the language of play is to read the minds and hearts of children. But we cannot say, "He who runs may read." The inner workings of young children have a philosophy and a poetry of their own and, like all philosophy and poetry, they can be appreciated and understood only by minds properly keyed and attuned to them.

Adults who would interpret the meaning of children's play must possess or develop the highest degree of sensitivity and sympathetic understanding of the basic emotional development of children and awareness of the difficulties to be coped with in the course of this development. They must learn to recognize, and meet *opportunely* (not just according to the routine of the school and home) the need which children have for time, space, and play materials and experiences. By developing an essential regard for the child's individuality they will refrain from imposing their patterns and ideas and will instead "draw out" the child's ideas and purposes. A child's actions are not necessarily the expression of intent or motive inherent in the same actions on the part of adults, and customary adult evaluations may therefore completely misinterpret the child's purposes and feelings.

Inevitably, all who care for young children come to realize that in play activities the child is engaged not in *self-expression* only but also, and this is most significant, in *self-discovery*—exploring and experimenting with sensations, movements, and relationships through which he gets to know himself and to form his own concepts of the world. It takes a long time for a child to organize his experiences, to fit people, objects, and events into categories and concepts so familiar to adults. His fumbling efforts often frustrate a child who lives in a world too big and resistant. But in play he can manipulate, organize, rapidly change and rearrange his smaller world of toys and materials; and, if given the time, materials, and opportunity to experiment in his own way, he finds himself, rights himself when he has gone astray, and gradually learns how to get along with himself and with others in a large and complex world.

LAWRENCE K. FRANK, DIRECTOR
CAROLINE ZACHRY INSTITUTE††

†† Discontinued, June 1, 1950.

ACKNOWLEDGEMENTS

WITHOUT the interest and help of numerous day care centers, nursery schools, individual volunteers, and manufacturers of toys and preschool supplies, this project could not have been actualized on as broad a base as proved possible. Therefore, we wish to acknowledge the cooperation of all those who helped and thank them for their aid and encouragement.

Our special thanks go to Mrs. Merl C. Hubbard, Mrs. Bess Haskell, and Mrs. Beatrice R. Lamm, administrative staff members of the Day Care Program, Department of Welfare, New York City. Also to the following of the centers' directors and teachers who gave unselfishly of their time: BETHANY DAY NURSERY, Mrs. Dorothy Beers and Miss Sally Knisely, Joyce Berlow, Marguerite Bird, Frances Bonoff, Louise Colven, Yetta Dober, Marguerite Gilbert, Janet Holzer, Mary Howard; BREAD DONOR NURSERY, Miss H. Gestel; EAST FLATBUSH CHILD CARE CENTER, Mrs. H. Rudolph; ELLIOT HOUSES NURSERY SCHOOL, Mrs. Gladys McElwee, Mrs. Frances Schoor, Miss Rosemary Edie, Miss Lorna Goudy, Mrs. Sylvia Moorman, Mrs. Any Pearman, and Mrs. Hannah Bardack, Secretary; FORT GREEN CHILDREN'S CENTER, Miss Eunice Max; GRAND STREET SETTLEMENT NURSERY SCHOOL, Miss Chester; HUDSON GUILD CHILDREN'S CENTER, Mrs. Ilse Mattick, Miss Maria Englehardt, Miss S. Leslie, Miss Blanche MacFarlane, Miss Virginia Moore; JACKSON HEIGHTS DAY CARE CENTER, Mrs. L. Crandel; JUVENILE HOUSE CHILD CARE CENTER, Mrs. G. Williams; MT. MORRIS CHILDREN'S CENTER, Mrs. Thelma

Adair, Mrs. Gausan, Mrs. Anderson, Mrs. Braithwaite, Miss Jackson, Mrs. Johnson, Mrs. Poole, Miss Shelton; OPEN DOOR CHILD CARE CENTER, Miss Ray Gaman, Mrs. Catherine Stokes, Miss Virgie Biggins, Mrs. Ellen Dennis, Mrs. Harriet Fuller, Miss Hildreth Jones, Miss Deanna Peddycart, Mrs. Stein, and Mrs. Adler, Secretary; St. NICHOLAS CHILDREN'S CENTER, Mrs. C. Gibson; UNION SETTLEMENT SUNNYSIDE NURSERY, Mrs. Margaret Michaelis; WESTERN QUEENS NURSERY SCHOOL, Miss S. Crosby.

We also wish to acknowledge the cooperation given us by the people in the following private agencies: COUNCIL OF CHILD DEVELOPMENT CENTER, Mrs. Herta Wertheim, Mrs. Fried, Miss Goldman, Miss Petscheck, and Miss Hunter, Secretary; BOARDMAN SCHOOL (formerly the HAMILTON SCHOOL), Miss Judith Gauman, Miss Janet Anderson, Mrs. Lydia Davis, Miss Sylvia Dudley, Miss Hannah Tyau, Mrs. Barbara Unger, and Miss B. Bradley, Secretary; HARRIET JOHNSON NURSERY SCHOOL, Dr. Barbara Biber, Mrs. Eleanor Reich, Miss Beatrice Bull, Miss Anita Barbaccia, Miss Margaret Tyler, Mrs. Dorothy Walker, Mrs. Vivian Yale; HUNTER COLLEGE MODEL SCHOOL, Dr. Florence Brumbaugh, Miss Providence Gambaro, and Miss Margaret Maybury; MIDTOWN CHILDREN'S CENTER, Miss Ethel Abrams, Mrs. Hilda Baum, Mrs. Barbara Bortin, Miss Arlene Sherman; NEW YORK HOSPITAL NURSERY SCHOOL, Mrs. Eleanor Gardner, Mrs. Jane Varian, and Miss Yone Endow, Secretary; THE NEW YORK KINDERGARTEN ASSOCIATION'S NURSERY SCHOOL, Mrs. Winifred A. Moore, Miss Gertrude Czinner, Mrs. Lucile Edmundson, Miss Helen Fischer, Mrs. Lillian Gelb, Mrs. Idie Goldberg, Miss Marian Hubbell, Miss Lyda Kassel, Miss M. McLean, and Mrs. Mary Vosges, and Miss Lear and Miss Morris, of the office staff; VASSAR COLLEGE NURSERY SCHOOL, Miss Hume.

We wish to thank the following people for their interest and cooperation in sending us students from their institutions: BENNINGTON COLLEGE, Miss Bertha Funnell; THE BANK STREET SCHOOLS, COOPERATIVE SCHOOL FOR TEACHERS, Dr. Barbara Biber; THE COLLEGE OF THE CITY OF NEW YORK, Professor Harold Abelson and Dr. Henry Miller; MILLS SCHOOL FOR PRIMARY-KINDERGARTEN TEACHERS, Dean Amy Hostler; THE NEW SCHOOL FOR SOCIAL RESEARCH, Dr. L. J. Stone; NEW YORK UNIVERSITY, Dr. Alice Keliher and Dr. Max Rosenbaum; TEACHERS COLLEGE, COLUMBIA UNIVERSITY, Dr. C. Del Solar, Dr. Roma Gans, and Mr. Meyer Rabban; VASSAR COLLEGE, Miss Hume.

Our sincere thanks go to the following people who put much time and effort into observing and recording the behavior of the children whom we studied. Without the cooperation of these people, who worked on a volunteer basis, we never could have gathered as much information as we did: Leone Adelson, Ella Aldrich, Shirley Alpern, Barbara Archer, Frank Arnhoff, Helene Arnstein, Leslie Atkins, Elizabeth Auerbach, Eleanor Barry, Hortense Barry, Leni Blumenfeld, Jack Blumenkrantz, Mrs. Schroeder Boulton, Mary Ellen Bowman, Evelyn Braff, Amelia Breit, Judith Brod, Shirley Brown, Phyllis Buckeley, Phyllis Burke, Michelina Capuano, Helen Carr, Patricia Carrington, Grace Chen, Shirley Chester, Sylvia Cohen, Viola Coler, Gertrude Colepaugh, Nancy Collins, Rose Cooper, Dorothy Corlis, Johnnye Cox, Sylvia Cramer, Eileen Cutler, Marie Disborough, Nina Diamond, Mrs. John Diggs, Dagmar Edwards, Henry Eldridge, Una Ellman, Lillian Evans, Irma Fensel, Helen Fischer, Louis Fischer, Everyl Fisher, Ruth Frazier, Ray Gedzelman, Alden Getz, Rebecca Haber, Mary Hartung, Henry Haskell, Marian Hays, Isidore Helfand, Leonard Hirsch, Oriole Hoffman, Gertrude Hyams, Norma Issacson, Henriette Janke, Betty Jennings, Joan Johns, Phyllis Jones, Judith Kallman,

Stanley Kaminski, Layne Kantor, Janice Kaplan, Naomi Kaplan, Barbara Katzinger, Sally Keliher, Mary Kelly, Ruth Korn, Julius Leopold, Arnold Lessard, Samuel Lewis, Clara Long, Clara Lovitz, Kathleen McCann, Madeline McDonald, Denise Martin, Barbara Michaels, Margaret Monroe, Lydia Munro, Helen Nagelberg, Barbara Negley, Simeon Neumann, Charles Ohrbach, Lucy Ortiz, Beatrice Persip, Rita Posner, Meyer Rabban, Miriam Reinhart, Naomi Robinson, Mildred Rose, Naomi Rosenberg, Seymour Rothman, Edith Rubino, Alvin Schiff, Herbert Schiff, Jo Sciacca, Yvonne Seal, Barbara Siegel, Sam Silverstein, Eva Steinhardt, Mrs. Henry Stimson, Dorothy Storey, Jackueline Taylor, Mrs. Abraham Tow, Sarah Townsend, Edith Toy, Vera Tracer, Regina Turk, Annette Uihlein, Jeannette Veatch, Robert Wallace, Joan Ward, Theresa Weil, Norma Westen, Nell Winn, Monique Winsten, Nien Hua Yao, Robert Zucker.

We wish to acknowledge the cooperation of the following people who took photographs of children using materials and equipment: Mrs. F. Arnoff, Mrs. Justen Harris, Mrs. H. Janke, Miss Cornelia Manierre, Marcus Neuhof, Mrs. Emma Z. Rodd, Mrs. Leslie Soper.

Our thanks go to those children at the Fieldston School who, during the spring term of 1948, made a family of hand puppets to be used in our project's work.

We wish to thank Mrs. H. D. Clark, Secretary of Toy Manufacturers of the U.S.A., Inc., and Dr. Grace Langdon, Child Development Advisor, for their cooperation in helping us procure many of the toys and materials we required. Our thanks go to the following manufacturing concerns which so generously provided us with toys and materials: Alrose Chemical Co., Providence, R. I., for bubble bath; Aluminum Goods Mfg. Co., Manitowoc, Wisconsin, for toy dishes; American Merchandise Distributors, Chicago, Illinois, for hand puppets; Milton Bradley Co., Springfield, Massachusetts, for hammer toys, mechanical sets, boats, farm animals, poster paints, finger-paints, clay, and paper; Bergen Toy & Novelty Co., Hackettstown, New Jersey, for miniature dolls; Carrom Industries, Inc., Ludington, Michigan, for hammer sets; Daisy Mfg. Co., Plymouth, Michigan, for pistol and holster sets; Fisher-Price Toys, Inc., East Aurora, New York, for animal cutouts and pull toys; Sam'l Gabriel Sons & Co., Clifton, New Jersey, for cardboard animals and dolls; Halsam Products Co., Chicago, Illinois, for plastic blocks and brick sets; The House of Dolls, Chicago, Illinois, for dolls; Ideal Novelty & Toy Co., Hollis, New York, for drinking-wetting dolls, stuffed animals, pistols, boats, letter and number sets, and miniature household toys and dolls; Mechani-craft, Inc., Woodside, New York, for mechanical construction sets; Newark Mask Co., Irvington, New Jersey, for masks; The Ohio Art Co., Bryan, Ohio, for drums; Parker Bros., Salem, Massachusetts, for paper doll sets; Plastic Art Toy Corp. of America, East Rutherford, New Jersey, for toy dishes and miniature household toys; Renwal Manufacturing Co., New York City, for miniature dolls and nursery furniture; Schindel-McDaniels, New York City, for cloth remnants; Shopsin Paper Co., New York City, for cardboard; Skaneateles Handicrafters, Inc., Skaneateles, New York, for train and automotive sets; Standard Toykraft Products, Inc., Brooklyn, New York, for finger-paints, poster paints, and paper; The Sun Rubber Co., Barberton, Ohio, for drinking-wetting dolls, toy nursing bottles, toy hot water bottles, and boats, cars, planes, trucks, busses, and ambulances; The Steel Stamping Co., Lorain, Ohio, for rocking chairs and toy phones; Strombeck-Becker Mfg. Co., Moline, Illinois, for miniature household furniture and trains; Transogram Co. Inc., New York City, for toy stethoscopes; A. C. Gilbert, New Haven, Connecticut, for toy broom, mop and dustpan sets; United States Travelware Corp., Manchester, New Hampshire, for laundry cases; Wolverine Supply & Mfg. Co., New York, for toy crane, shower and washing machine sets; Whitney Bros. Co., Marlboro, New Hampshire, for doll's bassinet.

NOTE: A related work by Eugene L. Hartley and Ruth E. Hartley, *Fundamentals of Social Psychology* will be published by Knopf in 1952.

CONTENTS

Understanding Children's Play

CHAPTER I

The Function of Play in the Child's Development

THE PROJECT on which this book is based was undertaken in order to explore the potentialities of play materials and expressive activities both for understanding young children in nursery and kindergarten groups and for providing them with opportunities for discovering and expressing themselves. The method of exploration was through intensive diary recordings (see Appendix) of children at play who were generally engaged with the more usual materials but at times were participating in experimental procedures. Since the purpose of the project was to foster healthy personalities through educational practices, all techniques and methods of study were adapted to the currently operating program in the schools. Except where specifically stated, no attempt was made to control the conditions under which the child played or participated in creative activities. Obviously such procedure would be very disadvantageous for a research project, but for such a demonstration program as ours it was not only a necessary but also a useful limitation.

Major emphasis in mental hygiene has been placed upon the interpersonal relations between the very young and adults, particularly parents and teachers. Without questioning the crucial importance of such relations, this study focused on how play as well as creative and expressive activities enable the child to translate impulses, feelings, and fantasies into action—to "play out" some of his problems; and on how such activities serve as sensitive indicators of the development of of the child's personality.

Play activities are equally significant for the relatively untroubled youngsters and for the many children who have suffered deprivations, frustrations, neglect, bad treatment, or exposure to crisis and disturbance in the family—for example, desertion, divorce, alcoholism, prolonged absence of the father in military service, or enforced absence of the mother for gainful employment. Children from disturbed homes may find in play and expressive activities the help they need in meeting their problems and releasing their feelings, especially if their teachers are aware of these possibilities and provide the materials and the encouragement.

The importance of creative activities and play opportunities within preschool and early school settings is recognized more and more by workers in many areas of human development. There is now a wider acceptance of the special function of the early years in the development of the individual's character structure, in the formulation of his expectations of the world, and in the molding of his approaches to other people. What is perhaps not so frequently emphasized is the great plasticity of the young during these years, their instant response to environmental impacts, their relative freedom from compartmentalization, and their consequent readiness to benefit from favorable experiences and to assimilate these into their growing concept of self. Likewise it has not been fully recognized that while the young child is undergoing many of the trial-and-error experiences that are crucial for his mental health, he needs an "educational therapy" designed to help him deal with his difficulties and conflicts while they are still in process. This, like treatment for mental and emotional battle casualties just behind the front lines, may prevent their fixation and permanent damage.

The desirability of providing channels of communication and means of expressing emotional difficulties for *all* children in the groups is supported by the findings of Jean Macfarlane,[1] who directed a study of the development of approximately 250 children and their families from birth through adolescence. Concerning the frequency of problem behavior during the preschool years, she reported, "We have found that *no normal child* is completely free of adjustive devices that are labeled as 'problem behavior'—the average number varying during the preschool years at any one age level from four to six per child," out of 63 descriptive and interpretive labels systematically covered at each age level. (Italics are ours.)

Lawrence Kubie[2] has stressed the necessity for introducing means of expression not usually available to most children, and for helping their teachers make the most of them. He says, ". . . we must learn how to free the child, *while he is still a child*, from his conflicts, his terrors and his rages. It is not enough merely to overpower him and to force his rebellious conflicts underground as we do today." He goes on to suggest that preventive treatment in mental health consists of handling every acute episode or disturbance in the child as an emergency, dealing with it as early and as intensively as possible. He implies that these difficulties are part and parcel of the growth process of every individual, and he insists that the child can pass through each successive phase of his development optimally only if the difficulties are handled in such a way that their roots are removed. The way to do this is to use "each episode as an opportunity for the child to *express all of his confused fantasies, fears, misinterpretations and misconceptions,* all of his painful, angry yearnings and conflicts, and all of his exaggerated fears and guilts." (Italics are ours.) He goes on to say that this process is one in which parents and teachers can, with appropriate guidance, assist in varying degrees.

Repeatedly Kubie[3] emphasizes the importance of exploring fantasy and giving the child the right to express his feelings without any sense of sin or danger. He says, "For instance, I can imagine honest discussion groups in the kindergarten and the primary grades in which children will be helped to think about and to discuss openly their real feelings toward adults and toward other children, both the adults and children of their homes and of the school. Group therapy we call it for adults: *group preventive education* it might well be called for toddlers. And the value of conducting such talks in groups is obviously that it *would help to lift the taboos* on secret feelings which isolation always imposes. It would help each child to feel his share in the common human heritage." (Italics are ours.)

While discussion groups such as Kubie suggests could be extremely helpful as soon as the children have acquired sufficient command of verbal symbols to project through them their emotional experience, for the younger children modes of expression must be offered which will be consonant with their experience and capacities. And if we are to be able to receive their communications, we must realize, as Margaret Lowenfeld has emphasized, that their experiences are inarticulate and complex and cannot be fitted into a scheme of communication based on adult concepts, biases, emphases, and taboos. (This may explain why, as Schachtel has said, amnesia for early childhood experiences is almost universal.) The very ways in which a child uses his senses, for example, differ from those customary to an adult. For the very young the proximity senses of smell, taste, and touch tend to be more important than the distance senses of sight and hearing, and it is therefore impossible for the adult to imagine concretely what the child is experiencing. If he is to understand the child and establish sympathetic contact with him he must put aside adult biases and concepts as far as possible, and observe him closely in activities that permit him the full use of the proximity senses as well as of the distance senses. But he must also remember that for the child, his body is an organ of expression as well as of perception, and that his attitudes toward himself and the world about him are expressed in the way he uses his body more fully than in his verbalizations. This point will be amply documented not only in the chapter on music and movement, in which the body is most obviously involved, but in regard to practically every play activity we shall consider.

Even when a child does resort to speech, the adult can understand him fully only if he understands also the desires and needs from which the thought springs. Vigotsky has demonstrated that the speech of early childhood, which is egocentric speech, depends on a grammar of thought and a syntax of word meaning that are not identical with the conventional socialized speech of adults. The meaning of the child's words is derived from the whole complex of subjective experience which it arouses in him, and one word in his egocentric speech may be saturated with sense to such an extent that it would require many words in socialized speech to explain it. It follows inescapably that any teacher who would comprehend his speech and foster his growth in the social world must be continually aware of his basic affective and sensory experiences as well as his attempts at nonverbal communication.

It may very well be that play experiences are so valuable to the child because they take an intermediate place between these inarticulate, subjective impressions and the structured language and prescribed conduct of adult social communication. Erikson[4] says the child uses play "to make up for defeats, sufferings and frustrations, especially those resulting from a technically and culturally limited use of language." He suggests that play offers the child direct, nonverbal modes of communication, as we have argued above, and he points out that "If we can establish the language of play with its various cultural and age dialects we may be able to approach the problem why it is that certain children live undamaged through what seem to be neurotic episodes and how early neurotic children have indicated that they have reached a deadlock." Although it is not the province of this book to offer extended case studies that might throw light on the problem of child neurosis, we shall cite many records of play sessions to show clearly how a child reveals his emotional reactions and handles his difficulties.

Slavson,[5] in discussing therapeutic play groups, emphasizes the role of the *group* in enhancing the value of the play process itself. Among other things he says, ". . . through play the child expresses traumatic fixations, conflicts and hostilities. . . . The child also uses play to disguise genuine conflicts and difficulties, or he may use play to relax tension and anxiety. Of greatest importance . . . is the fact that as the young patient discharges aggression and seeks to overcome traumatic anxieties through play, it acts as a regulative mechanism. . . . The service of play in finding permissible and acceptable outlets for primary impulses is of considerable value with which one must reckon." These functions of play will all be illustrated in the chapters that follow. In the centers investigated in this project, we also found ample evidence for the following statements of Slavson: "When several children play together, their interaction and mutual support help to employ the materials progressively, rather than to become fixed at one level of self-expression"; and, "In play groups, and this is to a great extent also true of other groups, children assign to themselves roles which are an expression or an extension of their basic problems. In such roles one either plays out the awareness of what he is or a hopeful phantasy of what he would like to be. . . . In a group such phantasies are reinforced and find easy and natural means of coming through in a variety of play forms and activity channels."

The value of multidimensional expression for young children is generally accepted by trained workers in related fields such as child psychology and psychiatry, psychiatric social work, and early childhood education. The importance of the teacher's acceptance and understanding, however, is frequently underemphasized. Some workers, indeed, question the appropriateness of attempting to induct teachers into the mysteries of children's nonverbal modes of expression. Some representatives of professional specialties feel that some teachers might misuse such information or that they do not have the background to assimilate it. We fully recognize that it is not desirable for teachers to try to be "amateur psychiatrists" and attempt to diagnose and treat individual children, since they lack adequate training for these functions. On the other hand, it is not necessary to acquire a professional vocabulary of psychiatric terms and categories or a set of therapeutic skills, to begin to understand what children are doing and what they are communicating in their various activities and forms of expression. This understanding is essential if teachers are to have insight and be helpful in what they do—and proof that it can' be acquired is shown by the increasing numbers of teachers who have learned to think and function in more understanding ways.

Already a start has been made in the use of so-called "therapeutic" techniques in the classroom. In an article in *The Nervous Child*, Emily Gillies[6] describes a use of dramatics in a first-grade classroom which proved to be effective in the emotional re-education of some children. She reports multiple values for this technique: "Both the classroom teacher and I checked and found that these dramatizations tended to be a good leveler, a good reducer of tensions in the group. The too-aggressive child seemed to become more capable of accepting others' ideas, and of working more pliably with the group; the inhibited and withdrawn children began gradually to volunteer and to voice their long suppressed ideas. In addition we felt that this honest talking over of upsetting feelings and ideas brought about a more honest give-and-take between the children, helped create a natural channel for bringing into the open a variety of subjects made taboo in their homes. Before the year was over we had met problems of sibling rivalry, of parents who are too domineering, of why some children grow into bullies, and of sex fantasies held by many in that group." Significantly, we found that a start could be made in many of these directions on the less articulate level of the nursery school child. The use of puppets and dramatic play would probably lead most directly to the techniques Miss Gillies describes, but other activities such as music and movement provided release of tension and encouraged elementary give-and-take.

This type of approach to the child's emotional life means a new departure for many teachers, and, as in all new departures, requires a period of orientation. In general, teachers who are attempting to understand their young pupils' play and use this understanding to aid them towards emotional re-education must (1) learn about the dynamics of behavior and the affective and emotional aspects of development, and

(2) come to know each child in the group setting individually and thoroughly.

It is encouraging to note that a start toward this approach to play has been made in several places. At one public school (P. S. 33) in New York city, a project for kindergarten children has been in operation for several years under the direction of Evelyn Adlerblum. As part of the project five children are taken from their regular classroom three times a week for one-hour sessions in a special playroom equipped with toys, books, blocks, and plastic materials for free play in the presence of a psychological counselor. These children are selected from among those who seem to need the warmth and relaxed pace of a smaller group: children from broken homes, from non-English-speaking homes, withdrawn children, etc. In another school a special group was formed for children ranging from the third to the sixth grade, who were delinquent, aggressive, or withdrawn. The group was limited to ten members, and art, handwork, music, and puppetry were used as the therapy media. Play sessions were held in a special playroom once a week for six months, with improvement reported for nine out of the ten. Both of these experiments point the way to the provision of play groups for children with special needs within the regular school program. At present, however, these stand as isolated and limited examples of what might be done. Means of including their benefits regularly in the on-going school program are yet to be devised.

From one "War Nursery" comes a report of procedures and techniques regularly employed which indicates what can be done in the daily program to meet the affective needs of children again made acute by the current defense program. Speaking of impromptu stories told to engage the interest of the children and to open the way to the free expression of their own feelings, the teacher, Gertrude Tipton[7] writes:

"Children like best the stories and songs about the day-to-day things they do. Like adults, they like especially well the stories that capture their feelings. These give them the re-assurance that their feelings are legitimate and understood by the adult. Even though they can't throw baby sisters 'in the ditch' they no longer have to be dishonest but can bring their feelings out into the open. These 'undesirable' feelings cannot be stopped by adult denials of their existence."

She offers an African folk chant as an example of the kind of "nursery rhyme" that really touches the children on a feeling level and releases both their unholy desires and their guilt about them:

> Siembamba, mommy's baby,
> Siembamba, mommy's baby,
> Twist his neck, hit him on the head,
> Throw him in the ditch
> And he'll be dead.

Miss Tipton's discussion shows that some teachers already are aware of the mental health implications of these procedures and of their own role in them. As a message from one teacher to her colleagues in the field, it is encouraging and instructive. Among other things, she says:

Teachers have usually accepted expression of pleasant and happy emotions, but there are other emotions that are equally strong and real. These other emotions have been almost universally barred from the classroom. Children should be allowed to express resentment, aggressiveness, and negativism. If the teacher cannot accept these feelings and provide suitable outlets for them, she forces the child to seek indirect and evasive ways of showing his hurt, or she drives his feelings underground to such a point that he cannot share his feelings with anyone.

The nursery school provides a natural setting in which to help the child to face his fears realistically. Through his play activities a child often displays his inner uncertainties. When fears come aboveboard, the teacher has an opportunity to help the child to do something positive about them. However, the teacher must lay the groundwork by letting the child know that "it's all right to cry" and that "some things *are* frightening."

These statements are strikingly parallel to some of Dr. Kubie's. However, he goes somewhat further in pointing to factors in the adult that need to be brought into harmony with their mental health objectives for children if their work is to be effective. Kubie's remarks concerning parents,[8] apply equally well to teachers:

Before undertaking the responsibility of parenthood [teaching], adults could be trained to understand something about how infants and children communicate their thoughts and feelings and needs and purposes, their conflicts and their pains. The language of childhood continuously coalesces and changes. It consists of expression, sound, gesture, and action long before organized speech occurs, and speech itself does not mean to the child the same things that it means in adult life. . . . Adults could be trained how to talk to children and to sense what children understand and also what they misunderstand from what adults say and do to them. . . . If in this way means of communication and of mutual understanding could be established between adult and child, a great deal of that which is now buried in unconscious processes could be brought to the surface for healthy ventilation. . . .

They [adults] will understand the dangers and frustrations of the physical world in which the child lives, the right of the child to feel even when he cannot act, the right of the child to explore, without guilt or shame, his own aggressive and lustful impulses in relationship to siblings and playmates. They will understand the right of a child to his fantasies; and they will be able to appreciate the significance of these fantasies and so to keep open constantly this avenue of contact between conscious and unconscious levels of the personality. The goal is not the elimination of problems nor the elimination of conflict, but rather to enable the child to live out his difficulties in the full light of consciousness.

To this happy future state we hope this report will make some small contribution. During the two years of the project, 180 children were observed, in 40 different nursery groups. They came from families of varied national and cultural backgrounds and ranged in age from two to six years, with the largest number concentrated in the three- to five-year range. For the collection of these observations, 98 observers were employed, most of them in a volunteer capacity. All observers used were given initial orientation talks which included specific suggestions for making the observations and recordings in the form of process-type diary records. (The specific suggestions are listed in the Appendix.) Each of the participating observers had already had some form of relevant training: some came from undergraduate courses in early childhood education; others, and these formed the greater part of the group, were doing graduate work in child development, child psychology, or clinical psychology. Many had had experience as nursery school teachers, and others were looking forward to such experience. The use of volunteer observers made it possible for the limited personnel of the project to devote a large part of its time to teacher interviews, to the collection of descriptions of the behavior patterns of specific children, to gathering facts about the home background of many of the children, and to collecting material on changes occurring in the behavior of the children during the course of their attendance in the nursery group. It was also possible to devote some time of the trained project personnel to utilizing the records currently being made in furthering the training of directors of nursery schools and centers and to disseminating the findings of the project concurrently with its operation through continuous contact with the educational consultants serving the cooperating centers.

As in all exploratory studies, we came to the end of our given time with regret for what was not done and with rue that we did not foresee some of the insights hindsight has given us. All in all, however, this has been an exhilarating experience, made so partly by our vicarious contact with the freshness of the world as it comes to children, and partly by the eagerness of teachers everywhere to grasp at whatever promises to increase their service to children.

CHAPTER II

Dramatic Play: Mirror of the Child

The Value of Dramatic Play

INTEREST in the spontaneous dramatic play of children has had a long and varied history. The meanings and functions of such play have preoccupied students of child development from the times of Groos and Spencer to the present day. While some observers have seen in it the recapitulation of the experience of the race and others have interpreted it as rehearsal of the future roles of the individual, little intensive empirical work was done before the last two decades. During this time, new and penetrating formulations of the service to which dramatic play is put by children have emerged largely as a result of the advances in depth psychology and the direction these advances have given to the study of child development.

Therapists and educational workers with a psychoanalytical orientation have seen dramatic play as a channel for growth in both individual and social areas. In particular, specialists such as Susan Isaacs, Erik Erikson, and Margaret Lowenfeld have found in it a means by which the child works out his difficulties for himself so that he can meet the challenge of his world with confidence. Although differently worded and based on independent observations, the statements of these observers are strikingly similar in meaning.

For example, Erikson[1] says ". . . *to play it out* is the most natural auto-therapeutic measure childhood affords. Whatever other role play may have in the child's development (and I do not think that these roles are adequately known) the child also uses it to make up for defeats, sufferings, and frustrations." Susan Isaacs[2] summarizes her observations in this way: ". . . Play is not only the means by which the child comes to discover the world; it is supremely the activity which brings him psychic equilibrium in the early years. In his play activities the child externalises and works out to some measure of harmony the different trends of his internal psychic life. In turn he gives external form and expression, now to the parent, now to the child within himself. . . . And gradually he learns to relate his deepest and most primitive phantasies to the ordered world of real relations." Margaret Lowenfeld,[3] in speaking of recurrent temporary neurotic episodes of childhood, gives a high priority to "symbolic play" as an agent for drawing off "some of the excess emotional energy which has become dammed up behind the neurosis." By permitting the child to play freely in a setting of security and acceptance, we enable him to deal satisfactorily and healthfully with his most urgent problems.

Susan Isaacs[4] develops these interpretations in vivid and memorable language. She points out that dramatic play not only helps the child understand the behavior of things and people, but "When the child plays at being father and mummie and the family of babies, the giant and the giant killer, the wild animal and the hunter, the teacher and the pupils, the policeman and the bus driver, he is externalizing his inner drama—the various aspects of his inner personality—in just the way in which the creative artist in literature or painting does. The tiny child has not only his own conflicting impulses to contend with, he has also to deal with his first pictures of the grownups themselves as well as of the other children; his first notions of mother and father, the great, the terrible, the loving, the deserting parents. When he can, through the happy cooperation of other children, express these phantasies in active play, his inner tension is eased and a new equilibrium of mental health and happiness is attained. . . ." She adds, significantly, that "In the nursery school, the greater number of children, the great variety of personalities and the lesser pressure of external life enable him to come more freely to artistic expression and so to mental health."

The same writer[5] maintains that the impact of dramatic play within the setting of the nursery school may take on critical importance not only for mental health but for the social development of the child. In the beginning this play may be purely individual or at most a temporary overlapping of make-believe, but "As the children get to know each other and build up a common history, the mutual adaptation of phantasy occurs more and more often. They gain the experience of doing things together in some way and some sense, and discover the benefits and delights of mutual support, both in imaginative play and in real achievement." In other words, dramatic play offers an intimate and personal means of communication and cooperation at an age when social growth is just beginning to accelerate. This "first effective social education," says Mrs. Isaacs, "is furthered not only by the necessity of recognizing other children and their phantasies, but by active cooperation in dramatic play." Even when one child imposes his will as leader he draws others into the play: "to be someone else's 'puppy' or 'baby' may not be as glorious as being the kennel master or the parent, but it does mean active cooperation in the game, and . . . the 'baby' of one group may become the 'captain' of another." Unlike the child who is left to his solitary phantasy or dominated in his play life by adults, the boy or girl in nursery school benefits from "the *real* clash of wills among equals and the *real* experience of mutual activity." . . . "He is, moreover, carried from his earliest and deepest needs for sensual satisfaction in actual bodily contact, to the non-sensual satisfaction of ordered social life." In a word, dramatic play helps the child develop from a purely egocentric being into a person capable of sharing and of give-and-take.

Research in child development within a more academic as opposed to a clinical setting has added further emphasis to the importance of dramatic play during the early child-hood years. In addition to its general utility in relieving tensions and externalizing inner experiences it helps the child set the boundaries between reality and unreality. This means that for the very young child play experiences have a greater reality value than they have for somewhat older children whose minds are not so amorphous.

Moreover, we know that the younger the child, the more easily he can accept substitute satisfactions when original objects are not available (he will take green cheese instead of the moon). Therefore, dramatic play can theoretically offset some of the inevitable frustrations of life and help him adapt to the real world.

Understanding the Child Through Dramatic Play

We turn from the value of dramatic play for the child to its value to the adult who seeks to aid him in his growth. For one thing, we can use it as a fairly good indicator of how life is going. Since children tend to regress in the presence of frustration, they can be expected to play at different levels of maturity when meeting adjustment problems of different degrees of difficulty. Naturally, appraisal of a given child requires a representative sample of his behavior, as well as a knowledge of normative standards of dramatic play. However, the teacher who is aware of the possible

meanings of fluctuations in level of play can, in the course
of her long-term contact with the child, become amazingly
sensitive to his reactions in special difficulties.

Most observers agree that the meaning of specific play
episodes is uniquely derived from a child's personal history,
the situation which confronts him, and his individual ways
of reacting and expressing himself. The literature of child
development, however, contains no concentrated discussion
to which teachers or parents might be referred for deepening
their understanding of this special mode of communication.
The few scattered references to the meaning of specific play
episodes as observed in individual children, however enlightening, are usually buried in strictly psychiatric discussions.
Erikson, for example, describes an episode involving a
four-year-old boy shortly after he had undergone an operation. Using very simple materials, the child reduced his
tension by playing out the role of the doctor, becoming, in
fantasy, master of the situation which in reality had made
him a helpless victim. Susan Isaacs[6] cites the case of a little
girl of preschool age who played at being a cat in a very
realistic fashion for several months, and interprets her play
in this way: "This little girl, thus, first solved her problem
of how to deal with aggressive impulses of various kinds,
which from her later phantasies we can see were, among
others, being dirty, burning things and wetting, by a complete flight to one particular phantasy. It was not safe to
be a little girl and to be aggressive. If one feels so aggressive the only thing to do is to be a cat. Cats are allowed to
have claws and to be greedy and to eat off the floor. They
are not hurt or destroyed for being so. Cats can even clean
themselves in a way that for a human child would be considered dirty, that is, by licking with saliva."

Markey shows how children use play situations to express
emotional impulses otherwise not perceptible. One little girl

pretended she was the mother of a household in which the refrigerator door was always kept open. Investigation revealed that in her own home the family refrigerator had been locked to keep her from raiding it. A rather circumspect child devised a game of mother and baby and "doggie," in which she could spank and bite the children she did not like. A third youngster, whose mother had recently given birth to another child, played at destroying babies with enormous zest; toward the real baby at home his behavior remained most acceptable.

In each of the above episodes the child gained satisfactions he could not otherwise achieve, and which would have produced intense anxiety if he had attempted to attain them in reality. This suggests that if adults are to make a fruitful study of children's dramatic play, they must first recognize that it reflects the interaction of their inner needs with external events; and second, have some knowledge of the real circumstances with which they have to cope.

Development of the Project

It was largely the emphasis which therapeutic workers have given to the values of dramatic play for both the child engaged in it and the adult observing it that led to the present attempt to study its functions in normal group situations involving young children. Since this type of play is one of the most common activities of little children, it seemed useful to find out to what extent its potential for mental health is being realized.

In planning the program, we hoped that observation on a fairly broad scale would suggest answers to the following questions: (1) How can spontaneous dramatic play help the teacher appreciate the emotional condition and needs of the child? (2) What information can it give her concerning his life outside of school, and particularly his family experiences? (3) How can it help to clarify the central problems with which different children are struggling? (4) Does it serve all children equally well under ordinary pre-school management, or do some children need special arrangements? (5) To what extent does it show the same qualities in the school situation that it has in the therapeutic situation? All in all we were interested in two main aspects of dramatic play: what it can tell the teacher about the child, and what the teacher can do to help the child utilize it fully in working out his own problems.

The basis on which we hoped to answer these questions were observational records taken on approximately 80 children, drawn from 33 preschool groups in 13 centers. We gathered a total of 260 records of spontaneous dramatic play episodes alone. The children had been chosen for observation because they fell into one of the following groupings: 21 were considered well adjusted, 33 aggressive, and 28 anxious and withdrawn.

It was hoped that by making this division in the selection of children to be observed, the recurrent patterns of dramatic play could be noted and common denominators emphasized. It was hoped, further, that the beginnings of a normative framework might emerge, and that in this way the study might contribute to a fuller understanding of children's play by the one adult who has the best opportunity to observe it during the day, his teacher.

The Problem of Norms

The importance of some kind of normative framework by which to examine the play of the individual child cannot be overemphasized. To assess any child's general or momentary status, his teacher needs to know what most children do at given ages or within certain age ranges. In dramatic play this would require norms for such elements as complexity, emotional toning, type of role played, variations in situations, levels at which the child participates, and other children involved.

Information about these factors would probably contribute not merely to our understanding of children, but also to teacher morale. For example, many teachers who cooperated with the present study were troubled by the high incidence of animal and "shooting" play. If they had access to objective evidence concerning the prevalence of these types of play and their relation to developmental needs and cultural factors, they might be able to function more placidly and more effectively.

Some standards have been worked out for other activities such as block building, use of plastic material, and painting, but for dramatic play the information available is comparatively sparse. We have come upon only one normative outline of dramatic play for the preschool years. Although tentative and limited to one aspect, it is well worth repeating, especially since it shows where dramatic play fits into the broader developmental scheme of play activities. Markey,[7] who made this analysis (here given in somewhat condensed form) lists the following types of activities in order of magnitude:

24–29 months: Make-believe uses of materials (3.6),[8] that is, simple pantomime, calling ladder a train, imaginative descriptions in terms of the attributes of the material: "The truck (toy auto) is starting," etc.; make-believe situations (1.7), more elaborate pantomime, and imaginative language, going to sleep, setting the table, shining shoes, games in which the attributes of the materials used are expanded and elaborated; games involving personification (1.6), imagined creatures, "the bogey man will get us," pantomime or language indicating that inanimate objects are personified, as in talking to dolls, stroking and petting toys, etc.

30–35 months: Characteristic patterns are the same, but there is an increase in all three types: make-believe uses of material (4.0); make-believe situations (2.5); games involving personification (2.1).

36–41 months: At this level, in addition to make-believe uses of materials (4.8) and make-believe situations (4.7), two different patterns are included in the typical repertoire of the child, namely: dramatic play (3.5), "We are bears," "I'm the cop and you're the robbers," "Mother and Daddy," etc., games involving the acting out of a specific role; construction activities (3.5), creation of imaginative products with raw materials (sand, clay, blocks, paper, and paints), "I'm making a barn," "This is a fire house". Identification of the product usually preceded or accompanied the activity.

42–47 months: The typical activities are similar but relative frequencies are somewhat different; make-believe situations (5.5); make-believe uses of materials (4.0); dramatic play (3.9); and construction activities (3.9).

48–50 months: The simplest pattern, make-believe uses of materials, is no longer included, but otherwise, the most frequent patterns are the same: make-believe situations (7.7); dramatic play (6.2); construction activities (5.6).

The imaginative behavior of the two-year-old with a set of toy dishes is quite limited in its scope: One may see him lift an empty cup to his lips, or pour imaginary water from an empty teapot, or possibly offer the cup to another child and say, "coffee" or "milk". . . . Some months later, nearer the three-year level, imaginative behavior tends to be more complex; the child begins to show appreciation of features less intrinsic to the material itself and to invent new attributes for the material. For example, cups and saucers may be combined with pegs and blocks for a breakfast or a "tea party." One child may appear to act as hostess, another may carry on a conversation about how good the tea tastes, and so on. At a still later level, the children assume definite imaginative roles more or less wholly independent of the attributes of the materials with which they are dealing, perhaps those of father and mother, and act out mealtime, departure for school, and so forth.

Markey[9] has also made some valuable observations concerning the role of cultural factors in determining the specific themes and symbols found in the play of different children:

Such everyday events as taking baths, having one's shoes shined, having one's throat examined, being a baby, being sick etc., comprised a good part of the imaginative games in the day nursery group. On the other hand, in guidance nursery group B, which consisted of children of more privileged socioeconomic status, train trips and construction activities, building of subways, taking an airplane ride, and the like, were typical of the topics dealt with in imaginative games."

Another revealing difference was the high frequency of the bogey man game in the day nursery and its total absence in the more privileged groups.

Beyond these observations by Markey there is practically nothing in the available literature on frequency of themes and roles assumed by children in dramatic play or the general emotional tone with which these roles are played.

One must, of course, approach whatever norms are available with the understanding that they can only suggest a general framework within which the play of the child may be viewed. Since play is an essentially idiomatic expression for each individual child, we would have to know not only how a particular child deviates from others, but also the *meaning* of the deviation for him specifically. Nevertheless a knowledge of norms is useful in bringing out this individual nature of dramatic play, as shown by the following record of a two-year-old.

Lola and Ralph go to the doll corner. They open the oven. Lola closes it. She runs back to the doll and bed which are in the climbing apparatus. She wraps up the doll and the duck. She takes the packages to the top of the steps. (She usually goes to places unoccupied by other children.) Ralph follows, saying, "Lion is coming." Lola repeats, "Lion is coming," and runs up the steps. Both get chairs and place them at the foot of the steps. Lola goes over to the oven and says "Let's see. Let's see." She opens the oven. "Turn off the gas, the lion's coming out." Both run upstairs and sit swinging their feet awhile. They then go downstairs to the oven. "He's screaming"—repeated several times.

This episode is very different from the kind of dramatic play generally produced by children between two and three years old, both in the type of animal fantasy and in the intensity of emotion centering about the imagined destruction of the animal. Lola had been making an excellent adjustment to group living, but this scene was not representative of her play in general, which was usually calm, matter-of-fact, and imitative of adult activities. The anomalies prompted the observer to inquire about her a year later. At that time, her teacher felt that she was not getting along well, that she had a tendency to be sneaky and to involve other children in mischief for which she was responsible. On the basis of this one example, it would be absurd to make any general claims concerning the diagnostic value of the normative approach. Yet it does suggest how a normative schema can help to bring behavioral cues into focus as indicators of "trouble spots" or difficult periods in development.

The following excerpts from the play of two other children will illustrate the characteristic flavor of a very young child's play in a somewhat less dramatic and more commonly observed manner.

Glen (age two years and two months) pretends to be a "doggie," crawls on the floor, and asks Jane for candy. She pretends to give it to him. He pretends to take it, then crawls away. He crawls under the table and says "Woof! woof!" To Vera he says, "Give me a bone." He crawls under the table and asks Percy for candy.

Hector (age two years) has been climbing and sliding off boxes. When this episode begins he is walking on a box. He looks at the teacher, smiles, and says, "Woo-woo-woo." He makes a face and looks upon the group. He says, "Meow! Meow!" and climbs up and down off the box. Then he climbs up and jumps down and says, "See." He rolls over on a wide ledge next to the box, smiles, and climbs up on the box, jumps down and rolls over several times on the ledge, falls on the floor, smiles and gets up.

Notice that although both small boys were assuming the roles of domestic animals, the function of the role was clearly different for each child. Glen used his impersonation to beg for gratuities for himself. Apparently in his opinion "doggies" got desirable things that little boys could not ask for. Hector, on the other hand, seemed to use his animal simply as a model to imitate. Fascinated by the supple agility of the cat, he took delight in the sheer sensation of acting out its movements. It will not be surprising to the reader to learn that Glen was considered an extremely anxious child who had to contend with a very difficult set of sibling and parental relationships, while Hector was considered a comparatively well-adjusted little boy.

Various Functions of Dramatic Play

We can speak with somewhat more confidence about patterns of play from our records of children falling within the three- to five-and-a-half-year-old age group. Within that age range, we distinguish eight functions that dramatic play serves in the usual group situation of the preschool center or kindergarten. Through this activity the child is given an opportunity (1) to imitate adults; (2) to play out real life roles in an intense way; (3) to reflect relationships and experiences; (4) to express pressing needs; (5) to release unacceptable impulses; (6) to reverse roles usually taken; (7) to mirror growth; and (8) to work out problems and experiment with solutions. Since the last two of these functions focus on the child's course of development we shall reserve discussion of them until the following chapter, in which we consider dramatic play primarily as an instrument of growth. We recognize that it is impossible to appreciate fully the unique quality of each type of dramatic play without repeatedly observing a large number of children engaged in it. However, it may be helpful to have descriptions of actual play episodes at hand as a guide to the functions just mentioned. Therefore we shall illustrate each of them from the records collected in the present project.

SIMPLE IMITATION OF ADULTS

These episodes are decidedly matter-of-fact, suggesting that children need the opportunity to play out what they have seen in order to understand it or at least to feel they are part of it. For example, a little girl who had watched an artist make a sketch at a street fair felt dissatisfied until she had played the part of the artist herself by sketching her friend. Imitation of this sort promotes not only understanding but also a feeling of identification between the child and the adult. The child of three, four, or five cannot discover what it feels like to be a mother except by going through the motions of mothering, and the son of a truck driver feels closer to his father by pretending to drive a truck. Moreover, lifted on the wings of "pretend," these children can assume the envied powers of strong adults and are encouraged to grow into the social roles prescribed by our culture. The following excerpt from the records of two three-year-olds will show the process of imitation in actual operation.

Excerpt 1. Each of three children is washing a doll in a bath tub. Perry is actively interested and very careful to wash the complete doll well. Upon finishing the baths they pick the dolls up and go over to the bed, sit in a row on the edge, and dry them with a bath towel. Each child then puts his own doll to bed. Perry stands still for a moment, then takes his doll out of the bed. He goes to the sewing basket, takes the tape measure, and measures his doll. He shows one girl how to measure the doll, being very careful to have the tape go from the top of the head right to the toes. He places the doll back in bed, putting it on its stomach, but before leaving it, he turns the doll's head to the side so that it doesn't have its face in the pillow. He was the only one to do this.

Excerpt 2. Kathie goes straight to the scrap box, digs in and selects a large piece of flowered material, a length of four-inch ribbon, and a hat; she then comes back to the teacher at the piano and follows the teacher across the room, seeking help. The teacher ties some material around Kathie for a skirt. Then the teacher ties Kathie's hat on with the ribbon. Kathie, smiling broadly, goes back to the scrap box, takes off her hat, puts on a feather hat. . . . Kathie says, "Sally, let's go for a walk," smiling cheerfully, holding her hat on her head with one hand. Sally does not accept the suggestion. Kathie goes for a walk alone. "Hi, Johnnie!"—as she passes the easel. She stops by a table where three are working, watches, smiles exaggeratedly as though imitating a social manner and says, "Now I have to go home."

INTENSIFICATION OF REAL LIFE ROLE

These roles may conceivably be assumed because they offer such satisfaction that the child does not wish to experiment with others. However, when the child is submissive both in life and in play, it is more likely that the role is imposed in the group fantasy for the same reason that it was adopted in real life—because of the child's helplessness to withstand it. This seemed to be the case with four-year-old Janie, who was considered by her teachers to be extremely withdrawn and fearful.

Doris is playing at the carriage. Janie, "I wanna play with you." Doris, "Only if you are the little sister." When she has completed fixing the carriage to her satisfaction she tells

Janie, "You're little sister. Hold here and help me push the baby. Now walk." Doris has arranged the carriage with a broom across it. Janie takes the broom away. Doris pulls her back ordering, "Stay here," and then, "No one touch the broom, nobody touch this carriage. No, no, no." They walk along, Doris pushing the carriage and Janie holding on at the side. The teacher greets them: "Hello! Nice baby you have." Janie, looking at Doris, says, "You play with me." But Doris quickly answers, "No, she's just the little sister." Ricky yells for no apparent reason and Janie still standing beside Doris imitates him. Doris hits her on the head. She offers no re-sistance. They walk back across the room, Janie holding on. Doris orders her, "Now turn, we have to go to the store." Janie says, "I wanna go to the park." She is told by Doris, "Well, you can't." Janie finally says, "I don't wanna play," but is told by Doris, "Well, you have to," and she continues.

The children in the following record were attending a guidance nursery because of special developmental problems. They were all noted for unpredictable and aggressive be-havior, and in dramatic play they carried their destructive urges to extremes not permitted them in real life.

Jimmy, Junior, and Gene were playing with blocks. They built an intricate and well-planned fireplace without much effort. Then they dashed to the shelf where the small toys were kept and, grabbing handfuls, threw them into the fire-place. From their remarks to each other, it was evident that this was supposed to be kindling wood. After they had finished with the kindling wood, they stepped back, apparently much satisfied. Then Junior, the smallest of the three, approached his teacher and said rather commandingly, "All right, Mrs. V., we're ready for you. Hop in."

REFLECTION OF HOME RELATIONSHIPS AND LIFE
EXPERIENCES

These episodes might be classed with the simple imitation of adults except for the intense emotion involved and the clear light they shed on the child's relationships to signifi-

cant persons. To see how the next records illustrate the
point, it is necessary to mention some facts about the child's
background. This little girl of three was originally referred
to the preschool group for observation because of persistently recurring minor ailments such as upper respiratory in-
fections. The mother was concerned also about her food
intake, elimination, and frequent constipation. Although the
mother seemed to have a basically good relationship with
the child, she habitually forced her to eat and often slapped
her for touching things and for getting her clothes dirty. The
child was customarily awakened at night to participate in
family parties and was frequently "shown off" to friends
and relatives. The following records demonstrate clearly the
relationship between her home life and her dramatic play.

Record 1. Mary begins to sweep vigorously in the doll corner,
accompanying her work with the following patter: "The party's
gonna be on at two o'clock and the company's gonna come.
Clean the house. Hurry up. Get that house clean!" Tim and
Polly sweep, too. Polly climbs into the big doll bed. Mary
covers her roughly, smacking her occasionally, and saying, "No,
no, no." Noticing Tim, who is picking up a telephone, she
says, "Your sister calling up." Polly pops up out of bed. Mary:
"Hello, my schicken. My schicken just got up." She gives
her a pat which is more in the nature of a smack. She starts
to put dishes on the table very vigorously. Out of the corner
of her eye she notices Polly crawling around. She slaps Polly's
hand, "Don't you bother anybody else." Mary puts some more
dishes on the table, then goes out of the doll corner and addresses the block-building group: "Who wants to come to my
party?" No one responds. She comes back, gives Polly a poke
and says: "Stay there now," and to herself as she fusses with
the dishes: "The company's coming. . . ."
(Mary is now using a doll as a baby.) The teacher suggests
that she get the baby some breakfast. She takes the plate and
puts it to the baby's mouth, then looks up with the most distressed expression, wrinkles up her nose, and says: "Dat vomit."
The teacher asks why the baby vomited and Mary says: "She's

a big pig." Her nose is still wrinkled and she clumsily and roughly presses the doll to her chest and says with great feeling: "Poor tootsie. I gotta call the doctor. Oh, my poor tootsie." Holding the doll with one hand, she picks up the telephone and says: "Hello, doctor? My baby vomit and my baby got a cold. Goodbye." To observer: "The doctor comes for my baby tomorrow. He says put nose drops"—and she points to the doll's nose. "Now her vomit again. Oh God! Get the doctor. Ooooh—." She gets a coat from the chest of drawers and sits on the bench, putting the coat on the doll.

Record 2. Today she was pushing Bruce on the swing when his hat fell off. Mary picked it up and attempted to put it back on his head, talking a mile a minute with much hand waving, to this effect: "You put this hat on your head, goddam! I spend all my money buying you a hat and you're gonna wear it. I spank you if you don't. Put this on! . . ."

Record 3. Mary has had a great deal of dramatic play at home to the effect that *she* (as well as her mother) is having a baby too. She apparently embarrasses the mother considerably by puffing out her stomach and announcing that the baby is growing. Only recently she told an observer in school that she was going to have a baby. The observer said, "Yes, your mommy is growing a baby." Mary was quite insistent, "No, *I'm* having a baby." Then she added, "It's going to be a boy." The observer said, "You wish it would be a boy, I guess, but sometimes it's a boy and sometimes it's a girl." Mary pondered for a moment and then said, "Boy—girl—what else can it be?" [The last episode also strikingly demonstrates how clearly a child's play can disclose current preoccupations and confusions.]

EXPRESSION OF PRESSING NEEDS

Some children sought in play the warmth and affection they failed to find at home; others, who were being insistently urged toward "mature" behavior, often adopted infantile roles. In the following record, Warren's actions speak eloquently though almost wordlessly for themselves. This four-and-one-half-year-old boy was described as withdrawn, constantly complaining of fatigue, uncooperative, generally hostile, and destructive. At the same time he was very dependent on adults and often clung to a teacher who resembled his mother.

Warren is in a crib in the doll-house corner almost completely covered with a small blanket. He is lying in a foetal position, with his legs folded and head forward, firmly sucking on a small nipple attached to a toy bottle. He shouts to the other children in the doll corner, "I'm the baby!" and returns to sucking the bottle.

The teacher now sets up a table and a large basin of water in the doll corner, for water-play. Warren watches this with interest and goes over to join in the water-play, holding his toy bottle firmly in hand. Sitting down at the table, he removes the nipple and, working carefully and intensely, he fills the bottle with water from the large basin. He puts both hands underwater and scoops up the bottle, all filled. Throwing his head back, he swallows deeply, then licks his lips sensuously. Filling the bottle again, Warren has trouble in replacing the nipple and asks Art to fix it. When it is fixed, Warren grabs it from Art, saying, "No, it's my bottle—I'm the baby!"

Warren gets up from the table and returns to the crib, still holding on to the filled bottle. He lifts the bottle to his lips and sucks voraciously. Brenda comes over to Warren and gently but firmly takes the bottle from him. Warren does not protest. Next Brenda gently pushes him down into a horizontal position on the crib. Warren seems to remain passive through this also, but when he has lost her attention for a moment, petulantly wails, "Cover me!" A little later he is sitting up and sucking his index finger furiously, when Bruce grabs the finger out of Warren's mouth and gleefully inserts the now filled bottle and nipple in its place. Warren sucks it vigorously until it is dry. Then the whole performance is repeated. At last he seems tired of it all and says, "I'm all finished with water; I'm not a baby anymore!" He gets out of the crib and follows Bruce.

Sometimes these impulses cannot be released completely even in play, but their existence is more clearly indicated in dramatic make-believe than in any real life behavior. The following records of Andy, a three-and-one-half-year-old, illustrate the fact that children frequently struggle against their own impulses. When this child first entered the center, he was referred for study because he seemed extremely withdrawn and disinterested. He rarely played with other children but when he did he was likely to become overexcited and destructive. He was unable to protect himself when attacked and seemed to depend on adults for aid. In his first dramatic play he frequently took roles designed to frighten other children or played the part of a creature that was killed. Andy's mother was reported to find the child a great burden. She was his sole support and had to do menial work to earn enough money to live on. (His father had committed suicide when the boy was only two years old.) Apparently his mother could give him very little affection and looked forward to the time when she could place him in a boarding school.

Andy is looking at his hands. He wiggles his fingers and continues to look at them. He walks over to a chair and picks up a broom with his left hand and uses it like a gun. When Leila walks over toward him he points the broom handle at her and falls to the floor pretending to be dead. Then he gets up and runs about making a sound like an "ack-ack" gun, points the gun at Jack and Jerry, and pretends to shoot them. Andy then walks over to the playhouse in another room and looks in. The broom is still in his left hand. He drops into a little rocking chair next to the playhouse. Right near the rocker is a table with a few small bottles filled with water. Jack, Jerry, and Tommy are standing around the table drinking from these bottles. Andy walks over to the table and picks up a bottle with his left hand, having placed the broom on the table, and drinks from the bottle. He smiles for the first time during the observation! He looks at the other children who are walking away, but he continues sucking on the bottle.

Andy changes the bottle from his left hand to his right, picks up the broom with his left hand and walks after the children. He has a worried expression on his face.

Leila walks over to the table and Andy follows her. He watches her closely as she picks up a bottle. She laughs; he laughs. He puts the bottle down and swings his left foot over the broom handle and gallops around the room on it. (He doesn't look as though he's having a good time. The observer thinks he looks sad.)

Andy then slings the broom over his left shoulder and marches around the room. There are a few colored boxes on the floor. He mounts one yellow box and straddles the sides as you would a horse and bangs away with his broom. He falls off the box and lies perfectly still on the floor with his arms outstretched and his legs spread apart. Jack and Jerry join Andy and they begin to ride the boxes. Andy gets up from the floor without any assistance from his hands—remounts and gallops on. Again he falls and plays dead on the floor. He picks up the broom with his right hand and points it at Jerry. Then Andy falls dead on the floor again. The child has a frown on his face throughout his dramatic play.

Andy gets up and points the gun at Jerry. Jerry turns on him with an angry expression. Andy appears quite frightened and backs away, then gets down on all fours.

Jerry says: "Look at the snake. He's a nice snake. Don't shoot him." Jack: "Are you a nice snake?" Andy: "Yes." Andy crawls up to Jerry and snaps his teeth. Jack says: "Bite him, snakie"—and Andy crawls after Jerry, in and out of the boxes. Jerry calls, "Nice snakie, come into my house." Andy precedes Jerry into a box. Jerry pats Andy very gently—"Nice snakie, you're my snakie, aren't you?" Andy says, "Yes." While Jerry and Jack argue over whose snake Andy is, Andy goes and hides under the table. He comes out, picks up the teacher's pocketbook and hits Jerry on the head with it.

This sequence of rapidly changing play episodes is particularly enlightening. The broom and the bottle serve as

perfect symbols of his dual problem: his powerful impulse
to hurt others and his enormous need for care and love. In
real life he cannot defend himself; in play he can exterminate
the population of the nursery. In real life he has to depend
on his teachers to protect him; in play he can incorporate
enormous power and destructiveness by straddling a box as
his horse and banging away with a broom as his gun. However, when he finds that aggression, even in play, can be
dangerous, he reverts to the role of "snake." In this role
he is immediately acceptable to the other children, although
he does not give up the need to attack them.

Sometimes aggressive impulses cannot be expressed towards
real people even in make-believe. Then the important role
of the object of aggression is assigned to some inanimate
creature such as a doll or a teddy bear. In the record below,
the little girl, Jane, had caused her teacher some concern
because she had seemed withdrawn and inhibited. The boy
was considered well adjusted and had been selected to play
with Jane because he was one of her special friends at the
time. The two children had been presented with a boxful
of "special toys," which included a toy stethoscope, rubber
knives, and baby nursing bottles. They were in their regular classroom and were free to play with any other toys they
wanted. Notice that while Jim begins the aggressive play,
Jane follows eagerly. (Incidentally, note Jane's joy in playing with the water and talking about the doll's bed-wetting—
one of her original difficulties had been fear of the messier
materials used in school.)

Jane quickly seizes the toys in the box, and since there are
two of everything, Jim also grabs some. They share and give
each other the duplicate of whatever they pick up. Jane sees
the knife and quickly takes hold of it. Jane: "What's dat
knife?" She puts it down and then takes it again, saying,
"That's a real one," and lunges it at Jim. Jane finds the

stethoscope, readily knows what to do with it and so puts it
in her ears. She laughs heartily and says, "Breathe." She
picks up a little box and says, "What's in here?" She opens
a small bottle and smells the inside. . . . Jim: "Take out
your kitchen knife and start working with it." Jane picks up
the knife, carefully feels it and bends the blade, but looks up
questioningly at the observer. Her tongue comes out of her
mouth and she wets her lips, then draws them in. She puts
her knife on top of the box, next to the stethoscope, and places
the bottles against the box in a neat row. Then Jim says, "We
need dolls." Jane jumps up very fast and says to Jim, "Shall
I get you a doll?" Jim: "Yes, get two dolls." Jane runs
over and comes back with two teddy bears. Jim: "Can I
stick a hole in him?" Jane takes the knife and tries to stick
a hole in the teddy bear. Jim, who is more direct, goes right
at his object and says, "I gotta hole in him. Operate on him!"
(He fiercely digs the blade along the belly of the teddy bear.)
Jim suggests putting some water into the bottles. They quickly
return from the bathroom and pour some of the water from
the bottle into the small pill bottles. Jane takes the big
bottle, puts it to the teddy bear's mouth and says, "Watch,
he drank some, see how much he drank!" She pushes the nipple against the nose of the teddy bear as she says this. Jane
laughs and giggles and seems delighted with everything. Both
children take up the knife again and Jim orders, "Cut him
open with your knife." Jane: "Look what I did," and sticks
the knife into the throat of the bear. She lays the bear down
and tries to pour water (by shaking the bottle which still has
a nipple on it) over him. Some water spills on her and she
giggles, "I'm all wet!" The throat cutting is repeated twice
more, each time followed by the feeding game. Then Jim
says to the teddy bear, "Don't you wet the bed tonight." Jane
repeats "Don't you wet the bed tonight." However, she repeats his words with great humor, or seeming humor. "Now
bed, now morning? He wet his bed, let him lie down. Let
him swallow the aspireene." She pretends to take out an as-
pirin and gives it to the teddy bear. She lifts the bottle to
her mouth and drinks the water. "Hee, hee, is it good? No,
I hate it." She bares her teeth in a wide grin which looks

rather forced. However, she seems to be having a wonderful time.

Aggressive play is by no means limited to children with special problems. The five-year-olds involved in the following record were not considered to be hostile or difficult by their teachers and got along well in their contact with others.

Paul and Jim each pick up a knife. Paul makes a lunge at Jim, yelling "I am going to kill you." The two boys start to wrestle and pretend to stick the knife in each other. The play gets very rough. Paul keeps yelling, "I kill you—where is that other knife?" Paul: "I am strong boy, I am a strong boy . . ." He walks around with the knife between his teeth yelling to Jim, "Come and kill me. I am going to kill you." Jim to Paul: "Don't use no knives, then, don't use no knives." Jim is apparently afraid of knives.

REVERSAL OF ROLES USUALLY PLAYED IN REAL LIFE

A very destructive child sometimes performs the role of a good and solicitous mother; a normally self-reliant child likes to play "baby"; and a timid, submissive youngster acts the dominating parent with great gusto. Through dramatic play these children are attempting to expand the horizons of the self, to break through the rigid and confining limits which circumstances have imposed on them. In some of these roles the child seems to identify with frightening or coercive parents as a means of tolerating them—perhaps by convincing himself of his ability to exercise eventually the same rights and prerogatives that are now inflicted on him. Other types of role reversal, in which the child plays a "good" part in contrast to his usual mode of behavior, suggest positive action on the part of the teacher. For if the youngster is able to *play* the role of a constructive and contributing member of the group, he has at least the germ of that conception of himself and proper nourishment may bring it to fruition.

The behavior of Della, a three-and-one-half-year-old was described as follows: "Observer rather than participant; fearful of new situations; rarely took initiative unless teacher was standing by; would hunch up when approached by children; showed affection toward teachers; did everything that was demanded of her; fearful of being dirty." Her change of pace in dramatic play is so extreme that were it not for her show of anxiety, it would be hard to believe that she is the same person.

Della is playing house with a group of children. She is the mother, while the others are her children. At the door of the house are protective, movable, wooden guards which she has placed there. Trina tries to get in the house but Della, in a belligerent tone, says, "You can't play in this house!" . . . . In the house, Jill, who seems to represent a special child to Della, asks her if she can go out. Della says in a dominating abrupt voice, "No! Get in!" Later Jill starts to climb on the house. Della shouts at her in her particularly screeching imperative tone, "Get down! Come in!" Pat, a spontaneous, bumptious fellow says, "I want to climb on here." Della loudly says, "No-oo-oo!" as if Pat had given her a personal affront. "Get in the house!" She continues to shout orders at Jill. Pat looks out of the barred side of the house and says he is looking out of the window. Della, watching him anxiously, says, "Don't look out of the window; *I* need to look out of the window! Don't climb, Pat!" Della has remained in the house continually and has been clutching her purse with adultlike motions since the play began.

Pat climbs on the bars on top of the house and the other children follow his lead. Della does not join them but remains passive, looking worried. She yells at Pat, "Don't do that! Don't do that!—I'll hit you if you do!" But Pat laughs and continues to climb. Suddenly Della becomes very active. She jumps up and down on the floor. Kitty, who is not a member of the group playing in the house, takes away one of the wooden guards at the doorway. Della frantically runs out, grabs the guard away from Kitty, replaces it and screeches, "Don't do that!" Back in the house she speaks to Pat as her particular

problem child: "If you're a monkey, you get out of my house!"
Pat goes out. Della begins to climb around the house with the
others. There is no spontaneous laughter or enjoyment as with
Pat, but she keeps a serious and anxious expression throughout.

Tessie, another three-year-old, had been described as "hostile," "aggressive," "destructive," "violent"—yet in the record
below we find her playing the mother role quietly and constructively. Brief as it is, the excerpt indicates that the child
is capable of relaxed, integrated behavior.

. . . . Tessie lays aside the colored paper and goes alone into
a small cubbyhole containing a doll carriage, some dolls, and
other assorted playthings. She first fusses with a doll in the
carriage, cooing affectionately to it and feeding it from a bottle.
Next she puts the nipple of the bottle into her mouth and
sucks abstractedly on it for awhile. Moving over to the shelves
lining the walls, she removes differently colored materials and
conscientiously lays them out. Intently she puts on a small
cloth jacket. The teacher calls her to come and listen to a
story. Tessie asks if she can bring the baby over. The teacher
calls again and Tessie answers, "I can't come, I'm busy putting her things away."

The Idiomatic Nature of Dramatic Play

It has long been held a truism that play is the natural
language of the child. What has not been emphasized sufficiently is the fact that each child uses this language in an
idiomatic fashion—that each word, each gesture, each action
has a significance peculiar to him alone. Some of the most
difficult and frustrating aspects of dealing with young children stem from this idiomatic quality of their behavior. We
must recognize that no matter how similar the behavior
patterns of two children seem to be, on a deeper *meaning*
level they may be quite different. And conversely, contrasting behavior may prove to be quite similar in meaning.

This idiomatic quality of play may be understood by re-
membering that the child himself gives the meaning and

emotional significance to his play. He makes playthings and activities and people mean what he personally thinks and feels them to be.

However, we must also recognize that children are influenced in their techniques of expression by the customs of the group in which they find themselves. They learn to express in the same way that they learn to conform. Yet, though any healthy young child will inevitably accept the play forms of his group, he will always mold them to his own special purposes. The media of expression are rarely original, but the use of them is bound to be. This is what happens with language. The child learns the words and phrases and their use according to the accepted vocabulary, grammar, etc., of his group, but he uses them in his own idiomatic way and gives them the peculiar meaning they have for him alone. That is why we may hear the words spoken by someone but may not understand what he is trying to communicate.

In dramatic play specifically, the medium of expression is the role the child chooses to perform or the theme he acts out. While this behavior may indicate what is of particular concern to him at his present level of development, it may, at the same time, reflect his response to the group. When we find in one center a constant repetition of fireman or cowboy roles, while in another there is a preoccupation with animal play and conductor roles, are we justified in assuming that these themes spring wholly spontaneously from within each child alone? Is it not more logical to assume that a child draws upon what goes on about him and reinterprets it according to his own understanding and his own needs? There is a good deal of evidence that children of lower income backgrounds differ from children of higher economic levels in their choice of play themes. While it is theoretically possible that these children differ in basic personality structure, it is also probable that they are simply using a different language for the expression of individual meanings that may or may not coincide.

Our records of animal play clearly illustrate the idiomatic nature of the language of play. Although the same general theme of imitation is found in all of them, each carries meanings peculiar to the child performing the role. The first record is that of a four-and-one-half-year-old-boy, Freddie, who seemed tense and fearful, somewhat withdrawn socially and unable to defend himself adequately against attack. His mother was known to be overprotective and showed a special concern for his health.

Freddie and Phil are stacking large building blocks on the wagon. Freddie: "Let's build a tiger house." He begins to stack blocks along the open side of a large box. Phil gets into the box. Freddie: "You want to be the tiger in cage? I'll build a wall up to the top so you can't get out." Phil tries to get out of the box. Freddie playfully pushes him back and continues to build the wall. He talks all the time: "You are the tiger, I'll build a house so you can't get out. You are the tiger, you can't get out, etc. etc." He is not engaging in conversation. He does all the talking. Phil comes out of cage, picks up the blocks, loads them on the wagon, and gets in. Freddie gets into the wagon and gets right out: "This is no fire truck."

Freddie goes to the "cage" and gets in. Phil begins to build the wall, saying, "You can't get out." Freddie pushes the wall over. Phil builds it back. Freddie sits quietly for about ten seconds and then moves about in the cage, saying, "I can get out, I can get out, I can get out." Freddie watches as Phil builds the wall. "I'm looking out window, Phil. We can bite everybody, can't we Phil?—Give me a chip to eat." "Tigers" roar as Phil moves the wagon away. Freddie gets out of the cage and watches as Ralph comes up. Freddie says to Ralph, "Get in cage." Freddie goes in himself and pushes down the wall and then runs over to get in line to go back into the room.

This play episode breaks naturally into two parts—the first when Freddie is walling up the tiger, and the second when he himself is the tiger. In the first part, when he is presumably in control of the dangerous beast, his continual assertion of power suggests that he is not too sure of himself. Exactly what the "tiger" represents to Freddie we cannot know from this episode alone, but since he later gets into the cage himself, it must be something to which he feels a close kinship. When he becomes the tiger he gives us a hint of its meaning by saying, "We can bite everybody, can't we?" Two things are therefore clear: from his play we know that he is primarily concerned with the "tiger" in himself, and from the teacher's report of his inability to protect himself, we know that in reality he cannot control this force in others.

In the following record, also, a timid child becomes a ferocious animal, but this time a young observer is the object of an unprovoked attack. To show how personal the language of play can be, the report will be given first and the explanation afterward.

I begin the game by making a slight growling noise. Marvin growls back and I ask him what he is. He says he is a fox. I ask him what I am. "A wolf." He growls, grabs my hand, bites my finger, but rather gently. I say a fox would bite a chicken, but not a wolf, because the wolf is bigger. He says he is a big wolf, and I'm a baby fox. He suddenly attacks me, opens his mouth as wide as he can, and bites my cheek. He is very intense, obviously wants to bite me really hard, but doesn't quite dare; he bites just hard enough to hurt. I pull away quickly, before temptation will overpower him. He grabs my hand, bites my finger. This time he bites quite hard, but is still obviously restraining himself with considerable difficulty from trying to give me a good chew. I snatch my hand away, showing him the toothmarks he has left. He is quite excited by now, and starts to slap my face.

There was nothing in the slight relationship that had grown up between the observer and the child to account for this behavior, and the boy himself was ordinarily unaggressive, even somewhat feminine in his play. However, it is easy to see why Marvin should vent his feelings on the observer, a young man. His father had been very important to him, but he had, from Marvin's point of view, apparently abandoned him, having left the home after divorcing the lad's mother. There was no other man toward whom Marvin could react either in his preschool center or at home. So, with his animal role to protect him, and with the receptive young man practically inviting attack, he could release his real feelings against a substitute.

The two following records illustrate the point that different children may assume the same animal role yet use it in ways that express their individual behavior patterns and basic needs. Both of these four-year-olds, Jay and Jackie, were described as more than ordinarily belligerent and destructive: both were vigorous and physically active, tending to dominate other children; both seemed to need a good deal of physical contact with their teachers. Their dramatic play discloses not only these similarities, but reveals differences as well.

Jackie is lying on the floor pretending to be dead. Whenever someone comes near him, although his eyes are closed, he kicks with both heels on the floor. He runs to join a small reading group, sits at the table for a moment, then says, "I'm a dog, I'm a dog," and climbs on the radiator. Another boy joins him and the two shove each other to get more room. The teacher lifts Jackie down. . . .

He goes over to the construction corner, suddenly drops down on his hands and knees, playing "kitty" and making pitiful meows. He crawls over to a train, where the boys are playing, gets up and pulls one boy's hair and thereby upsets the whole train. The whole corner is in an uproar. Jackie does not appear to be affected and merely throws himself on the floor again, mewing like a cat. He goes over to Billy and pulls his hair, then hits Tod, throws a big block at Billy, and runs away.

Note that Jackie's animal play is consistently aggressive. Through his roles he destroys group stability and group play. Jay, in the next excerpt, attracts a variety of attentions and plays his role in such a way as to gain both an outlet for aggressive impulses and satisfaction for passivity needs. While Jackie's role puts him out of the group, Jay's role becomes the focus for the group.

Jay lost interest in the wagon and began to crawl around on the ground. Suddenly, he dropped flat on his stomach, and lay perfectly still. Another boy came over and lifted him back to his hands and knees by his stomach. This procedure was repeated ten or twelve times, and then Jimmie shouted that he was a cat. Whenever any of the boys touched Jay, he got up from his prone position and started to crawl again. Finally he got up on his feet and started to walk around with the boy who had been lifting him up throughout the cat play. For no reason that I could see Jay suddenly struck out at this boy, who then went away. . . . He went over to Jimmie. They placed their heads together and then they both lay down on the bench and acted as if they were asleep. Jimmie "woke up" first and got off the bench. Jimmie and his girl friend went over to wake Jay up. Jay pretended to claw at them; off they ran, but they came back soon after. Then the three played together, all of them acting as cats, meowing and clawing at each other.

What accounts for the differences in the animal play of these two boys? Again the reason is to be found in specific life situations. Jay lives at home with his mother, with whom he has a very warm relationship. His aggressiveness stems mainly from her easygoing lack of control. Jackie, on the other hand, was abandoned by both mother and father, who are divorced. He spends one day a week with his mother, but lives with his grandmother, to whom he is obviously a burden. Moreover, he has been the victim not only of a broken home, but also of several older children who resent taking care of him. His attitude towards other children may well be a reflection of his feelings toward his brothers and sisters. Little wonder, then, that his play is not only aggressive but hostile in nature.

The foregoing accounts contain evidence of a good deal of released aggression. However, this is by no means the only function of animal play. As some of our other records indicate, children often impersonate animals for the sheer joy of experimenting with different patterns of movement. Frequently, too, animal play is a transparent substitute for household play, in which "lions" and "tigers" are treated much like children. Just as little girls alternate between "mummie" and "baby" roles, little boys play "animal" or "keeper." Occasionally the keeper turns into the hunter, and occasionally the wild animal eats or pretends to eat his keeper. But by and large this play is calm, jocular, or simply imitative, and derives from visits to the zoo in much the same way as household play derives from living in the home. Playing animal is also associated at times with playing "big men" or with simply the assertion of being big—for example, "I am the biggest one in this group." A rare use of the animal role is to get into a cozy place; for example, when the child crawls under a table or into a packing box in lieu of a cage. The variety of purposes to which the single animal theme is put is testimony to the ingenuity of children in bending whatever they find at hand to their own individual needs.

In addition to finding that similar roles have very different functions for different children, we have found that different roles convey similar meanings. In one of the groups observed, two boys seemed outstandingly stereotyped in their play. One was continually occupied with trucks and trains.

He built elaborate railroad yards, garages, and cars out of blocks; he painted trucks almost exclusively and made complicated bridges out of clay; his outdoor play was confined to wagons and tricycles, which always represented cars or trucks in need of attention. The other boy played in more varied fashion, but over and over again assumed the role of a doctor about to "operate" on someone. This lad usually played with girls rather than boys and always took a dominating role. The first boy, on the other hand, was always the center of a large group of other boys who were attracted by his skill in creating elaborate receiving stations for vehicles and by his interest in "driving" and maintaining them. Superficially the play of the youngsters was quite different, yet in terms of their inner dynamics, similar purposes were served. Since the first boy's father owned and operated a truck and the second boy's was a surgeon, their play was obviously imitative. However, this was not the basic likeness. Their real similarity lay in the fact that both were preoccupied with their relationship to their fathers and their desire to be close to them.

General Observations

To this point we have been stressing the value of dramatic play as an individual expression of the child's inner needs, strivings, and concepts. We now add a few general observations on the way it reflects sex and other group differences among children.

SEX DIFFERENCES IN DRAMATIC PLAY

As early as three years of age there seems to be a marked division in the type of roles played by little girls and little boys. The girls engage in house-play almost exclusively, but within this apparently restricted area the number of roles they play is surprisingly large. They take turns at being mothers, nurses, neighbors, and visitors; they cook food and care for children, walk in the park, clean the house, wash and iron clothes, dress up to go out, etc. The boys, for the most part, play variations on the one limited theme of mastering vehicles. They are captains of boats, pilots of airplanes, drivers of cars and busses; and on occasion they minister to these vehicles as garage men and mechanics. The comparative sparsity of roles among boys may be due to a lack of direct contact with these jobs, since they have experienced them only as spectators. In contrast, the girls have not only lived through an enormous variety of domestic situations, but have been encouraged to assume many of the roles in real life.

These observations raise a question of some importance: Why does this male—female division occur at such an early age? If the answer is offered that early childhood is a time of identification par excellence, when the children are asserting their kinship to adults of their own sex—then why is it that the boys so rarely play fathers? Does this mean that our boys do not identify themselves with males as fathers, but only with males as workers or as "bosses" of machinery? Does it mean that they cannot conceive of a satisfactory role for a man within the household? These questions in turn suggest that they actually do not experience their fathers to any great extent in their parental roles, and what is more, do not picture themselves as future fathers. Of course, in many cases the father makes his contributions to the house only when the children are asleep. Yet even where they do participate in child care and homemaking, as more and more younger fathers are doing, the boy very seldom takes the father role in his dramatic play.

The implications of these sex differences for both domestic and social relations are grave indeed. If boys do not learn to see themselves as fathers, will they ever become real family men? And when the division of the sexes occurs at such an early age, how are we to make room for genuine sharing and communication later in life?

Seeking a fuller explanation of these divergent play patterns, we discussed the situation with a number of preschool center supervisors. They re-examined the housekeeping corners in their schools and discovered that the materials were usually designed to suggest female household duties rather than appropriate male activities. Due to the predominantly female personnel of the schools, little thought had been given to the possible inclusion of boys in house-play. However, as soon as items of men's clothing, such as shoes, jackets, and caps were included in the doll corner, as well as tool boxes, lunch boxes, pipes, and other masculine paraphernalia, the boys participated far more frequently. When, in addition, water-play was introduced in relation to household equipment, such as egg beaters, pots, muffin tins, mops, and dishes, the attraction of domestic play for boys increased still further.

The importance of props and materials available for play has perhaps never been sufficiently appreciated. The possibilities of opening new play vistas, and new opportunities for identification, through the introduction of new materials was impressively demonstrated in one group of rather hardened six- to seven-year-olds from a "tough" neighborhood. Because this group was mainly male, the housekeeping corner had been neglected almost completely by teachers and youngsters alike. The director of the center, however, knew from the background records that most of the boys had baby brothers and sisters. She therefore suggested the addition of more doll-house equipment, including drinking and wetting rubber dolls, doll-bathing apparatus, and full-sized baby bottles. Some of the teachers objected, since the group seemed more interested in exhibiting their physical prowess over each other than in any other kind of activity. Nevertheless, as soon as the doll-house equipment was introduced, an immediate and dramatic change came over the group. Aggressive behavior fell off sharply, with a parallel rise in the number of "mothering" activities. A few, it is true, pounded the rubber dolls—but spared their playmates for the first time. Most of them enjoyed hours of washing, feeding, and diapering the "babies," and occasionally took to the nursing bottles themselves.

One teacher discovered that when the group was either quite large or predominantly male, a sharp division between the boys and girls generally occurred—but when it was relatively small and fairly equally divided between the sexes, such a division did not occur. The surplus of males probably evoked the masculine world of work where "fathering" activities did not seem appropriate. Two practical solutions, therefore, suggested themselves: first, to set up more than one housekeeping corner so that when girls usurped one, the boys would not have to oust them to get their turn; and second, to divide groups so that they contained the same number of boys and girls, and to keep the groups small enough so that neither sex could overwhelm the other by banding together.

This brings us back to the young child's concept of a sharply divided world of work. Outside the home he sees a public world dominated by masculine figures; inside, a private world where women carry on. Would it not be salutary for little girls to learn that women may also share in the delights of subjugating machines, and for little boys to know that activities very similar to those carried on at home are respectably male? Visits to bakeries, tailor shops, cleaning establishments, and offices—where both men and women contribute—have as much to offer the children in the way of role material as the more usual excursions to library, wharf, and firehouse. Furthermore, the lives of their parents will begin to take on new meaning and acceptability through just such simple contacts with everyday activities outside the home, and the opportunity for identification with other adults is also extended. If flexibility is a virtue, why not give our children the material with which to be flexible? Why not break the narrow mold of their thinking by widening their experiences in a realistic fashion? The ideal instrument for absorbing these experiences is dramatic play. Why limit it?

OTHER GROUP DIFFERENCES

It is noteworthy that in addition to the sheer imitative activity of children who are comfortable and happy in their growth, three different motifs can be found occurring over and over again in the dramatic play of little children. These we might call a need for protection (for mothering, babying, being cared for), a need for power (over things and people), and the need to attack and destroy. Youngsters with difficult problems tend to be preoccupied with roles that express one of these qualities exclusively. Well-adjusted children, on the other hand, adapt more flexibly to the suggestions of others, play a greater variety of roles, and slip from one to the other with relative ease.

Certain more specific qualities appear to differentiate the play of well-adjusted youngsters from the play of children who are having marked difficulties. Although shooting and "cops and robbers" games are common enough among both well-adjusted and ill-adjusted boys, they occur more frequently among the overly aggressive. Moreover, for the well-adjusted child these games seem to function rather as an outlet for energy than as a channeling for feelings of hostility. They shoot for the sake of shooting, for the motor activity and the noise, and they generally shoot into the air. On the other hand the deeply aggressive boy almost always shoots someone, as if the real reason for the game lay in the object against which the activity is directed.

Anxious and withdrawn children tend to take on either very dominating or extremely passive roles. They rarely show aggression openly either in play or fantasy. However, the discriminating teacher can detect this need in its rather subdued and subtle form. The following two records illustrate the expression of aggressive impulses at different levels of intensity. The first presents a sociable, spontaneous lad who has no difficulty in asserting himself at any time, while the second depicts an extremely inhibited and withdrawn youngster who apparently needs help in recognizing and acknowledging his hostile impulses.

Jamie was in the process of playing soldier all by himself. For this purpose he had secured one of the toy mops and was carrying it around on his shoulder. He stoutly marched up and down the room, shifting the mop from one shoulder to the other, calling out commands, executing marching maneuvers, etc. Naturally he was quite noisy and he accompanied his shouts with vigorous stamping. Evidently he had somewhere gained the impression of a soldier as a pompous individual, for he had his chest stuck out and a somewhat arrogant expression on his face. Cary was evidently impressed by Jamie, for he picked up a broom and also played soldier. For a few moments the two were engaged in parallel play, but then Jamie challenged Cary to a duel. The two quite energetically crossed swords. The action moved from one end of the room to the other, but finally Cary tired of it and left the field of battle. Jamie returned to his solitary play, charging up on to a table and jumping off.

Compare this free and easy activity with the constricted play of Tip.

A group of boys go over to the storage shed and eagerly get out more boards. Tip follows at a distance and comes out carrying a short board carefully and tensely under his left arm. He sings softly to himself: "Ahhhh!" Playing alone, he approaches a wooden box, still holding the board. He says "Brrrr-ah!" in a quietly guarded tone of voice as if shooting; then he goes over to the wall and repeats this performance. While the other boys play noisily together, Tip stands aside pretending to shoot the wall.

While certain group differences become apparent and certain roles are found again and again, it would be a mistake to assume that any theme or role is in itself indicative of any particular group difference or any specific personality pattern, preoccupation, or problem. The theme is simply the raw material that seems appropriate to the child in expressing what he needs to express, either because it is opportune at the moment or because of the quality of the feelings it invokes in him. If we are to be alert to the peculiar meaning which any sample of dramatic play has for a particular child, we must observe when and how it occurs, its emotional quality, and whom it involves—and we must relate these observations to our knowledge of his background and relationships. This effort at understanding will invariably prove rewarding to both the teacher and the child.

CHAPTER III

Dramatic Play: Instrument
for Growth

WE HAVE ALREADY suggested that even limited observation of a child's dramatic play may reveal a great deal about the relationships, people, needs, and impulses that preoccupy him. Now we should like to demonstrate how continued observation will corroborate or illuminate fragmentary flashes of insight derived from single incidents and reveal the sequence of the child's growth. An isolated episode is frequently like one movement of a symphony: one must experience the whole in order to understand the part.

General Functions

We shall first present the general functions of dramatic play that are primarily concerned with the sequence of the child's growth. Illustrative records will be cited to show how this type of play (a) reflects and encourages changes in attitude and adjustment, and (b) supplies a laboratory in which the child may experiment with possible solutions to his problems. It will be recognized that these two aspects were included in the enumeration of functions in Chapter II.

REFLECTION AND ENCOURAGEMENT OF GROWTH

It is rather difficult to find play excerpts sufficiently brief to be included here, yet full enough to picture a child's growth in process. This is particularly true in view of the fact that validation of any interpretation in the play material would depend on some knowledge of the child's behavior when engaged in other than dramatic play. However, this aspect of play seems so important as a clue to social growth that it seems worth demonstrating, even if the effect is somewhat diminished because of lack of space. Because it will be necessary to present several episodes to demonstrate the trend of development, we will limit these illustrations to one child. Perry, the child in question, was described originally as "quite restrained and inhibited." His teachers said, "In his dealings with people and in his body movements, he never appeared to relax. He always seemed under a strain. He did not seem to trust adults. He was very cautious, did not come to people easily." He could not fight back when attacked, and played for the most part with little girls. When hurt, he would not cry but would grit his teeth and clench his fists. He used paints and clay only occasionally and meagerly. His dramatic play seemed to center around house-play, in which he was the father. He seemed slightly prissy when observed.

About eight months later, he was freer with adults and played with a larger number of children, including some boys. He began to cry when he was hurt, and would seek out adults at these times. He was able to protect himself against attack and began to use curse words. In general, he seemed less restrained, less inhibited, and showed much more variety in his play. He even became somewhat assertive and finally achieved a leader role. His teachers felt that he resorted less to fantasy and was able to meet the world on a more realistic basis.

These changes did not come about without the expenditure of a good deal of thought and effort on the part of his teachers to give him the kind of experience he needed. Knowing that the father was rigid and demanding in his relations with Perry, they encouraged the boy to express hurt and angry feelings. They provided toys to help him identify with his father (a surgeon) and were careful not to discourage displays of "toughness" on his part.

Episode 1. .·. . Perry to Jane: "Let's play house." Jane: "No, let's play bridge." They don't notice Carol, who is standing near them and watching. Carol slaps at Jane. Perry to Carol: "Afraidy-cat." Carol drops to her knees near the sawhorse. Carol: "I'm a pussy." Perry points to Jane: "She's the mamma pussy cat." They pick up a board and carry it back between them. Carol: "Meow, meow, I want food." Carol points to the paper bag. Jane—"No, no." She takes her paper bag and runs off for a short distance. Perry quietly sits on the ladder and watches Jane.

Note that it is Perry who suggests playing house and, although he does not contribute to the play, he remains with the two little girls. In the next episode his tender solicitude for the doll is more characteristic of feminine play than of masculine play at this age level. Although he turns to the blocks and begins to occupy himself with trucks and trains, a more characteristically masculine interest, he returns to house-play via the blocks.

Episode 2. Perry, Jane, and Carol are washing small rubber dolls. They dry them and put them to bed. Perry goes to the block corner, starts to take out several blocks at a time and puts them in a pile. Carol comes up to him with her doll dressed. Perry returns to the doll corner and takes his doll out of the bed, turns the head to the front, and then returns to his pile of blocks, putting the doll down beside them. He starts to build a bridge, stops, picks up the doll, and hands it to Carol. Jane helps Perry build. He glances at Carol as she puts the doll to bed. Perry and Jane now build a long road with square corners. Perry tries out a small wooden train on it. He cannot keep the train on the track while going around the corners so he now adds curved blocks. . . .

Perry and Jane each take a full armful of blocks and start to build houses with them. Carol takes a wooden train and crawls around Perry and Jane. Perry stops and watches her, then dances around his building, adds more blocks, and calls it a house. He decides that Jane is the mother; Carol is the child; he is the father. He returns to his building and adds an archway for the door. He helps Carol park the train beside the building. He returns to his building and adds a window.

In the third episode, which takes place two months later, we find a dramatic change. Although he is again playing with little girls, the role he takes is a more aggressive one, and he is beginning to express in fantasy some of the impulses which must have preoccupied him earlier when he seemed timid and inhibited. Although the play is clearly influenced by the motion picture *Bambi*, his interpretation is definitely his own. Notice that, in spite of his new daring, he is still "Little Thumper" and needs a hole to hide in.

Episode 3. Perry notices two girls and starts to chase them. "When I shoot, you must drop dead. I am a hunter." He shouts, "I killed a bad beast! I killed him already. I kill you, too." "But that is *bad*," says Jane. "You must drop when the car goes away," he says. Biking again with John, he starts to sing, "I killed the beast." Jane, holding the doll in her arms, sings back: "Don't kill the baby." Perry: "Kill all deers in the forest." Jane: "Are no deers." Perry: "I am going to kill you as big as you are." Jane starts to cry when he pushes her quite hard against the wall. He goes away on his bike. Jane complains to the teacher who asks Perry, "Why did you knock Janie?" "She threatened me," he lies, and then says, "My car has to go. I have to go with snow.—John, why don't you come? I'll run you over—peep, peep."

Later to Jane: "You must go in the thicket, and someone must shoot you, and you must be walking like this." (He goes on four legs and then starts to hop like a rabbit.) He goes on: "Bambi was not with his mother. He was with Thumper when they want to kill him, want to kill them." —And he hops along. When Carol wants to join them, he says, "We don't like it here any more. Let us fly away." He moves like a bird and says to Jane, "You must say Flower. I don't mind if you call me Flower. What do you call me?" "Thumper." They start to stamp hard together while going around. "Look at this deep hole," says Perry; he sits down and goes on, "Bambi, let us hide in the snow. Nobody comes to the hole. This is a lion's hole—weasel cats won't come here." Jane: "Weasel is coming after us." Perry: "Then he wants to eat you, too." Jane: "It is big enough for you." Perry: "It is bigger than me. I am a *little* Thumper. I could go into such a little hole. Let's hop to the hole, Bambi." They hop away and then sit down together on the ground. Perry: "I like to get wet. My mother does not mind. My poppy minds. So my mommy and poppy start to fight!" Jane: "What do *you* do?" Perry: "I push him down in a chair. I put a brace around him so he can't get up till I let him go." Jane looks at him with big eyes.

The fourth scene finds Perry playing with boys and blocks and dealing with airplanes, a favorite instrument of power among normally masculine little boys. He seems well on his way toward achieving the male role.

Episode 4. . . . Tip and Melvin have each made a beautiful plane out of blocks. Perry goes over and does the same. He tries to fix some blocks on the tail and three smaller ones on top. Everything falls down and he starts again, completely undisturbed. Crawling on his knees he pushes his plane slowly forward, saying, "Prrrr! Prrrr!" Melvin's and Tip's planes start to move also; Perry's is faster and he now races Tip's. "Look at this," he says, "this is the propeller." It falls down and he fixes it quickly again. He laughs when other boys start to throw blocks around and says, while moving it slowly forward: "Mine is a fighter plane! Mine will be beating up the whole world in a few minutes. Burr! burr!" Melvin, John, and Perry start to fight jokingly. Perry kneels again and fixes something on his plane. "Look at this, my airplane." He turns it around: "A crash at the airport happened. Three million people died." Melvin: "Mine is a hospital plane." Perry reports: "Mine too." Alex's long train bumps into his plane. "You bumped into mine," Perry says, but he repairs it carefully and diligently without any resentment. "This is a fighter double-decker," he says again. Then he notices four of the girls and goes over to them and invites them to come over and admire his plane. He says to Carol, "Here is my plane, Carol. See my plane. It is a fighter!"

WORKING OUT PROBLEMS THROUGH DRAMATIC PLAY

In this category we include single play episodes in which children indicate their difficulties and actually try to *solve* them—as opposed to play which is simply a *reflection* of changes taking place within them. Our illustration here is drawn from the play behavior of a four-year-old named Jackie who was described as quiet, tense, withdrawn, and rather timid. When he entered his preschool group he was extremely neat, conformed to routines, and spoke in an almost inaudible voice. At first he had trouble parting from his mother and could not cope with the aggression of other children. During the year, however, he became freer, more vigorous, very sociable, and began not only to defend but also to assert himself. He then started to use materials with almost carefree abandon, and conformed to adult demands less meticulously. In the following account we watch him venture haltingly, then more boldly, into these new roles.

Jackie runs out to the playground and finds Morris at once. They set a tire upright and together start to roll it. Jackie stops to look through the bars into the playhouse where two girls are playing. Jackie tells Morris to put the tire inside. Morris tries to and can't, so Jackie gets down to help him. They can't get it into the desired place; Jackie tells him to get it in the other side. They work to get it in, but it's too big to fit. Jackie pushes, Morris pulls. Jackie then pulls it out entirely. "Come over here, Morris." Morris to observer: "Teacher, get this up." The observer puts the tire on the roof. Morris: "Get me up." The observer does so. They work to get the tire up on the next height, and the boys succeed by themselves. Jackie to observer: "We got it." "Good for you, Morris," he says in a triumphant tone of voice. Morris: "We're big strong boys." Jackie repeats this. Morris now tells Jackie to get another tire, so he runs off and gets it from Louise, hitting her and taking it by force. They lift it up to the next height by themselves. Then they ask for help. Observer: "You can do it." And they do. Morris tells Jackie to get a third tire from John and Louise. He goes over to them and talks to John, but can't get the tire from them. He hits John who cries. Jackie comes back, climbs up on the structure, and says to the observer: "We're strong guys, eat a lot." Morris goes over to John; then Jackie swaggers up, too. The teacher says that they have enough with two tires. They come back to the structure. Morris throws one tire down; then throws the second one down. This one hits Jackie on the head. The teacher is right there and comforts him although he doesn't cry.

Jackie moves a block of wood which Morris had been pushing and tells Morris to "Catch it." Morris answers, "Got it," as they stand it on roof. Jackie: "O. K., Morrison." He runs off and gets a second wooden piece from a younger girl, who cries as he takes it from her. He moves it over by throwing it on the ground, over and over. Two other boys come along and throw the first wooden piece from the roof, and then try to take away the tires. Jackie runs over to the observer and cries, clinging to her skirt, and says, "Taking away tires." He then stands with his finger in his mouth. At first Morris cries for the teacher, then stands by the tires. The teacher interferes, and the two boys go off and leave Jackie and Morris alone. They move the wooden piece up again. Morris gets on the roof and helps Jackie lift it up.

Notice Jackie's repeated assertions that he is "a big strong boy." (The fact that he was actually smaller than many of the other boys in his group may account for his comparative lack of ease.) So far he needs the help of adults in protecting his materials from the other children. As the play goes on, however, after impersonating a "strong" individual, a truck driver, he finds he can protect himself. Also, he apparently incorporates the children who interfere with him into his fantasy and expresses his rage against them within the structure of the play episode: "I got so mad at that man I could have killed him."

As the play continues, Jackie gets out from down below. "I'm driving, Morris, OK?" He stands up in the front part of the structure and pretends to steer. Morris gets a block and puts it up front. Jackie then goes off, returns with a block also, and says, "Make it higher. . . ." They fight over the blocks on the seat, and Jackie knocks a block into Morris; they both come over to the observer. Jackie holds on to her skirt, and then they hit each other violently. "Damn." "Bastard." They walk about two steps from each other for a second, then both go underneath the structure together and they are friends once more. A girl comes over and interferes with their play. Jackie hits her violently, saying, "Get off of dere." She cries. Jackie says to Morris, "I'm strong." A third boy comes up on the structure. Morris to the observer: "Teacher, get him off." Jackie swaggers up fast, comes to the observer, clings to her skirt, and, as if crying, says, "Get him off." When the observer does nothing about the situation, he goes to the regular teacher, who helps them. Jackie climbs up, then Morris. Jackie: "Here water for dis truck." They talk and laugh together, then climb down. Morris puts his arms around Jackie. Jackie: "I got so mad at dat man, I could've killed him."

Another boy passes. Jackie shoos him away, and a battle ensues. They tear each other's hair and clothing, but neither cries. Then the fight is over. The other boy leaves. Morris to the observer, "Teacher, you can sit down now." Jackie, "We're going in a little while." The observer sits. They sit on a block and turn the bars of the structure, as before, as if driving. "Er-rr errh. Peep, peep." Observer: "I'll get off here." Jackie to the observer: "It'll be finished in a little while." A bigger boy rolls a tire into the truck. Jackie watches; the boy leaves. Larry joins them. Morris lets him play, saying only, "He'll get all wet." But Jackie tells him to get off and hits him.

Looking back, it appears that through his manipulation of the large outdoor blocks and the tires Jackie first assured himself of his powers, and then proceeded to exercise them against his rather aggressive playmates. The episode shows vividly how a child will seesaw back and forth between fantasy and reality in his dramatic play, each time bringing into his real relationships some strength that he has developed during the performance of his chosen role.

Using Brief Notations to Understand the Individual Child

A series of observations taken day after day will often give us a bird's eye view of a child's adjustment and the direction in which he is headed. Surprisingly simple notations, recording only the theme of his play, his relationships to others involved in it, and the emotional tone of his role, will frequently show up the "sore spots," the undigestible elements in his life. Children who are functioning smoothly, whose life holds no problems they cannot solve with comparative ease will be found to perform in a variety of roles involving different kinds of relationships. Not so the troubled children. They generally cling to one or two types of role with grim tenacity, and when these roles are concisely recorded and reviewed in sequence, they tend to fall into a single emotional pattern. A glance at the notations of the play of three children made over a seven-day period will illustrate this point.

Perry

Sept. 22: Plays role of father with wife and child. Bids family good-bye as he leaves for the office.

Sept. 23: Role of doctor operating on patient.

Sept. 24: Role of ice-cream man selling by the gallon.

Sept. 26: Role of policeman arresting man for fighting; role of angered father who spanks baby for wetting diapers.

Sept. 30: Role of American soldier shooting Germans and Japanese.

Oct. 1: Role of father who prepares baby's milk.

Oct. 2: Role of doctor who operates on child.

For Perry the father figure is the important one. However, there seems to be more variation in his play than there actually is, because his father is a doctor and he is identifying with him in two different roles—that of the family figure and that of the professional man. The reader will not be surprised to learn that the way in which Perry's father actually performs his father role invites confusion between the "doctor" and the "father" functions. A concern about aggression is also revealed by the boy's policeman and soldier roles and by the fact that the doctor—his father—is not shown caring for his patients but cutting into them.

Lola

Sept. 22: Plays role of a little pussycat who belongs to a lady who leads her by a string.

Sept. 23: Role of an angry mother who spanks her child for wetting herself.

Sept. 24: Role of a housewife who becomes upset because her children won't eat their dinner.

Sept. 26: Role of a baby being pulled in a wagon by her mother. Role of a ferocious tiger in the zoo.

Sept. 29: Role of a mother who takes her children on a picnic and is chased by a tiger.

Sept. 30: Role of a mother cooking dinner who forgets she has no milk in the house.

Oct. 1st: Role of a doctor's nurse who tends the patients.

Oct. 2nd: Role of a child who cries for candy and is spanked by its mother.

It is significant that Lola has an extremely irritable and impulsive mother. As with Perry, there are reflections of opposing tendencies—in this case to be cared for as a baby and to express ferocity as a tiger. We find out rather clearly what happens to the child who cries for candy or wets her clothes in Lola's family. We also discover what forms her fantasies of revenge take.

Michael

Sept. 22: Plays the role of a ferryboat operator. Resents any children riding other than those he chooses.

Sept. 23: Role of a train conductor who does not let anyone ride with him.

Sept. 26: Role of a fireman who saves children from a burning house. Role of a taxi driver with no passengers.

Sept. 29: Role of a bus driver.

Sept. 30: Role of a ferryboat operator who takes children for a ride.

Oct. 1st: Role of a pussycat being pulled around in a wagon.

Oct. 2nd: Role of a vicious dog who tries to get out of his kennel. Role of a pilot who has a wreck in his plane.

We see at a glance that Michael's central problems take a different form from those of Perry and Lola. Although he, too, occasionally reflects the presence of a shadowy threat (i.e., the pilot whose plane is wrecked), nevertheless, he feels sufficiently self-assured to operate a ferry and rescue other children from a burning house. On the other hand, the fact that he excludes others in so many of his roles clearly indicates some difficulty in his relationships. This puzzled his teachers until they discovered that he was never permitted to play with any children in his neighborhood because his parents thought they were too rough for him.

Obviously, these brief notations do not present a very full or rich picture, since their brevity eliminates all nuances and shades of feeling. Nevertheless, like black and white line drawings, they bring out distinctive patterns of play with impressive clarity and economy. The value of this technique of interpretation will be more apparent if we now summarize similar notations on four other children from the same group who have no outstanding difficulties.

The first child, Paul, plays a great variety of roles. On succeeding days he operates a train but yields this central role to another child; plays a lion who attacks and is chased away; pilots a plane carrying two passengers; plays pussycat on a leash; initiates a ferryboat captain role and invites teachers along; plays a fireman who saves children from a burning house; drives a taxi into a streetcar and kills his passengers; plays a cop who is shot by robbers; unwillingly takes a baby role and abandons it; plays he is a vicious dog. These roles are notable for the wide range of feelings and relationships they portray. Paul can be submissive as well as dominating—yielding as well as assertive. His flexibility in the play situation indicates less pressure from within and more adaptability to circumstances than are shown by the three children discussed above.

The next child, Jennie, took the role of a mother who goes to the park with her husband, holding hands; played house and school; initiated fire-engine play but told another child to drive; played train—drove, collected tickets, let down bunks, sold food; played mother; played house and school again; played school and pussycat; pretended to go to the beach where she sold food and rode on the carousel. Although house-play predominates, note the liberal sprinkling of other roles. Tragedy is noticeably absent from her dramatic play, while pleasant and stimulating things that can happen to a young child in the course of a fairly varied family life are distinctly present.

During five days Zephyr took these roles: a child in house-play, a ferryboat passenger, a pussycat, a baby who fights back when spanked, an airplane passenger. Although many of these were comparatively subordinate, she was actually quite able to stand up against a "bossy" mother and showed the best self-acceptance of any in the group. To be positive and well-poised a child does not need to assert control over others.

The fourth child, Teddy, exhibits both variety and sameness in his roles. On succeeding days he plays a cowboy, a bus driver who forces passengers off the bus, a pilot who fights and shoots down Japs and Germans, a doctor who inoculates his patients, a ferryboat operator who collects fares and forces some children off the boat, and a storekeeper who sells candy and ice cream but will not accept any competition. Here is a child who can play many dominant roles appropriately, and one who cooperates with most children, yet is able to eject those he doesn't care for. There is no need to resort to animal roles to be assertive or to baby roles to be submissive. This boy is ready to meet his world squarely and is confident enough to insist on his own terms.

The foregoing illustrations were used to emphasize how much insight even a few brief but consistently recorded notes can yield. These records and the fuller accounts given before together suggest four general aspects of a child and his world which are most strikingly and consistently revealed through his dramatic play: (1) the characteristic "flavor" of the world from his point of view; (2) his own pressing needs (without necessary reference to the basis of these needs); (3) his conception of himself; and (4) the specific problems and preoccupations with which he is concerned at a given time. Some of these aspects have been discussed briefly in Chapter II. Here we shall develop each of them further in order to bring into focus the less obvious clues to the child's experience contained in dramatic play.

Sensing the Flavor of a Child's World

In constructing a full picture of any child's world, we must discover which of his experiences are having the greatest impact on him and which are hardest for him to assimilate. For these purposes dramatic play is unexcelled. One of the best clues, here, is sheer repetition—of theme, of relationships or simply of general flavor as demonstrated by the following two excerpts from the records of Lilly, aged four. Although this little girl does many different things in the course of her play, she does all of them in a certain way, presenting a picture of rather distraught domination. The reader might try to visualize her family life from these play episodes and compare the image that results with the information given later.

Lilly has built a car out of some horses and planks and three children sit passively on it. Lilly seats herself beside Mitch saying: "You're the father, Mitch." She jumps up immediately, saying, "I always have to jump up," darts around into the sand pit, scoops up dirt with both hands, and piles it onto the floor of the car. She says to Penny, "Penny, you're very foolish." [So far as the observer knew, Penny had done nothing.] Penny sits there looking dreamily away. Lilly announces: "Now I'll go"; [to Mitch] "Start the motor." She climbs up on the wire mesh fence near the head of the car, jounces up and down making motor noises. She jumps off and runs out into the middle of the play yard, jumps up and down, wriggling her body and waving her arms. She comes back to the "car," and pulls at the floor boards. Penny and Joyce seem to ignore all this frantic activity, but Penny moves her leg and in doing so pushes one of the wooden horses a little. Lilly hits her, "Get out now, Penny, get out." Penny does not move. Lilly rushes down to the end of the car and piles three loose boards into a haphazard crisscross arrangement, saying, "I'm getting angry." She comes back to the car saying, "Now there is room for me to get in." Gets into the "car" saying, "I'm the mother." She jumps up immediately, shouting to the children who were about to move the boards she had piled up a moment before, "Leave the boards there." She turns and says to Mitch, "Mitch, look, I have us good now." Then she darts around into the sand pit again and scoops up more dirt onto the floor of the car, saying, "That's all we need for tomorrow, cause we going today away." Then, "Hey, poppa [Mitch], where we going today away?" She looks eagerly into Mitch's face and repeats this question three times. Mitch does not respond. Lilly then says, "Hey, Florida, O.K." Penny suggests, "Jamaica." Lilly says emphatically, "Jamaica we don't go. We just go———" leaving the sentence unfinished.

She clutches at Mitch who has started to climb out of the car saying, "What shall we do now? You're the father, don't you know?"

It will probably come as no surprise that Lilly is an only child who lives with two very managing females, and that her relationship to her father has never been well established. Her mother is described as high-strung and hysterical, always hurrying the child and pushing her around; her grandmother also seems to be dominating and demanding. The little girl's actions, full of "busy movements" without apparent plan or purpose, show the influence of a tense, poorly organized individual, and her management of her "babies" reveals the kind of training to which she has been subjected.

After some experience in matching children's play with home relationships, it is not too difficult to reconstruct a child's conception of his more influential parent. Although this picture is occasionally distorted by wishful thinking, it tends, in the main, to be accurate. From a glance at the following dramatic play of a rather belligerent four-year-old girl named Cathy, it might be possible to guess that she comes from an upper middle-class group where "refined" behavior is the rule, that she is subjected to many social pressures, and that she is handled inconsistently by her mother.

Cathy sat on one of the bars of a Jungle Gym and kept saying: "Look at me, honey!" Then: "I am in the house, and my both children are outside. Come in this very moment, you are both very naughty children!" . . . "Josie, you're my child now, and you're always bad." She hits her to "make her good." "I will take care of you, Josie." "Let's make a pie for dessert," she orders. Beth is the cook, but Cathy supervises and then takes over because "I'm not very pleased." She makes "pies" for a while, and has Vivian "stay home." Beth asked Cathy if she could play with Leila, another three-year-old. Cathy: "Yes, only if you and she play with me." Beth agreed. When we had to go in she said: "Oh dear, good-bye my lovely children," and then proceeded to instruct the others that we "must go inside now. . . ." Cathy then walked around the room wheeling the doll carriage, interrupting conversation or play to say "don't" or "You mustn't." Rory "came home from work," and Cathy ordered him to get the "sisters" for supper. She ordered them to sit down and eat.

The reason for a child's assumption of roles is not always so apparent. For example, little girls who appear to be extremely well adjusted and spontaneous sometimes take the role of a dominating mother. Investigation often reveals, however, that they are exposed to parental demands and standards that are inappropriate to them—but they have come to nursery centers at an early age and have been very fortunate in the groups which they attended. Although they have successfully learned to get along with others and to regard their pleasures and desires as legitimate while at school, their home pressures are, nevertheless, reflected in their dramatic play.

Noting the Child's Needs

Dramatic play reflects not only the flavor of the child's life but the needs which his experiences generate. We have already illustrated its value in disclosing needs that do not come to light in other preschool activities—for example, the passivity needs of Teddy and Warren or the aggressive impulses of Perry in the "Bambi" episode. Now we propose to show how brightly it illuminates many needs that *do* appear, more or less darkly, in the child's behavior at other times.

Bobby, a three-and-one-half-year-old who could not be persuaded to leave his mother's side, played out the following incident one day.

"You know, this is a ferryboat,"—leans over to tell mother who has been joined by teacher. He adds: "Only for trucks.

Only for trucks." Rex hovers over Bobby. Bobby pushes him away, then encloses himself behind sawhorses, watching three children at dramatic play on the other side of the roof. He lays his head down on the wagon. He wiggles his foot, hums, and moves his knees. He has a black toy dog in the wagon with him. He chants: "Fenced in. Fenced in."

Bobby's eloquent satisfaction with his fenced-in state suggests an enormous need for security and a fear of the world beyond the "fence." Observation of his mother throws light on this behavior. Within a few minutes we find her insisting that he cannot have a wagon if he does not play with it—criticizing him for getting dirty—refusing to interrupt her knitting when he asks for attention—quickly demanding that he show her something he has picked up from the floor. In view of this constant vigilance and reproof, it is quite understandable that he seeks the safety of being fenced in and at the same time needs the reassurance of his mother's physical presence. Furthermore, being fenced in may symbolize self-protection against a very real desire to reach out, since any venturesomeness has consistently brought disapproval in its wake.

The play of Harvey, a boy of almost four, tells another story, and one that is different from what it at first appears to be.

Harvey was playing with Karen, his twin sister. Karen began to push the carriage. Harvey said, "Let me be the baby, Karen," and started to talk like a baby. He got into the carriage. Karen pushed him around the room as he squinted his eyes and cried. She stopped the carriage, patted his shoulder, saying, "Don't cry, baby." He squirmed around, put his thumb in his mouth, and swayed his body.

Josie came to the carriage and wanted to push Harvey. He jumped out and hit her in the face. She walked away almost crying. He went to her, put his arm around her and said, in a sympathetic manner, "Come, you be the baby, I'll push you in the carriage." She climbed in. He ran and got the dog and gave it to her, saying, "Here, baby." She smiled and began to play with the dog. He went to the housekeeping corner, got a cup and held it to her mouth. He smacked his lips, looking at her, smiling. He pushed her around in the carriage. Karen ran to him and said, "Harvey, let me push the carriage. I'll be the mamma, you be the daddy." Harvey said "O.K.," and reached his hand in his pocket and gave her money. He said, "Bye, baby," waving his hand. He went to the shelf, took a hammer and a bed, then sat on the floor and vigorously nailed spokes in it. Karen pushed the carriage to where he was. She said, "What are you doing, Harvey?" He said, "I'm making a bed." He looked at Josie and smiled.

This episode proves—if proof be needed—that the understanding of children's dramatic play is no simple matter. On the surface it appears to be a direct reflection of a rather congenial home life. Yet other observations belie this interpretation, for time and again Harvey's play records reveal immaturity and tension, constant recourse to "baby" play and overweening delight in the aggressive use of water. In addition, it was discovered that his mother paid scant attention to him, leaving his father to supply whatever "mothering" he got. Seen within the framework of this kind of information, this dramatic episode takes its place not as a picture of what Harvey's parents are like, but as a revelation of what he thinks they should be like.

A fragment of play that occurred later the same morning seems to reflect this boy's real world more accurately. Compare the casual quality of the attention that he, the "mama," gives to his "baby," with the concern he had showed for her earlier:

Harvey ran to the carriage and said to Karen, "Come on, mother, take the carriage and teddy bear out." Karen said, "Harvey, you be the mother, I'm the baby." She climbed into the carriage and he pushed her into the gymnasium. Karen was crying like a baby. He stopped and gave her a stick for a bottle, then left her in the carriage and went to the wagon. He filled it with blocks and pulled them saying, "Peep, peep," jumping up and down. When he ran by Karen, she called, "Mamma, mamma." He stopped abruptly, ran to her and gave her a piece of paper, pushed her for a minute, and went back to the wagon. Later he passed the carriage again. Karen was screaming, "Give me a pencil." This time he did not stop. . . .

These contrasting scenes make it clear that in sensing needs through dramatic play, we must distinguish sharply between play as a projection of actual situations and as an expression of the wishes or hopes of the child. Occasionally these two facets may be blended into one episode, but generally they come to light at different times. This is another argument for continued observation of the child rather than emphasis on one or two samples of behavior.

Discovering What the Child Thinks of Himself

Many fleeting incidents in dramatic play combine to give us information concerning the child's ideas about himself, his role in life, and what others think of him. Consider, for example, the behavior of Donnie who lived alone with his mother and was treated more like a girl than a boy. He consistently refused to play father and spontaneously chose motherlike roles instead. Apparently it was easier for him to think of himself as feminine than to attempt a real masculine identification. Like other boys in similar circumstances, Donnie was unable to protect himself when attacked, and shied away from aggressive play. The upshot was that he played with little girls like another little girl.

The record of Jackie, described earlier in this chapter gives us an instance in which the child's conception of himself emerges in new and vivid form. In building and manipulating his truck it is evident that he is testing himself against a threatening environment. As he succeeds in holding his own in handling heavy blocks and tires and in competition with assertive playmates, his self-confidence grows and he becomes bigger and bigger in his own estimation.

In another vein, many instances from the play of Tessie, a rather destructive child, reveal that she has all but accepted the name of "bad girl." Given the choice of Hallowe'en characters to play, she wants to be the witch. When asked to choose a mask, she picks a threatening one. When her group is engaged in rhythms and her teacher announces that they will all play rabbit, she casts herself as a "bad bunny." You may remember that Tessie's play was cited earlier as an example of reversal of roles. Happily, her constructive playing of the mother role in that episode indicates that she still can think of herself as something other than "bad girl."

It seems to us that the teacher has a golden opportunity for correcting the child's misconceptions of himself. (Of course, she must be able to recognize them first.) The techniques of the psychodrama were worked out precisely for the purpose of demonstrating to individuals their own unsuspected capacities. Our own observations of the formation of limited and rigid self-conceptions within the nursery school age range suggest a fruitful field for the application of psychodramatic techniques. When children show these faulty self-estimates, it might be useful for the teacher to assign roles requiring behavior not habitually shown—a "good" mother for a "bad" girl, a bold and "bossy" policeman for the timid lad, a "fighter champ" for the fearful one. This procedure has not been widely used with very young children, and it must be applied with tact and skill. But the fact that it parallels so closely what children do spontaneously under favorable circumstances suggests a wealth of promise for the future.

Detecting Children's Preoccupations and Problems

There is little need to present fresh examples of the ways in which children reveal their specific concerns, since we have already touched upon this function of dramatic play in almost every other approach to it. But there is one question that deserves special attention: How can teachers use dramatic play as a clue to the child's life outside the nursery group? In answer, we should like to offer several selections from the play of Julie, a three-and-one-half-year-old child.

A few facts about Julie will facilitate the interpretation of her play. The little girl first aroused her teacher's concern by her egocentric, destructive, and aggressive behavior. She masturbated excessively during rest periods, and was extremely negativistic: "One sure way of getting Julie to say 'no' is to ask her to do something." She lived alone with her mother, an embittered woman who had borne her out of wedlock. The mother's vowed ambition was to "harden" little Julie so that her daughter would not suffer as she had.

In the first record cited below, note Julie's insistence on playing the part of the "father," a nonexistent figure in her life. The way in which she plays the role indicates what she thinks fathers do in families and what children can expect of them. Observe, next, her eagerness to take the place of the baby when that role is vacated, her mounting pleasure in the attention she achieves from wetting herself, and finally, her restort to masturbation when the attention of the "mamma" is taken away from her.

Julie watches mother—baby play and then says, "Knock knock, I'll be the father." Lola, "Well, get off the bike then." Julie: "How is the baby today? I'll get something to eat. I'll go in my car." Lola: "Could you get some baby food?" Julie: "No, I can't because they don't have any but I'll see if I can get some other kind." Julie rides to one corner, and says to herself, "No baby food." She rides to another corner and picks up one of the rectangular blocks, then rides back to the "house" and gives it to Lola, pretending it is a box of baby food.

Bud, the "baby," cuts his finger on a ladder and runs into the nursery. "You know what? I'll be your baby," says Julie, "Do you know what I'm gonna do? I'm gonna ride my bike in the house." Lola says, "No, baby, you are going to have your supper now." "No, ride the bike first," says Julie. Lola turns about and looks at Julie in a very annoyed manner. Her hands are on her hips and her lips are tightly squeezed together. Julie says, "Mommie, I wet my clothes—change the baby's diaper." Lola puts her arms around Julie and attempts to carry Julie into the house. She rushes to an imaginary room and snatches a diaper off a line, then tells Julie to hold her hips up and slips the diaper under her, and pretends to powder her. Pantomime of fastening the pins is very realistic. Julie smiles (the first time I have seen her smile) and says with bright eyes, "I wet again." Lola goes through the same actions, grumbling a little to herself and says, "Bad baby." As soon as the procedure is completed Julie says with even more joy, almost a giggle, "I did it again. . . ." Lola is distracted by the other children. Julie is inside the play space and is apparently enjoying the chance to lie down. She rubs her eyes. . . . Her hands now approach her genital area. She is lying on her stomach now and swaying her hips back and forth.

Julie occasionally wet her bed during this period. While it did not happen often, it must have been significant to her, since six months later she greeted a former playmate with "Remember when we wet our beds?" and then giggled delightedly. Undoubtedly it had served as a means of annoying her mother as well as of capturing attention. Her conception of a father, while meager, is related to the service that he can render his child. At a later date it became clear that she fantasied the father as the "all good" parent, who would support her in her hatred of the mother and give her everything she failed to supply. Since the little girl had no real father, she could hardly be expected to test this unrealistic conception.

The highlights of a record made about six weeks later indicate a continued preoccupation with many of the same ideas.

Julie and Addie are planning to play house and Addie says, "You don't need a daddy." Julie insists that you do. Addie: "I had two daddies and one died. Do you have a daddy?" Julie replies, "No," and rides away quickly, saying, "Let's race—Yahaaaaaaa." She overturns her bike and has some difficulty in extricating herself. . . .

Now Teddy is being drawn around in the wagon, whining periodically. Julie speaks to him in a pampering tone, "Does the baby want a toy—Does the baby want another toy?" As Teddy replies "yes" to every suggestion, she picks up things she finds on the ground to take the place of toys—paper, rope, etc. "Have you got to go to the bathroom, little baby? Baby, you can wet your pants like that, bumpty bump." (She has just gone over a bump, and as she says this to him she looks back and smiles such an affected overly protective smile, it is comical.) "You know what, we're going visiting on the train. Mommy has the tickets." Julie takes Teddy's hand, then suddenly plunges forward and says, "Oh, here is the train. Come on, baby." Julie and Teddy now sit in the wagon and Julie stares into space. "Now we are here." Teddy says, "I don't have nothing to play with." Julie picks up a piece of paper and says, "Here read this. You know your daddy does that. He's at work. He's sick." She puts her arm protectively on Teddy's shoulder. "Tomorrow is your birthday. You sit in your carriage now." Julie walks away for a second and then approaches Teddy, singing, "Happy birthday to you." (As she does this she is clapping her hands and marching with a hopping rhythm.) "Daddy is going to send you a present." Julie takes Teddy's hand and says, "Hello, little baby, two years old. Here comes your daddy now. He brought a new shirt for you. Maybe we'll go to the show, me and daddy."

As this record indicates, Julie's play is beginning to reveal both her concern about where her daddy might be and her expectations of what would happen if he should appear. The intensity of her pleasure in what the daddy will bring is pathetic in relation to the facts and suggests how keenly she feels what is lacking. Again we find that she believes urinating in one's clothes is a special "baby" privilege, and that a "good" mother would permit it.

A month later Julie expresses the same themes through the medium of miniature life toys as well as dramatic play. She makes a trip on the train and again brings the "daddy" into her play. This time, however, she grows bolder and fully assumes the part of the baby, playing it through in a very realistic fashion.

Julie takes out various toys, showing special interest in the train, into which she puts a nude adult doll. She puts the baby in a play pen. Observer: "Who's the baby living with?" Julie: "The daddy and the mommy." (She goes on searching through the box.) "Where are they?" Julie: "They're at home." (She points to the "house" where there is only the baby doll.) "There they are." (She puts the trains together again.) Observer: "Who's this in the train?" Julie: "That's the girl." "Where is she going?" Julie: "Her going shopping." "Alone?" "Yeah. Her going to get her mommy some wax." (This refers to a "shopping" trip Julie and the observer had taken that morning.) . . . Observer: "Where's the daddy?" Julie: "He's at work." "What kind of work does he do?" No answer. "What's the little girl going to do downtown?" Julie: "Her's the baby. I'm the baby and you're the mommy. AHnnnn." (She pretends to cry.) Observer: "Don't cry, little baby. What's the matter?" Julie: "I want my bottle." "All right, baby, I'll get it for you. (Goes to kitchen to get bottle from sterilizer.) Here, baby, here's your bottle. Do you want to sit in mommy's lap to eat?" Julie sucks on the bottle and climbs into the observer's lap and lies back.

This went on for a few seconds and then Julie jumped up and went over to the toy shelf and brought back a purse for the observer. Then she brought another. Observer: "Two pocketbooks." "Yes, I buyed them for you. Here's your pocket-

book, mommy. Here's your 'nother one. You got another one.
You buy so much for yourself. Here's another one. Here's
another one (about four purses piled up). So much you buy.
Why do you buy so much, mommy?" Observer: "Because I
have to feed my little baby." Julie: "Here's some money,
mommy. Do you need some money?" "Yes, I need it to go
to the grocery. . . ." Julie (reaching over and getting a magazine to look at): "This is you, mommy (pointing to a picture
of a woman). And that's my daddy (pointing to a picture of
a man). When's my Daddy coming home?" Observer: "Pretty
soon. What are we going to do when daddy comes home?"
"I'm going to sing "Happy Birthday" to him because he has
a birthday. . . ."

Julie got into a carriage and was wheeled back home. She
opened her purse and said, "I want some money, mommy."
The observer offered her some pretend money which she put
in her purse saying, "This is my purse." Then Julie handed the
observer a toy phone: "Your phone is ringing." The observer
answered and asked whether "they" wanted to speak with
Julie and handed the phone back to her. She picked it up
and said, "Hello, daddy. What do you want? Do you want
mommy? Here's mommy." She handed the phone back to
the observer who told "daddy" to be home in time for supper
and hung up.

Julie repeated the baby play with various teachers after
this episode. They later learned that she had been asking
questions about her father, and that she may have over-
heard her mother discuss a trip that involved a possible
marriage. The episode also foreshadows a development which
took place several months later, when the separation between Julie and her mother seemed imminent. She then
began to steal pennies from the other children. The meaning
of money to Julie as something your mother gives you and
the timing of the stealing are both significant in explaining
her behavior.

Sometimes the importance of a simple episode remains
unrecognized until it is related to other samples of play be-

havior and evaluated in the light of the dynamics of development. Jackie, the little boy whose aggressive animal play was discussed earlier in this chapter, furnishes a case in point. At one time he seemed to be seeking the kind of constant and exclusive attention adults give to babies—help in putting on his clothes, putting his things away, etc.—at another time he seemed intent on establishing his power over others through negativism, destructiveness, and especially through annoying those bigger than himself. It therefore seems reasonable to suppose that his need to be a baby was somehow dangerous to him, a sign of weakness against which he had to protect himself by demonstrating strength. But why is this child afraid of being weak? What threat does babyhood with its implications of weakness hold for him? One answer is suggested by the fact that he is the youngest of four children and therefore may have had to exert himself constantly to keep from being exploited and overlooked. However, further inquiry into his play furnishes clues to another and more specific source of anxiety, as indicated by the following excerpts.

The group was playing a game in which each child took a turn running behind an easel, pretending it was a door. When he knocked, the teacher invited him to come in and asked his name, then pretended he was a turkey. When Jackie knocked the following incident took place. Teacher: "Who's there? Come in. Who are you?" Jackie: "I am Jackie." Teacher: "We are very hungry. Let's eat Jackie for breakfast." But Jackie did not consent and ran back to the door again. After going through the same procedure once more, he came to the teacher and lay across her lap. She pretended to put him to sleep and explained to the children that they were going to celebrate by eating a turkey. Teacher: "What part do you want?" Children: "I want the nose"—"I want the mouth"— "I want the legs." Jackie wriggled uncomfortably and ran away. When another child took his place, he joined the game as one of the "eaters." The game went on. Charlie: "I want the heart of the turkey." Jackie: "I want some too." Charlie: "I want to eat the whole belly." Jackie: "Bang! Bang! (with his gun). I want a big slice. I want the pee-pee."

Somewhat later Jackie was playing with Lola. Lola: "If you give me your gun, I will be your friend." He ignored her remarks, and placing his gun suggestively, announced: "This is my pee-pee. I broke my pee-pee and put it back again. My pee-pee is sticking out dis way." A few minutes later Jackie was calling for help because Lola insisted on playing with the gun. Pointing to the gun he said, "Dat a turkey, dat a black turkey." Lola (cajoling), "Let me play with it." Jackie (generously), "Wrap it up so no one will see it." He handed her the gun with a napkin. "Now I can play with your toys."

Whatever the origin of his apprehension might be, it is clear that Jackie is preoccupied with thoughts of a detachable penis; that he is uncomfortable when put in the position of a possible victim of the kind of thing he would like to do (i.e., to eat the turkey's pee-pee); and that he cherishes his gun, which he has used as an extended penis. When he does permit Lola to have the gun, notice that it must be done secretly. Obviously, these are the events of only one day and thus only suggestive. Their importance, however, is underlined later on, when he makes a snow man with a huge penis out of clay, announcing, "This is a daddy one." Immediately afterward, he makes what he calls a "little tiny one" without any penis.

Several months after this incident, Jackie went for a walk with his class and stopped to admire a horse. He crowded very close to examine him, then remarked, "He ought not to make a wee anymore. He can't." Another child countered with, "Oh, yes, he can because there's his hole." Jackie insisted that he could not and left the horse very reluctantly. Clearly he was still preoccupied with anatomy and anatomical differences and seemed to have some very confused ideas about them.

All these bits and pieces from Jackie's behavior suggest, first, that he has compared his own anatomy with that of an adult male and wondered at the differences; second, that the loss of a penis and urination have been associated in his experience (perhaps in a threat to his own penis if he does not stop wetting himself); and third, that he is wondering how penises might be removed—whether it might be done, perhaps, by biting. Is this not enough to make a child worry? If this is a world in which a boy can lose his penis because he wets himself, is it not important for him to prove his strength by aggressive behavior, and by so doing, to reassure himself that he can retain his body intact?

A kindly and understanding teacher, sensing a need for reassurance, could surely help this boy. Actually, Jackie gave his teacher many openings—for instance, he never left a clay session without having made something with a very emphatic penis. If nothing more, these incidents could have formed the basis for tactful inquiry about his experience at home, perhaps through the grandmother or an older brother or sister. In the hands of an experienced person, the boy himself might even have been the source of information.

In Jackie's play there were many other intimations of confusion about bodily functions; for example, fantasies concerning feces and food.

On one occasion Jackie was playing with another child in the doll corner and pretended to call up the doctor on the telephone. Jackie: "Hello, doctor, can you come up now?" Other child: "I am coming up." Jackie: "But are you the cop or the doctor?" Other child: "Hello. Get out." Jackie (unperturbed): "I am talking to you. I am a bogey man. Here is some cocky for breakfast. . . ."

On another occasion, taking the part of a cook, he poured water out of some tins, giving each child a bit, "There's some cocky in it."

The repetition of these themes suggests that the boy was asking for help. His teacher, however, tended to ignore his references to body parts and body functions, believing that he would get over it. If the basis for his original aggressiveness had been a generalized one, such as a need to defend himself against brothers and sisters, or a lack of adequate mothering, he probably would have responded simply to the calm and secure atmosphere of the Center. But the real problem was not touched by ignoring it, and we can surmise that it was based more specifically on fears or fantasies of attacks on his body, and therefore required special attention.

Jackie's case clearly indicates that, before a teacher can understand the meanings in a child's dramatic play, she must be willing to accept these meanings, whatever they are. As it was, his teacher either overlooked or rejected an opportunity to be of service to the youngster. And Jackie is not an isolated instance. Many other little boys give evidence of confusion about their anatomy and their sex roles. If female teachers cannot handle this problem with equanimity, perhaps it would be wise to have at least one well-oriented male available in every group dealing with young children. Or perhaps women teachers need to be told in a very matter-of-fact manner that little boys do sometimes suffer threats to their persons, that they worry about these threats, and that a reassuring word from an adult can do much to help them cope with this potentially damaging experience.

Time after time, dramatic play incidents yield clues to the meaning of puzzling behavior. One three-year-old boy who lived in a fatherless household frequently played a mother role with little girls. Occasionally he said he was the father, but the way in which he acted this role was definitely feminine. His confusion as to whether he was a boy or a girl was demonstrated in the following scene.

He was playing with a little girl out-of-doors, when he turned to an observer and remarked, "You can't see her pee-pee." Then the observer asked, "What are pee-pees?" He replied, "What all girls have." He unbuttoned his pants and showed his penis, and permitted the little girl to fondle it saying, "Don't tell teacher." He needed help in getting his pants buttoned and approached the observer (a man). When the observer asked why he had unbuttoned his pants, he said, "We show our pee-pees now." The little girl said, "He'll tell teacher." But the child replied, "No, he won't. He likes it too. . . . He better not tell." Then he turned to the observer and said in a threatening manner, "Don't tell." As the observer started to leave, the little girl called to him, "We have nicer things than you."

Several things are clear from this incident and from the character of the child's dramatic play. It seems somehow better to him to be a little girl than to be a little boy. However, he is definitely confused by the discrepancy between his self-identification and his anatomy. He has something little girls don't have, but since he wants to be a little girl he gets around that by denying the difference and asserting that little girls have "pee-pees"—but one simply does not see them. A lurking sense of kinship with male creatures, however, is also indicated when he says, concerning the observer, "He likes it, too," implying a difference in point of view between the female teacher and the male observer. All this indicates why it was necessary for the child to repudiate his masculinity. He clearly implied that his teacher, a woman, did not "like it," and knowing, as we do, that little children frequently expect from their teachers the same kind of treatment they get from their mothers, we might venture the guess that he believes his mother did not "like it" either. If this is so, his determination to be a little girl rather than a little boy, in spite of anatomy, becomes understandable.

We do not suggest that this interpretation is, in any sense, conclusive. Our object is rather to show how observation of dramatic play, taken in conjunction with other incidents, can suggest reasonable hypotheses which call for further investigation.

In general, the most frequently expressed conflicts in children's dramatic play refer to their dual need to receive comforting and to express aggressiveness. They alternate between the small and weak baby and the big and powerful pilot or cowboy. Sometimes the power figures are emphasized while the desires for babying are indicated only in subtle and subdued ways. At other times the longing for mothering is uppermost, while the aggressive needs find obscure and tortuous outlets. In any case, judging from our records, children need reassurance concerning both their desires for protection and warmth, and their needs to express rage and hate. They must be helped to see not only that each of these is acceptable in itself, but that they are not incompatible—that the youngster who sometimes wants to hurt and destroy is still considered worthy of being loved, and that wishing to be cared for and cuddled is not an indication of weakness and unworthiness. But before these attitudes can be conveyed convincingly to the children, the teachers themselves must be fully and sympathetically aware of them.

Progress through Dramatic Play

In the second chapter we referred to the value of dramatic play in bringing together the child's unverbalized fantasies and the demands and offerings of reality. It was suggested that in the course of his play he could restructure the world closer to his heart's desire, and possibly free himself from some of the limitations imposed by personal history and circumstance. As we have examined record after record, we have witnessed the mirroring of the child's world and we have seen his attempts to gather the strength to cope with its pressures. But a two-pronged question still remains: How well do children succeed in the attempt to use dramatic play in assimilating life, and does the group give the individual child the freedom he needs for growth?

To answer these questions, we propose to follow one child through several play situations. Donnie, a boy of four, lives at home with his mother and a female lodger, but there is no father in the family picture. His teachers describe him as a "quiet and scared kid, shy of children and adults." When he joined the group he would not take part in any of the usual activities; when messy play was in progress he would say, "My mother does not want me to do this; I will get my clothes dirty." Though he conformed to the letter in routines, he was a poor eater and seemed to move slowly in every way. The only things he enjoyed were the doll corner and "walking around with a gun."

Donnie's mother complained that he was "stubborn and contrary" and asked the teachers to break him of these habits and teach him to get along with other children. He had never been separated from her before he came to the Center. She reported that he was allergic to dust and cat's hair, and "very sensitive" to strong winds. Several times she was observed to admonish him about cleanliness. To keep his hair out of his eyes she used a "bobby pin."

From this brief description it is evident that this little boy had much to confuse and oppress him—a fatherless home, exacting standards of obedience and cleanliness, a possible nudge toward femininity.

Let us now watch Donnie as he tries to tackle some of his problems in play. In the first record we find him playing gently with a little girl, apparently assuming a feminine role.

Donnie and Alice are pushing two doll carriages round and round the room. Donnie seems to be very happy this morning. As he pushes his carriage into an enclosure, he turns to Alice, saying, "Bring yours in this way—this way," indicating the opening. She continues on, however, and he follows her to the enclosure on the other side of the room. They stand inside. Donnie goes over to the stove and puts a block in the oven without saying anything. They go out again and push their carriages across the room to the enclosure. Donnie lies down on the play bed for a moment, then gets up and they walk back to the house holding hands. They sit down there for a moment and, holding hands, walk back to the enclosure. They sit on the bed and whisper.

In the next episode, recorded five months later, he joins a group of boys in much more exciting play. However, though there are indications that he would like to do a little destruction, the enthusiastic creation of the "fire" by the other children proves too much for timid Donnie. Alone later, he fulfills himself in a milder fashion.

When asked what he wants to do, Donnie says, "Just play." All the children have left the table but he sits there slowly sipping his juice and eating his cracker. He goes over to join his friend Rex who, with Eddie, is building blocks. Donnie kneels and watches them, saying nothing. The two other boys make a ramp for a car to glide down and Donnie makes a humming sound and then, "Be-eep, beep," as the car slides down. Jackie has now joined his group. Donnie picks up a small square block and puts it on Rex's head and says, "I wanta bump you on your head." Jackie grabs the block away and has a tussle for the block with Donnie, but Donnie quickly gets it as it falls down. The three children pile blocks on top of the car and Donnie says, "Put 'em all in the garbage can, Hee." Next they pretend they are burning the car up. Rex is the leader in this play. He announces, "I'm goin' in the fire," and lies down over the blocks. Jackie follows suit. Donnie is somewhat hesitant about getting in and draws back. Jackie: "C'mon, Donnie, let's burn him [Rex] up." Donnie starts to whine about the car which is under the pile of blocks and tries to get it out: "I want it *now*." The other children excitedly drop bricks on Rex, and Donnie half-heartedly does the same. He says to the teacher, "He's burned up," and points to Rex. Donnie still is most anxious to get the car, manages to get hold of it, but it is soon taken away by Rex. He scratches his head and gives up, then picks up two blocks, puts them on the floor, and says to no one in particular, "These are my skates." He repeats this several times and says, "Get out of the way," then puts the blocks away.

Although Donnie was quite ready for some private release, as he indicated by bumping a block on Rex's head and suggesting that they put the toys in the garbage can, he was not yet sufficiently sure of himself to join the other children in their fantasies of destruction.

In the third record we have evidence of an attempt to change his conception of himself.

Ivan, Rex, and Donnie have made a large block structure in a sort of square. The observer asks what this is and Donnie replies, "A jeep car." He is standing looking at the car when Buddy comes along and tries to knock it down. A few of the blocks tumble and Ivan yells; Donnie and Rex build the car up again. During all this Donnie has said nothing. Suddenly, as if he had been thinking it over all this while, he says in a plaintive way, "I have to drive, let me in, let me in!" Despite having said this he does nothing about it, probably because he is afraid of being pushed away. . . . Donnie gets some long blocks to add to the "car" and Buddy tries to snatch them away. He hangs on to the blocks and yells; the teacher comes over to the rescue and Donnie quietly continues to build. Again, as he is holding on to the long block and trying to bring it over to Ivan, Buddy tries to take it away. This time Donnie cries out to Ivan for help. Buddy goes away and Donnie gives his block to Ivan.

This episode takes on real significance when we recall that for many young children a car symbolizes an instrument of great power, and that to drive it is to be in a position of mastery. However, Donnie's attempt to overcome his helplessness is still in the realm of fantasy.

In the next episode the boy's needs are still more fully revealed and we clearly see that the so-called "car" serves a dual purpose—to aggrandize and to protect. It gives him at once a "cozy" place away from the encroachment of others and an instrument of power through which he can realize his hidden longings. Moreover, the achievement of building a car emboldens him to the point where he can at least begin to defy an old enemy.

Again Donnie says, "I wanta play with the car." It seems as if he is the "boss" as he says to Rex, "Get me two blocks to put here." Rex complies and Donnie says, "Get in the car." They both climb in. The two boys continue building their car and proudly display it to the teacher. Donnie: "We could sleep in the car, couldn't we?" He seems very satisfied.

They sit inside their "car." Donnie to Leila: "You can't come and get us." He says this in the rather plaintive way that is characteristic of almost everything he expresses verbally. Buddy, who is in a very aggressive mood, comes along to disturb the peace. As Donnie watches him come over, his whole face puckers in fear. Bud pushes him; Donnie gets quite red and tries to push him off. He whines and sticks out his tongue (which is the first sign this observer had seen of an attempt at aggressive defense). Bud spits in Donnie's face and he continues to whine. Bud is led away by the teacher. Donnie and Rex continue to play and discuss their "car." Bud comes along again and knocks down the car. Donnie quietly and patiently starts to rebuild it. Again Bud comes over, and this time Donnie moves away abruptly. Then he sits on the side of the "car" and plays with Rex there.

Unfortunately the enemy thwarts Donnie in the end and he again exposes the impotence which haunts him. But when he is free of other children, in the next scene, he effectively implements his power fantasies. Then, backed by the strength thus gained, he is able to oppose interference with genuine tenacity and bring his play to a successful conclusion.

The children are having their free play in the big gym hall. Donnie sees a small ladder and props it up against the radiator. Oblivious of the others, he climbs it and says to the observer, "Who wants their windows cleaned?" He makes a few cleaning gestures, comes down, holds out his hand and says, "Here, thirty cents." Then he goes off by himself but comes rushing back, his face drawn in anguish, as he sees another child trying to move the ladder away. He manages to get it back, this time without whining or crying for help.

Donnie is now playing another game of his own making. He puts the ladder against the water fountains, above which is a ledge piled with big square blocks. He climbs the ladder, lifts the blocks off one by one and moves them to another place. He tells the observer they are ice. Since they are big and bulky and Donnie is rather small, he strains as he carries them but seems rather proud of his success, looking at the observer as if to say, "Look what I'm doing!" Bud and Donnie have a tussle over one of the blocks. To the observer's surprise, Donnie clings to it with all his strength and manages to keep it (without calling for the teacher). The other children want to join in this game and Donnie readily lets them.

This series of observations shows how persistently a child will struggle to realize himself through play. It also throws light on the forces that oppose him in an arbitrarily organized group, and suggests the importance of the teacher as protector of the interests of the individual child.

Other children may not be so fortunate as Donnie in dealing with their attackers. When groups contain strongly hostile or dominating children along with the weak and timid, the latter are almost invariably blocked in their attempts to play out compensatory roles. Having been overwhelmed from infancy by controlling parents or by older and resentful brothers and sisters, they must continue to knuckle under to aggressive playmates or withdraw from the group's activities. This happens frequently when groups are conducted largely on laissez-faire principles. It is quite possible that a child's development may be retarded if we allow him to be continually dominated in dramatic play.

But when arrangements are made to protect the play of the inhibited child, a startling change frequently takes place. In nursery schools, it may be possible to provide opportunity for more protected play between two low shelves—about 30 inches high and 6 feet long, projecting out from the wall. In this space children needing some protection can play with less interruption and still be in the room, always visible to the teacher but not exposed to other children. The shelves should be on casters so that they may be rolled away when not needed.

One child who might have benefited from such an arrangement is Donnie. He was included in a small group of children, rarely more than four, who were encouraged to stay in their room, while the others were outside, and play with the box of "special toys" mentioned before. Compare the following report of his behavior with the records presented above. Note his boldness with the adult, his insistence on the role of authority, and his self-confidence in dealing with Rex.

Donnie is playing with Rex and says to him three times, "I wanta be the cop, O.K.?" Donnie takes the handcuffs. Suddenly he says to the observer, "Come on. You're going to get locked up." With a serious expression on his face, he leads her off to the block corner. Rex gets up on a chair to look at the fish bowl and Donnie runs to him and says, "Come back here." Donnie pulls him down. . . . They go to the observer and Donnie says to her, "All right, you can come out. You have been in there long enough." He tries to put various children in jail. Suddenly he comes to the observer again and tells her, "I have to put you in jail." Observer: "Why, what did I do?" Donnie: "You hit somebody." He takes her by the arm and leads her to "jail," saying, "Now you stay in there." He goes through the motions of locking two doors and then leaves. He goes to the teacher and tells her that he will have to lock her up too. He returns to the observer and says, "You can go now."

Donnie gets the pliers and says to Sally, "I'll pinch you." He puts the pliers near her but doesn't touch her. Then he turns to Tim and puts the pliers on his shoulder straps and pinches them. Leaving the children, he returns to the observer, again telling her he has to put her in jail, saying, "I am going to make you nervous and I won't let you out for a long time." He says, "Bang, bang." But the observer shakes her head saying, "You make me nervous." Then Donnie gets the hammer and pretends to hammer the observer. She pretends to cry, says she is very nervous. Rex comes to watch. The observer says she needs a doctor, so Donnie tells Rex to be the doctor. Rex approaches the observer but Donnie closes in, still making loud "banging" noises, and swinging the hammer. Rex loses interest and leaves. Donnie starts to run after him, and the boys run around quite a bit.

It must be recognized that the new assertiveness shown in this scene occurred only under special circumstances. Donnie is still a boy who, in ordinary play "screams in a whining tone: 'I didn't do anything to you,'" when Rex blocks his car. But the scene does prove that dramatic play is a valuable learning experience and that he has within him the potentiality for change.

The Teacher's Role

Subtle, unobtrusive guidance from the teacher can make dramatic play an instrument of growth, not only for the timid, hesitant child, but for the scattered, aggressive youngster as well. The capacity of this child for constructive functioning is often overlooked and, without the help of a perceptive teacher, may remain completely hidden. In this connection, consider the following scene involving a child, Jed, who was so disturbed in his relations wtih others that he was receiving psychiatric attention.

. . . . Jed now gets the wagon and comes back down the roof. The teacher says, "Are you a delivery man with Christmas packages?" He gets a small box and then a big one and asks the teacher, "Will you help me lift it?" The teacher says, "Yes," and helps him load them onto the wagon. He pulls the wagon with the boxes to the top end of the roof. The teacher goes with him. He gets another load. Julie, watching, asks him to extend the square of elevated boards which she now calls a bedroom. He helps, taking some of the big boxes that he has brought in the wagon. She says delightedly, "He's helping me make the kitchen." Jed goes back and piles three "horses" and a big box on the wagon. The teacher asks, "Do you want help?" "No." Then he finds that his wagon is caught, so he says, "You can turn my steering wheel." He works hard to put the boxes on the wagon and draws them up the roof. Julie jumps up and down as he comes saying, "He's making a kitchen," and repeats it over and over again. Everybody watches Jed build the kitchen. Jed says to the teacher: "I'm going to change it," and with her encouragement, he goes ahead building. . . . Julie is in the kitchen with him now. Jed says, "Shall I build a garage for cars?" At this point the teacher says, "We'll have to go downstairs now but you can build a house down there." At the elevator, Jed says to Julie, "You're going to play with me."

Downstairs, with the help of the teacher, they build a house with the shelves as one wall.

Notice that the play might have disintegrated several times when the teacher recalled it, knit it together, and sent it onward. Her suggestions, however, were made in the spirit of what was going on; she simply offered herself as a helping hand through which the children's own desires could be realized.

Dramatic play can sometimes be extremely useful as a means of integrating a child who does not fit easily into a group—whether because of inner pressures or cultural differences. The technique a teacher uses must obviously be tempered both to the individual child and to the particular group. Nevertheless, some specific examples of the use of dramatic play as a kind of "social cement" should suggest its possibilities.

In the record below, we find a teacher luring a grief-stricken child into group activities. She uses fantasy to get him to accept reality. With her help he discovers that participation in the group has as great a reality value as the situation which caused his grief. Notice how ingeniously she makes Rex the center of the play, gradually induces him to move out of his seclusion, and then leaves him free to continue on his own.

Rex was standing with his face in his coat locker, crying. He turned away when anyone came near him. The children went out on the playground, and he went with them. But he immediately lay down in a corner with his face to the door, kicking his toes on the steps. Allan and Fabian ran to him with toy pistols and tried to get him to play by prodding him. He kicked at them and said, "Go away," in a muffled voice. The children left him alone after that. He lay on his side, sucking a lollypop, and talking and singing to himself, but too low to be heard. He then banged his feet on the door. His teacher went over and shook him gently. She said in a very fierce play voice, "Where did you get that sucker? Give me one at once, do you hear?" Rex: "I got it from the wall." Teacher: "Open wall, and give me a sucker." She banged on the door. Rex: "He ain't got any more." Teacher: "You mean to say you ate the last one?" Rex nodded his head and kicked at her half-heartedly. She boxed with him for a moment. Teacher: "When I come back, you'd better have two suckers ready, understand it?"

Rex curled up again on the step. When the teacher came back with six other children, he paid no apparent attention to them. She banged on the door, and so did Lola and Annie. They yelled, "I want suckers," and the others took it up. Rex (without turning around): "No more." The teacher said in a fierce voice, "What do you mean, no more? I'm going away, and I want some when I get back." To two of the children Rex said, "I got them from the wall." Teacher: "Rex, are you in there? Where are the suckers?" Rex: "No more." He smiled at her and curled up again. The teacher went away with all the other children except Bud, who stayed by Rex. Rex to Bud, without turning, "Is she coming?" The teacher rushed up, followed by more of the children, and said, "Hello. Are you listening?" Rex said, "I haven't got them no more." Teacher: "Did you eat them all up?" "Yes." The teacher said more fiercely, "I want an orange, a big one. Do you understand?" Rex said, "Yes." (He had a big orange in his coat pocket.) The teacher went away again and then rode up on the back of Bud's trike, "We are looking for something. Where are the oranges?" Rex: "I ain't got any." He turned his face to the door again. The children went off. Rex said to the door, "Hop dee, hop dee. Oh-h-h," in a sort of chant or incantation. The teacher, returning, "Have you any suckers or oranges today?" Rex: "No." The teacher, "But we are very hungry. We want some potato salad." Rex said: "We ain't got nothin'." Teacher: "Well, you'd better." They went away. Rex peeked behind him and said to Eric, who had stayed with him, "Now they are coming around again. You sleep over there. Oh boy, I'm going to sleep." The teacher came up and said, "Any suckers?" Rex: "*No*, ain't nuthin'." Teacher: "Nuthin' again? When I come back I want a nice turkey, you understand?" To Bud she said, "Go way down, and we'll get some cranberries." Rex lay down and said, "I'd better turn over." He peeked behind him to see where the teacher was. When she came back he said, "No, nuttin'." She said, "Throw the cranberries on him." The others pretended to and Eric pretended to protect Rex. Rex now followed them out of the corner, and the teacher chased him back, saying: "You've got to stay in this house, and you'd better not come out. Hear?" Rex marched after the teacher, his arms flying, and his chest thrust out, but she chased him back. "Make him stay in here, and don't let him follow us, hear?" Rex to Eric: "Let's go follow them, hear? Let's go." They ran over to the other end of the court, then ran back when they were chased. The teacher said, "I told you to stay in your house and not follow us, hear? Understand that?" Rex said to Eric, "Let's go." He repeated it to the other children who had stayed behind with him. Teacher: "Hold him here. I've got something to read to you." She hunted in one pocket after the other for a book, which she drew out with a flourish. "Rex, you are to stay in this house and not follow us. It says it right here, see? Understand? Come on girls." Four boys stayed with Rex. Three of the boys now pointed toy guns at each other and danced around. Rex was still a little more subdued than usual, but was smiling. He danced a sort of rhumba, pointing the gun at his hips. They sat on the step. Eric: "I'm going to get candy and I'm only going to give Allan any." Allan said to Rex, who was still sucking his lollypop, "You've got candy. Are you happy?" Rex: "Yes. When I get a huge box of candy I'll give you any."

The above record centers around a child who has been accepted by his group but at the time needed persuasion to participate in it. But what of the child who is not accepted by the group, and who, for emotional reasons, is unable to contribute anything to it? This presents a far more exacting problem. While many teachers realize that some children are not yet ready for group life and would profit from solitary attention, they rarely have an opportunity to be alone with them. To illustrate one way of handling this difficulty, we should like to return to Julie, the fatherless child whose play so poignantly revealed both her longing for a father and her need of genuine mothering. The little girl found some of these needs fulfilled through her relationship with her teacher. However, she tended to be insensitive to parallel needs on the part of other children and tried to monopolize attention. In the following protocol, note how the teacher went several steps beyond simple acceptance of Julie's needs and the use of her fantasies to help fulfill them. She successfully combined fantasy with reality in such a way that the child could participate on both levels at once and learn that she need not either ignore or withdraw from the world in order to gain satisfaction.

When Julie arrives back at the plank where the teacher is sitting, Rex and Allan have gathered around. She plops herself in the teacher's lap and says, "Mamma." The teacher immediately follows this lead and says, "Oh, this is my baby." She cuddles Julie and sings a song to her. Julie says: "Mamma, I'm sleepy." "Oh, my baby is sleepy," says the teacher as she puts her on the plank and covers her up with her sweater. "Now I'm the mamma and Julie is the baby and Rex you can be the papa, and we are downstairs sweeping and the baby is up here sleeping." "I'm hungry, mamma," says Julie. Teacher: "I must go downstairs and get you a bottle." At this point Julie has to go in.

The teacher, standing in the center of the small group, sees Julie come out, stretches out her hand and says, "We missed you." Julie now smiles a great full smile. "We are going to play ball," says the teacher. Julie, in a mimicking baby voice: "Oh, are we going to play ball, mamma?" They all sit on the ground and spread their legs wide apart. The teacher is on the ground with the children, instructing them: "I roll the ball to Julie and you roll it to Donnie, and he rolls it to Larry, and he rolls it to . . ." Julie looks over at the teacher and her mouth is puckered as she imitates a baby, "Am I still your baby, mamma?" "Of course you are." She reaches for a teddy bear and props it up beside Julie, then rolls the ball to Julie. Julie catches it and with her eyes shining brightly, says, "I'm going to roll this to the teacher." As she does this, she smiles a broad smile, then claps her hands in glee. Larry rolls the ball to Addie and Julie tries to get in front of her. The teacher sees this and says, "We need a bigger circle." The children follow her to the center of the yard and she tells them where to sit.

This teacher's techniques bore further fruit later in the day when the children were left with another teacher. Then Julie not only organizes the play, but is willing to act the "baby" role in relation to a *child's* "mother" role. She no longer needs to be the constant center of attention. Although nominally fulfilling a baby role, she actually acts as leader in the play and gives Teddy some of the care she had received earlier. Moreover, she falls in with another child's suggestion, and, in general, shows a new and promising flexibility.

Julie walks over to Sally and Teddy and says to Teddy: "You are going to play with me 'cause I'm your friend. I gave you peanuts." Sally: "Shall we play house?" "You be the mommy and Teddy and me will be the babies," answers Julie. "You must have your supper now," says Sally. Teddy, "I don't want any supper." Julie, "But, baby, you must eat 'cause you'll be hungry." Julie finds a dirty popsicle stick on the ground and gives it to Teddy. "This is your spoon, baby." Julie, "I'm such a good baby, mommy, take me and baby brother for a walk." She says this in a tone imitating a baby as she walks with a mincing step.

The three arrive back at the plank and Julie says. "Are we going to the movies?" Sally says, "All right, if you babies get dressed quick." The three pretend to change clothes and walk to the step. They sit in a row. Julie is in the middle. They all stare ahead of them for a minute as if there were a screen. Julie bobs up and says, "All right, it's all over now."

These records illustrate a point made by Susan Isaacs[1] in her discussion of the teacher's role in the social development of young children. She says:

In social matters, the educator cannot teach the child, nor can he learn for him. All that he can do is to create such situations as will give the child opportunities to learn for himself. In this regard, he has to control the social environment of the child as well as the physical, in order to make it possible for the child to learn. The child can, however, learn only by his own real experience, whether social or physical, and the educator must not stand between the child and his experience.

In other words, to free the child, it is frequently necessary for the teacher to support him in situations where he has not yet enough courage of his own, and help create an opportunity for him to play a hitherto avoided role. This does not mean that a teacher should push the child into a role he cannot play—that would only reinforce the feeling of helplessness and failure. She must rather find out why he cannot function in a group, discover where he has been damaged, and help him to strengthen himself. This she can do only if she gives him full reason to believe that she can understand him and his feelings. One main road to such understanding, lies in the sympathetic study of his dramatic play.

In conclusion, it seems to us that spontaneous dramatic play in preschool and kindergarten groups is as promising an instrument for growth as the play within the clinician's office is for therapy. The teacher alone holds the key to this constructive force. Only through her sensitivity to the individual child, her insight into the basic processes of living, and her skill in group management can the potentialities of dramatic play be realized. There is still much to learn, but of all people, teachers are not the ones to shirk learning.

CHAPTER IV

In the Block Corner

BLOCKS are probably the most widely accepted material for the use of children in the preschool age range. Any school that pretends to an educational philosophy includes opportunities for block-play in some form. What is more, blocks have the clear stamp of approval of the children themselves, since they use them more often than any other playthings. For these two reasons—and many more—they deserve our special attention.

When teachers and those engaged in training teachers speak about blocks, they emphasize the contribution of blocks to the child's growing skill in manipulation and imagination, as well as the assistance they offer him in integrating his observations of the world with his own activities. The focus of their discussions seems, in general, to be on development and learning in relation to physical abilities, interpersonal relations, and the child's growing awareness of his powers. Dramatic play with blocks is occasionally mentioned, but its potentialities are not explored. In the main, there is little awareness that block-play offers more to the child than sheer cognitive development—although we do find Harriet Johnson[1] calling block building "an outlet for the manifold experiences through which children are living, whether they are the intentional experiences of the school or those that life itself thrust upon them."

A few psychologists and psychotherapists have recently suggested new insights into this medium of expression. Alschuler and Hattwick,[2] in their book on painting and personality, speak of the importance of blocks for those children who are emerging from the magical thinking of early childhood into a sharpened awareness of everyday realities. In their words, "Their developing interest in building with blocks was paralleled by a keen interest in discovering and interrelating facts in the world about them." These writers also point out differences between well-adjusted and poorly adjusted children in their use of blocks. The poorly adjusted children tended to use blocks in solitary rather than in cooperative or parallel play situations; they were wont to build the same structures over and over again far more than did the better adjusted children, who used blocks in a variety of ways; and they showed a more extreme reaction to their own products, such as long-continued and vigilant protection of their products without using them, extreme disturbance if products were destroyed or touched by other children, or else, as happened in the case of some children, they got intense pleasure from destroying their own products. It is significant that they conclude, "Because self-expression is often more specific in blocks than with easel painting, blocks may offer a simpler method of understanding what is going on within the child than do paints."

These observations suggest that a teacher with a reasonably keen eye can readily spot youngsters who need special attention by watching their block-play—a point we shall have to check against our own investigations.

Two investigators whom we have cited before have also made highly suggestive statements that bear on our subject. Margaret Lowenfeld[3] observes that all play has both an outer aspect and "an inner or psychological aspect, which is the meaning that the type of play has to the child." She points out also that "Children appreciate the materials they find at hand, and invest them with imaginative qualities that make them a vehicle for the concepts, wishes and phantasies that surge within their heads." In somewhat similar vein, Homburger[4] points out that children "express their vital problems in the metaphoric language of play—more consistently and less self-consciously than they are able or willing to in words." Focusing these ideas on block-play specifically, he goes on to say, "If . . . the child weaves fantasies around the reality of objects, he may construct a small toy world which is dominated by the laws of his own growing body and mind. Thus, he makes blocks 'grow' by placing them on top of each other, and with obvious pleasurable excitement in repetition he knocks them down, thus externalizing the trauma of his own falls. Later the blocks may serve as the building stones for a miniature world in which an ever increasing number of bodily, mental and social experiences are externalized and dramatized."

It is both revealing and amusing to compare this last quotation with the following lines on block-play from an early manual written for teachers: "The only restriction placed upon the use of the materials is that they are not to be thrown and that structures are not to be knocked down." But the real question is, how far have we ourselves gotten away from imposing our adult standards on the child's play, as this older book does? Have we sought with an open mind to discover the meaning which block play has for the *child*?

A statement of Lowenfeld's[5] contrasts even more vividly with the restrictions laid down in the teacher's manual: "Exercise of the body, of the voice, of the whole person in production of the maximum possible commotion is an absolute necessity at some time or other to every healthy child.

Noise is necessary, movement is necessary, and to be healthy these must be allowed to be exactly what they are—shapeless explosions of an overplus of energy. . . ."

The more violent release of energy has a further function, she maintains: "Risk and danger are normal elements of adult life, and the ability to cope with dangerous situations is a mark of successful adult character. Every child has a hunger to emulate in this way the adults who surround him, and every child, if left to itself, will create games in which the element of risk appears."[6] Such play is "the bridge between the helplessness of childhood and the possession of power and skill for which he longs."[7] But again the question is: To what extent do we actually permit blocks to be used for such purposes?

Our interest in re-examining the potentials of the block corner in this project arose from the three considerations just mentioned: the ready availability of blocks, the unambiguous enthusiasm that children display for them, and the apparent gap between the educator's approach to the use of these materials and that of specialists who have had the opportunity to study children more intensively.

The subjects of our study were 97 children engaged in spontaneous block-play in normal preschool group situations. They ranged in age from 2.6 to 5.6 years and presented all kinds of behavior pictures, from very well-adjusted youngsters to those who were deeply troubled. In all, 152 records were made of the block-play of these children, drawn from 27 different groups, in 20 preschool centers. Along with the protocols of block-play, we were fortunate in having available teachers' descriptions of the behavior of our subjects in relation to other children, to adults, and to other kinds of materials; diary records of their behavior in a wide variety of situations; and in many cases information about their family backgrounds.

There was no attempt to standardize the physical situation in which the play took place. In some rooms floor space was so limited that blocks could be taken out only on certain mornings. At the other and more fortunate extreme was a huge playroom one end of which was entirely given over to blocks. Here the block shelves partitioned the space into sections so that several groups could play comfortably at one time and even leave their structures standing indefinitely. Intermediate between these two were the rooms that offered adequate building space but necessitated putting away the blocks at the end of the play period to make way for dining tables or resting cots.

However, factors other than the physical plant determined the availability of the blocks for the children. Attitudes of teachers toward freedom of use differed almost as much as the room situation. One, for example, assigned special children to block-play during "work period"; she also demanded that all blocks be placed neatly on the shelves at the end of the period. Another encouraged the children to use blocks whenever they wished, even between wash-up time and lunch, and did not demand that they pick them all up afterwards. In general, most teachers seemed to be fairly relaxed about their use, within the very real limitations that lack of space frequently forced upon them.

It might be helpful to give a slight statistical summary indicating the comparative popularity of blocks during the periods when our observers were studying certain designated children. Of the 217 children observed during the two-year period of this project, 97 chose to play with blocks while observers were present, 83 chose the easel, and 75 went to the clay table. Only dramatic play ever approached blocks in general popularity.

These figures alone are impressive evidence of the importance of block-play to children. But to discover the specific services it renders, we must turn to the protocols we have gathered. Through them we may find out whether the potentials mentioned by Lowenfeld and Homburger are now being realized in block-play as it is ordinarily conducted in preschool groups, and what further opportunities this medium might offer the teacher in discovering children's needs.

One word of caution. Since this was not a statistical study, no effort was made to find out how many children showing certain characteristics did certain things with blocks. Our major approach to the protocols was to ask, "What qualities do the children seem to perceive in the blocks and to what service do they put them?" We assumed that if youngsters use them for some unexpected purposes, they perceive qualities in them which are somehow congruent with their inner needs—no matter how incongruent with adult predilections —and we simply asked why those particular aspects appealed to them at that particular time. Also, it should be emphasized that these reports show a predominance of emotional release in use of blocks and do not reveal adequately their contructive use for learning spatial relationships.

Blocks as a First Medium

The following account is a sample of many similar experiences reported by teachers.

Amy was an only child, three years old, whose relationships with her parents had somehow 'gone sour' in spite of their excellent intentions. In school she apparently considered all adults her sworn enemies, especially when they desired a given kind of behavior from her. While her large muscle activities were performed adequately, all creative effort seemed to be outside of her interest until she engaged in block-play. Her first attempts were only pilings of the blocks, but she was able to accept a little help in this area and her constructions gradually developed into quite elaborate buildings.

This appeal of blocks above all other materials is common though not universal. Their flexibility and ease of handling have often been mentioned in explanation, but they have another characteristic which has not been sufficiently emphasized. In contrast to finger-painting, poster painting, and water-play, block-play seems to be completely nonthreatening to the child who comes upon it for the first time. In addition, blocks are obviously sturdy, so that children who have been somewhat damaged by parental admonitions about breaking things need not be afraid of handling them. The appeal of their cleanness is also important, especially when many children in preschool groups have already been taught to identify dirt with wrong.

Blocks are an excellent medium for helping a new or timid child feel comfortable. In the block corner he can work alone, in parallel fashion, or in active cooperation with others, just as he chooses. He may hide behind a rampart of blocks, or if he does not yet trust the teacher, he can refuse her aid without obviously depriving himself. Children who are fearful, preoccupied with cleanliness, or wary of adults as a consequence of excessive demands made on them, profit particularly from the ease of achievement that blocks afford. By simply removing them from the shelf they make an impression on the environment; by merely piling one on top of another, they gain the satisfaction of creating something without evoking anxiety.

To lure the timid child into further activity, blocks should be stored near materials that can be readily used for elaboration of the play. Sawhorses, boards, large packing cases, and wooden cartons are particularly helpful, but many smaller objects should also be accessible. These might consist of the usual wooden figures of animals and people, as well as such miscellaneous objects as empty spools of various sizes, large wooden beads, small tree models, squares of cloth, etc. By the same token it might be well to store blocks in places where they will attract interest to other types of play— especially in the doll corner. We observed children using them as food, baby bottles, guns, and as nameless "little things" which can be "tucked in" and hidden.

The unique combination of creative expression and mastery that block-play affords seems to be practically irresistible. We witnessed one example of this in the case of Billie, a five-year-old boy, who was considered withdrawn, apathetic, and inhibited in relation to materials. He could not cope with the natural self-assertion of other children, spent a great deal of time listening to the phonograph, and was able to establish rapport only with his teacher. His facial expression was usually "flat," sometimes downright unhappy. Only when he had access to the block corner did he seem to come alive. His complicated creations there gave evidence of intense concentration and high intellectual ability. The following brief excerpt from the record illustrates his absorption in the problems of dynamics which the blocks presented and his pleasure in achieving control over them.

Billie forms an arch of two big blocks; he experiments, putting a smaller curved block on top (see p. 107). He concentrates on the new project, does not even look at the fort on which he had been working. Then he puts long blocks on each side of his structure, but finally removes them. Sits back to decide what to do. He gets a fresh idea, attempts to balance a long thin block on top of his structure. It is not firm, so he selects a shorter one which stays in place (see p. 107). Then he adds a wider short one on the start of the curve of the arch, looks pleased at this difficult balance.

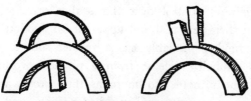

BILLIE'S BLOCK PATTERNS

Block-play not only stimulates children to perform their first creative activity, it also helps them grow in their own estimation. They realize suddenly that they are capable of doing things that are worthwhile—which is a steppingstone of no mean value in the direction of maturity. The following quotation from a summary record of a three-and-one-half-year-old boy illustrates this process. "Jerry was apt to sit with a few blocks lined up as a road and watch other children. Prodding or suggestion from his teacher usually elicited a negative response and sometimes resulted in abandonment of block-play entirely. Recently, however, he has been able to sustain more interest in his own play. This seemed to date from one morning when he built a house, the first he had made in some time. He remarked excitedly, 'I didn't make a building in many days!' On the days that followed Jerry created other types of construction with the teacher's help and cried out again and again in real pleasure at his creations." It is not unusual for children to shout spontaneously, "I made it, I made it, I made it! Just what we needed!"—or to clap their hands and even break into a dance of triumph.

Power Through Blocks

The sense of achievement and control expands in some children to a genuine feeling of power and escape from limitations. When they build airports, skyscrapers, etc., they are not merely reproducing objects—they are, at least in fantasy, gaining control over things that ordinarily dwarf them. But their very real and apparent satisfaction in building these models probably has a further source. Gigantic structures symbolize release from a physical world that is cramping them more and more as they grow, as well as escape from an interpersonal world of parents' and teachers' demands that becomes more confining as their psychic horizons expand. Listen, for instance, to the conversation of two well-adjusted boys in the record below. Their defiant air of braggadocio seems to fling down a challenge to a constantly shrinking world.

Timmy and Martin size up their collection of things. Martin: "I'm gonna get the teacher to get more blocks." Timmy: "We'll build a big one." Martin: "Bigger than this school." The teacher has brought seesaw boards. Martin runs to get one, carries it over and leans it against one set of steps. Timmy does likewise. Martin: "Start building the airport?" Timmy: "Ya, the airport." Martin: "Gonna make a big one." He gets a sawhorse and starts to place it. Timmy fixes two sawhorses with a long board across the top. Martin tries several places, can't decide where to put his sawhorse. Finally puts it in line with Timmy's. Martin: "Let's make a high one." Timmy: "No." Martin: "Let's make a little high one, O.K.?"

For boys especially, the creative possibilities of blocks seem to be related to the magical power of modern machinery. Through building and controlling airplanes, cars, trucks, and trains, they participate in the extraordinary potency of the real world and express their desire to control things and people that dominate their lives. In other words, blocks serve as an effective link between the observed magic of the external world and the wishful magic of their own fantasies and desires.

Sometimes we find that little girls as well as little boys transfer these feelings of power to their relations with people. We witnessed this process while watching four-and-one-half-year-old Bessie build "a great big house that will go to the end of the room." She was an anxious, frightened child, the victim not only of a broken home but of her mother's brutal treatment. In the following record note how she seems to grow in her own esteem as her ideas about building expand, until she feels big enough to tease her teacher and even to order her out of the way.

Bessie, sitting on the floor, puts the blocks in a row around the toys, and says, "Now look what it is, Effie." "What is it, Bessie?" "A train." She stands and watches Joe and Amiel. She adds a few more blocks, "What is it now?" "Tell me, Bessie." "A train—a house—and I'll add a few more blocks and it will be over to there, and to there." (Points around the room.) She goes to the block corner, takes a few more blocks out and says, "Now it will be beautiful. She stands with her mouth open and looks at the blocks, then stands them in a row, and says, "A great big house. It's going to be a great big house, a dog house." She builds up and then pushes them down; then she starts to rebuild. She says, "It will be a little tiny house." She knocks the building down and starts to rebuild again. She says to the teacher, "You don't know what this is going to be." Teacher: "I can guess." She takes one block up and puts it on the teacher's knee, and says, "Boom," and smiles. She starts to rebuild again and says, "Pretty house. Teacher, my building will be all the way down to the door." Amiel says, "My name starts with an A." Bessie: "My name starts with an A, too. I'll make my house to the end of the room." She tells the teacher, "You better move, I can't build near the chair." She pulls out her skirt and says, "Dirty." She finishes up with the building and then goes over to the teacher, who lifts Bessie up and Bessie says, "Look at my beautiful big building." She stands near Tillie, and says, "Look at my great big building." She hugs the teacher.

Blocks for Release

So far we have been discussing constructive and imaginative aspects of block-play that are quite familiar to teachers, but we have endeavoured to emphasize its contribution to the child's self-regard in a way that is not common in educational literature. Now, however, we come to a function of blocks that is either ignored or definitely suppressed. Both from a perusal of literature designed for teachers and from our own observation of their techniques, we have been driven to the conclusion that unfortunately many teachers consider the aggressive use of blocks inappropriate to their educational function. In the following two records, which are not at all unusual, we see children making tentative movements in the direction of "commotion" and "explosiveness" and being definitely stopped by their teachers. Both of these four-year-old boys are considered "difficult." Tuffy is described as "aggressive" and William as "anxious," but we do not know what specific tensions they are trying to relieve by throwing the blocks instead of building with them.

Record 1: Tuffy got two chairs and pushed them over to the large building which a group of children were making. Tuffy and another child stood on the chairs and added more blocks until they could not get any more on. Then they began to throw blocks inside the building. Tuffy laughed and jumped as he threw them. The teacher told the children to put the blocks away. "Hahaha," he laughed uproariously, but he scrambled up on a chair and started to hand the blocks to the teacher. Then he threw some down. "If you can't take them off neatly, then you don't have to help put the blocks away," the teacher said sternly. Very contritely and meekly he handed her another block and said, "Here, teacher."

Record 2: William is piling red and blue blocks symmetrically. Bill comes over to the table and takes some of the red blocks. William is annoyed and grabs them back, saying, "You better not take some of mine!" Another boy comes over to the table and belligerently grabs at some of the blocks in front of William, saying, "Gimme my blocks!" William seems stunned and stares at him. Then he seems afraid and pushes *all* the blocks before him to the belligerent boy, sticks his index finger in his mouth, and watches him. This boy now gets up and Bill returns to the table. William stands up and looks at Bill for a moment. Then he says to Bill, "Let's push all the blocks off the table." A teacher reprimands him, however, and he docilely begins to put the scattered blocks back into the boxes.

But why permit children to use blocks for "explosive" purposes? This undeniable need must be examined in the light of the tasks that face them during the early years. Constant and inexorable pressure is being exerted in the direction of conformity to adult standards which have little intrinsic meaning to them. Moreover, in an effort to answer the pressing question, "Who am I, and what is my place in this world?" they are constantly impelled to explore the limits of their strength and to test and reassure themselves in the face of people and things that frequently threaten them. We know, too, that in many cases "explosions" are like safety valves and that people, like engines, break down when pressures build up too high and there is no way to relieve them. Therefore, it would seem to be a highly salutary precaution to permit the growing child to blow off steam when he seems to need it.

For those who question whether youngsters need these outlets in the course of normal development, we should like to offer the following record of a child considered to be well adjusted. It can be matched by any number of others.

. . . . Carl (three years old) places blocks inside the box in a neat pile with a resounding thud. He waits for the noise expectantly, closes his eyes in anticipation, and smiles when it comes. . . . Now he is showing great delight in piling up the blocks and throwing them down. He runs around very energetically, climbs into a locker, jumps down, and resumes throwing blocks down. He bangs a block with his fist very viciously, using a great amount of energy. Very softly while doing this he says, "F - - - you, f - - - you." Gets up quickly, looks around and runs over to the teacher and hugs her; he runs over to where the easels are and plays with the covers of the paint jars, rearranging the bottles. He leaves this quickly and runs back to the blocks. He dances around the blocks in boxerlike fashion with fists held up and clenched, although not directed at anyone. Then he lies down in complete relaxation, rises gracefully but quickly, and runs around the room. He unloads blocks from a large box, piling them very high. The teacher places her hand on top of the pile and explains to Carl that they are going to fall and hurt other children. Carl listens attentively and says, "No." The teacher allows him to throw the entire pile down. He does so with utter delight, jumping up and down. He builds it again. The teacher tells him it is too high. He stops and she leaves. Again he throws the pile down.

Youngsters who are under great internal pressure often feel compelled to use blocks "explosively" before they can use them constructively. Like the pegboard and workbench, they become instruments of relatively safe destruction. The following record of a three-year-old is an example of behavior frequently observed in children who seem diffusely hostile and aggressive.

Jules immediately goes over to the shelf and removes some of the long blocks in a very violent manner, throwing them on the floor. He looks up rather cautiously to see if the observer is going to say anything (perhaps restrict his activity?). Then he continues and takes a small pail full of tiny blocks and dumps them upside down. Next he goes to the peg-work bench and hammers at the pegs with great vigor and energy. However, he quickly leaves this game and picks up three of the large boards, arranges them in a haphazard fashion and says to the observer, "I build a house tunnel." Again his attention quickly diverts to something else and he takes a red truck off the shelf. He says to the observer, "What does dis truck do?" He doesn't wait for an answer but moves the truck around. He returns to hammer at the pegs again, stops abruptly, and builds an alley with the blocks—saying to the observer rather proudly, "Look at *dat* one!" Talking in a low voice to himself, "Go dere," he puts himself into the "alley," then suddenly kicks the arrangement wide open. Immediately he looks up at the observer with an expression of questioning. He goes back to more building, then back to the pegs again, hammering with the same decided vigor.

When a child's ability to utilize his own safety valves has been impaired by overrestrictive parental handling, he will often show evidence of conflict even when block crashes are accidental. This was true of Hal. In the record below, he retreats to the safety of a "cozy place" after enjoying an inadvertent crash. With this boy, the permission to crash blocks as much as he wished might well be salutary in itself, since it would show him that there is nothing reprehensible about the impulse and that there are channels through which such urges can be safely released.

. . . . Hal finally concentrates on two small blocks and one long one. He lifts one end of a long block onto a small one, then runs to the other end, lifts it as he straddles the small one, and pulls. The far end slides off with a crash. Hal squeals, dances up and down, and throws his arms about, dropping the end he was holding. This makes a nice loud bang, and there is more dancing and laughter. He makes another attempt to get the long block up on the two small ones, but this is only half-hearted and he is unsuccessful. He leaves the blocks as they are. His right thumb goes into his mouth, his other hand into his trouser pocket. He strolls over to the group in the center of the room who are playing with a wooden box, curls up in one corner with knees bent under his chin, and continues to suck his thumb as he watches the activities of others.

Sometimes children give the equivalent of lip service to the teacher by building things up—with the intention of pushing them down later. In the guise of building acceptably, accidents, too, are often "arranged." It seems to us that a teaching approach which provokes this devious method of achieving satisfaction must encourage hypocrisy.

Here is a striking example of building for the purpose of destroying. It is part of the record of Cathy, four years old, who is considered well adjusted.

Cathy started to build a structure on the floor near Vera. She stood two five-inch blocks on end opposite each other and a little apart. Then she placed another five-inch block across the top. She continued building in this same way, but one block kept falling down. Finally she slapped it down hard on the floor and exclaimed good naturedly, "Every time you fall down." Then she put it in place very carefully and it stood firm. She kept building. As she reached over past the structure and into the shelf to add another block, it suddenly fell down. Cathy and Vera squatted on the floor mixing the blocks and pushing them gaily in all directions. Cathy, on her knees, began to build the same structure again. As it got higher she called out excitedly, "Oh, look," and reached faster and less carefully for more blocks. Again the structure fell as she reached across it for more blocks and the two girls laughed heartily about the whole thing, and soon commenced their work anew. When Cathy's structure fell a third time she laughed hysterically and excitedly pushed Vera's down. Still laughing, she and Vera built two more structures near each other. This time Cathy let her hand knock into Vera's blocks, and when both structures began to tumble, she gave them a kick and jumped up and down, yelling and laughing. Then the two built their structures back to back. Cathy built hers faster than Vera, and while she waited for Vera to catch up, another girl came up and asked, "Gonna let it fall again?" "Oh yes," Cathy answered happily. Vera finished and they both dived into the structure knocking the blocks about, laughing more heartily and louder than before.

It may be that knocking over block structures has still other values. It is a way of controlling the environment and asserting possessiveness: what one creates, one has a right to destroy. It may also show the satisfaction a child gets out of process as opposed to product. While the teacher may value the final structure for certain elements of symmetry that she sees in it, to the child the experience of constructing it successfully may be the more important aspect—and he may be expressing this feeling by knocking it over. Below we offer an instance where pushing down a block structure is a gesture signifying possession.

When I arrived, Bud was playing with blocks with two other boys. They had built a high wall in a corner of the room and were behind it looking over the top. Jeff pushes a block off and Bud says, "Don't do that." Jeff: "I *made* it." Bud: "Perhaps we could push it all down." They push the wall with both hands and most of it falls down.

There is yet another consideration. We have ample evidence of the excitement and pleasurable release that children experience when they destroy their own buildings. We have seen that often they build only to destroy. Now we may ask, "What motivates this pleasure in destruction?" For one thing, blocks undoubtedly offer children a chance to do, without the usual consequences, precisely what is forbidden in other areas. For another, we believe that through this repeated destructive play they are trying to reassure themselves about the relatively innocuous character of their own destructive impulses. In the process of growing up, they are constantly warned to be careful, not to throw things, not to break things. They are punished, often harshly, if they do destroy, even when the destruction is accidental. Yet they are constantly surrounded with a host of apparently fragile objects. The net result is that their own ineptness and their experimental impulses may acquire an aura of limitless threat. Where then, except in the world of the block corner, can they destroy and repair, destroy and repair, to their heart's content, until they reassure themselves that they are not the completely destructive forces they have been made out to be by the intolerant adults about them? If they can accomplish this purpose, they have taken a long step forward in the direction of self-acceptance, which is an important prerequisite for mental health.

Blocks as Substitute Objects of Hostility

Blocks have two values as substitutes for persons against whom children would like to vent their anger—they save the prospective victims from bodily hurt and they allow an outlet for hostility without irreparable consequences. We are not recommending that blocks be offered for this purpose, since there are other materials which may be found more suitable; we are simply drawing attention to the fact that a well-equipped block corner may prevent more serious forms of violence. For example, two four-year-old boys who resented the presence of an observer, carried some long blocks to where he sat and banged them on the floor at his feet, remarking succinctly, "There's that same bad man." After that they were able to return to their play and seemed to forget his presence.

A somewhat similar incident occurred during the observation of an extremely anxious and aggressive four-year-old, whom we shall call Bud. Notice how he expresses resentment by attacking blocks instead of counterattacking his provoking playmate.

Bud makes a tunnel with three cars all headed in the same direction. A little girl watches him, and he says to her, "Would you like to play in my tunnel?" Just then Joe races over to the tunnel and breaks it. Bud runs after him, carrying part of his damaged property, strikes out at Joe, then returns to the tunnel. The little girl is still watching him and she lifts one of the largest blocks, saying, "Can you do this, Bud?" Bud says, "Yes," and picks up a very large block and throws it. . . . Again Joe tries to fight Bud. Bud pays no outward attention. Joe hits him with a large block. Bud tries to retaliate but the teacher intervenes and tells him he was a good boy to ignore Joe's persistent disturbances. Bud now gets a wooden hammer and strikes each block in turn.

A similar incident occurred when one child unintentionally began to destroy another's block building. Instead of indulging in a free-for-all, the children concerned in the incident were able to give vent to their feelings by turning them against the blocks.

Rex has built a complicated structure. Across the partition others are singing to guitar music, and he joins in, "Oh where, oh where can she be?" Alfie starts to put Rex's blocks away. Rex: "You are breaking up my things, ohhh, ohhhh!"—waving his arms in wild gestures. Then he proceeds to kick his building all to pieces and pushes Bud's. Bud rushes over and pushes Rex in the stomach. Then all three boys kick the blocks until Rex begins to put his blocks away.

The significant aspect of the situation described next is the anxious little boy's ability to establish constructive relations with other children only after relieving his internal pressures against blocks.

Henry pulled and pulled on the gate trying to close it, but couldn't. He yelled for Ronnie and said, "Come play over here." Ronnie didn't come, so Henry ran to the wagon and tried to take it from Calvin. Calvin screamed. The teacher said, "Don't do that, Henry, Calvin had it first." Henry poked out his mouth and hit at the teacher. He ran to the sliding board and tried to push Irene off. She kicked him on the shoulder. He cried. The teacher made him sit on the step. She talked to him. He stopped crying and said, "Shut up," in an angry voice to the teacher. Then he looked up at the observer, and said, "Shut up, shut up." He jumped up, ran to the blocks and kicked them about. He climbed on the tricycle and rode very fast.

Ronnie came up. He asked Henry to let him ride the tricycle. "No." Ronnie said, "Yes." Henry rode around making a song of "No, No, No, etc. . . ." Later he got off the tricycle again and went to the corner where the blocks were and suddenly ran to another teacher and put his arms around her. Mafalda was playing with blocks. Henry said, "I'm making a building." He arranged several blocks in a semicircle. Kitty was pulling a wagon. She came to where Henry was playing and started to pull the wagon over the blocks. Henry: "No, you can't do that." He pushed her in the back saying, "Get out of my building," in a high-pitched voice. Henry was still putting blocks on his building when Ronnie climbed up on them to sit down. They tumbled over with him. He jumped up laughing. Henry laughed too. They picked up the blocks and put them on the building. Henry knocked the building down. He ran to the wagon and pulled it over to the blocks. He put five blocks in the wagon and sat on top of them while Ronnie pulled him around.

Sometimes a child's reaction to teacher-induced frustration takes the form of block crashing. If he is permitted to acknowledge the real object of his hostility at the same time that he takes it out on the substitute object, this may mean the beginning of mature emotional control.

In the following record of Hal, whom we met earlier in this chapter, the teacher's techniques for diverting the play seem clever enough, but the lad apparently feels their basically restrictive quality and eventually expresses himself in a violent manner.

Hal spies a straight chair from the office and pushes it. As he goes up and down the length of the floor, the scraping noise is apparently fun for him since his face is one broad grin. The teacher is attracted by the noise and takes the chair, and talks to him. Hal heads for the blocks. He climbs up onto the large blocks when the teacher returns and tells him, "We are not playing with blocks this morning." He then wanders into the doll house and is immediately attracted by the teacher's coat and pocketbook which are on the partition. He puts the bag on his shoulder and marches around the room. The teacher speaks to him but he runs down the corridor. She does not give chase and Hal returns. . . . The teacher talks to him and lets him go—with the bag still hanging from his shoulder. He picks up the telephone, dials and then holds a quick conversation—"Hello, ya ya, goo'bye." Turning from the telephone, he knocks over the wastebasket, and odds and ends tumble out. He seems a little upset, exclaiming, "Oh, all the spools are falling out." He stoops, rights the basket, and replaces the spools. Larry picks up the basket. Hal is excited and, jumping up and down, urges him to "Empty it out, empty it out!" The teacher arrives at this moment and speaks to the boys, apparently asking them to help her put away the coat and pocketbook. They carry her coat and all three go to the coatroom and return without coat or pocketbook. Running back from the coatroom, Hal and Larry go to the chest and each takes a pocketbook. Hal races to the stacked blocks and quickly climbs up, Larry folowing him. He throws his bag and directs Larry to do the same. He really seems happy at this point. He then starts to throw the blocks, picking each one up in one hand and carefully aiming it into the center of the room. There is a terrific noise as each block lands on the floor. Hal is putting a good deal of energy into this and is quite intent on the activity.

Finally, we must speak of the rather subtle ways in which some children use blocks to attack other youngsters without provocation. Many "accidents" in the block corner are the result of such hidden intentions. Moreover, children who wish to destroy are especially quick to protect their own buildings and to complain of other children, since they suspect them of having the same intentions. In the next record Jon, a fearful child who distrusted adults and rarely played with others, uses rather obvious "accidents" as an outlet for hostility. Notice how he gives himself away through his eagerness to protect his own buildings when other children merely approach him.

Jon chews on a cardboard crayon box, then returns to his blocks. His block building is of a much simpler design than that of the other children. The teacher tries to take the crayons away from him and tells him, "These are to take home." When he resists she says he can keep them in his pocket. In going over to the shelf to get additional blocks, he accidentally knocks down the block tower the others have built. He makes two more trips to the shelves and accidentally knocks down the other children's blocks each time. Then he knocks down his own block structure, takes two blocks across the room, and starts another pile. A girl, in passing, stops to touch his blocks. Jon quickly says, "Get outa here." He picks up a block and chases her.

Joe, the same child who annoyed Bud in the play record cited earlier in this chapter, offers us an even more illuminating example. As the youngest child of a large family, abandoned by both parents to the more or less casual care of a harassed grandmother, this youngster had plenty of cause for resentment. Two years in a play-school group, however, taught him that bold and undisguised attacks were not looked upon with favor by the teachers. As a consequence his hostility seemed to "go underground" and become more devious. In the following record he very cleverly assumes an interested air while effectively managing to frustrate his little playmates. This kind of behavior should be a signal to the teacher that a child needs individual attention—perhaps outside the province of the school.

Doris calls Joe to look at what she's building. He kneels down and then sits on her structure completely destroying it. He says, "It's broke," and without another word gets up, goes over to Max's "house," sits down on it, and also breaks it up. The teacher tells Joe to build it up again. Max is very careful as he plans and piles the blocks but Joe takes all kinds and sizes of blocks, mumbles to himself, and quickly puts one on top of the other. Max watches Joe, looks up at his face and quietly says, "He's making it crazy!" Joe laughs, showing all his teeth in a wide grin, and repeats with much pride, "I'm making it crazy." Finally Max announces that he wants to build his house up again by himself. Joe then goes back to Doris, annoys her by adding bricks to her structure where and when she doesn't want them, and continues in his way to disorganize their work. However, he teases them in a way which doesn't really make them angry and ingratiates himself by saying, "Look, I want to show you something!"—thereby distracting them. He continues this way for five minutes when he is asked to go with the teacher to the store to buy something.

Blocks Offer Safe Adventure

We have quoted Lowenfeld's statement to the effect that every child has an urge to emulate the risks and dangers in adult life and to prove his ability to cope with dangerous situations. When children play with blocks and block accessories, especially out-of-doors, it is as if the whole world were beckoning and daring them to "come and conquer me." Usually they respond to this invitation by trying themselves out in slightly risky but essentially safe situations—thus intuitively following the accepted maxims for acquiring confidence.

The following brief record suggests this type of fate tempting among a group of four-year-old girls. Their impersonation of powerful animals reveals the exhilaration and feelings of strength they gain from climbing their complicated structure.

Laura: "Come up this way." (She motions Daphne to come around and up the dais steps.) Daphne: "Can I come up dat way?" (She points to the planks and bars.) She jumps up and down and giggles at the idea. Laura: "Yeh." Daphne climbs the steps. Once atop she giggles again. She crosses the plank on her hands and knees, then crawls across the bars and over the rail of the dais. Cora calls Laura a tiger. Laura growls. Daphne growls. All the children taunt "Tiger, tiger."

Daphne swings her mittens at them, goes off the dais, and chases them.

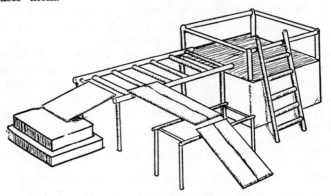

OUTDOOR PLAY APPARATUS

Youngsters occasionally miscalculate and bite off more than they can chew in their impulse to master situations. When this happens it is important to give them unobtrusive aid so that they will be willing to undertake further experimentation. Sometimes, however, the child will work it out for himself, as in the following record of an anxious boy of four and one half.

Art and Walter turn the box upside down and build it up higher and higher by piling blocks on it. They get chairs to stand on, to facilitate building it still higher. Laughing, they get up on top of the box and blocks. Walter jumps down, leaving Art on top alone. He appears afraid, is not smiling now, looks down at Walter and says, "Get me offa here, Walter." Walter laughs and runs off a distance to look at him. Art looks toward the descent and shrinks back again, calling, "Walter, I don't like up here. I wanna get down now." Charlie comes along, "You scared, Art?" Art says, "Go way. I want Walter." Charlie shakes the box on which Art is perched. Art screams, "G'wan away, you." Charlie gets up on the chair and pushes Art off. He tumbles down, then gets up behind

Charlie and pummels him in the back. His eyes look defiant and his face is very red. Charlie kicks at him and he runs. Walter comes over and climbs up on top of the blocks with Charlie. They both jump down, pick up large pieces of board to act as guns, and chase each other around the box. Art looks on excitedly, picking his nose and smiling.

The consequences of these triumphs over physical obstacles are frequently impressive, as indicated in the following two records. The protagonist of the first, Donnie, seemed most fearful of aggression of all kinds; he could neither protect himself when attacked nor witness fights among others. Yet, as the action shows, all he needed was to assure himself of his own strength before he could be as freely aggressive as his group mates. Notice too, how his triumph over blocks leads to an indiscriminate eruption, as though he had been waiting for an opportunity to release impulses long held in check.

Donnie gets some big square blocks. "I wanna make something." He piles two blocks, then four. He climbs up and says with great pride, sticking his chest out, "Look, I can jump down." However, the top block slides down each time and he doesn't complete his jump. Once the block stays in place and he grins and says to himself, "This time I didn't fall." He gains more confidence and becomes very excited and energetic. He fairly yells, "Out the way," to the children who are crowding in. Then he shouts about how high he can jump and says, "Don't do anything, take your hands off," and gets more daring. . . . Suddenly, for no apparent reason he lashes out and pushes Rex, saying, "Bang, bang, bang, ha, ha," and then he gives full vent to his aggressiveness by pushing all the children who are in line. He shuts his eyes as he hits out violently on all sides and suddenly there is a free-for-all fight until it is quieted down by the teacher. The group leaves quietly. After following them into the other room and seeing that all, including Donnie, had new interests, such as putting on masks and pretending they were scaring each other, I left. At this point Donnie's behavior seemed very like that of the rest of the group and he was fully joining in.

A similar incident led to quite a different course of behavior in the case of Bud,[8] a little boy who frequently expressed his anxiety by unprovoked and unpredictable attacks upon other children. Watch how his conquest of the blocks leads through a rather violent route to much more integrated behavior and finally to a retreat inside a shelter.

Bud runs around the room with four of the other children, yelling. He jumps up on a block in the corner and stamps on it and then jumps up and down on it to make more noise. He piles up three blocks and jumps from them to the other blocks. Beth comes over and they do this together for quite a while, laughing and yelling. Beth leaves and he continues by himself, stamping, jumping, and throwing blocks on the floor. He runs to the cupboard, squeezes himself onto the shelf, and slams the door shut, and then opens it. He repeats this over and over and smiles at me each time he opens the door. Tiring of this, he runs all around the room; he jumps on a doll's cup and breaks it. Some other children are making a house and for a while he adds a block here and there to the structure, quieting down as he becomes more interested. He shouts to the other children, "John, put it in this way." He crawls inside the house, then crawls out and puts more big blocks around it.

Because of its potentials for offering children "dangerous" situations which they can control, the block corner holds special promise for those who are fearful and lacking in self-confidence. Certain accessories can aid the teacher in this task. With fairly short planks and large blocks, it is possible to build ramps and bridges that resemble many of the real situations that inspire fear. Beginning with these, it is possible to develop more and more daring structures until the child is fully confident of his ability to handle the hazards of his environment.

Blocks and Cozy Places

Our discussion here will be in direct contrast to the last section. This should not be too surprising since many of the values of blocks derive precisely from the fact that they can be used by all kinds of children to satisfy all kinds of needs. They offer youngsters a chance not only to test their strength against the world but also to retreat from it, particularly when they are used in conjunction with such materials as boxes, screens, and shelves. Unfortunately preschool and kindergarten groups seem to be planned on the assumption that all young children are, or should be, constantly gregarious. They must play together, eat together, and sleep together, with little cognizance taken of the very real service to growth that solitude can offer. However, they often find ways of making up for this lack by crawling into empty boxes, by nestling in closed cubbies or on shelves, cots, or tables, or by building ramparts behind which to hide. While this tendency to withdrawal and relaxation is seen more frequently in the younger age groups, from two to three and one half years, it is encountered often enough among the older preschool and kindergarten children to suggest that even they need to "get away from it all" at times. The following record of Polly, a well-adjusted child of three and one half years, is fairly representative of the way in which blocks can serve passivity needs.

Polly rests one long block over two others and sits and rocks on it like a seesaw. She gets up and arranges the blocks into a lopsided pentagon and stands in the middle, saying proudly, "Look at me, teacher." She carefully selects more long blocks and some smaller ones and fills in the center of the structure, placing the blocks in symmetrical order. Lorene takes a block from her building. Polly looks after her and wails but sheds no tears. Observer tells Lorene that it's Polly's block and Lorene throws it down. Iris, crawling by, accidentally knocks over part of the building. Polly lets out a whiny groan, mutters something to herself about "doggie," followed by "not gonna bite me." She fixes the building, turns to the observer saying in a proud tone, "That's my house." She gets in and sits down. A block falls over and Polly grunts "Uh-oh," gets out, fixes the block, gets back into the house, and sits down. She adds more blocks and gets in again. She addresses the observer— "Look at me." Now she lies down inside of the house, curling up small, and looks up at the observer, grins with pleasure, and then sticks out the tip of her tongue. A little later she pretends to sleep.

Because of the evident need for places of retreat, it would be well for the teacher to have some crates or empty cartons put in or near the block corner. When they are available they are used as much as the blocks themselves. When they are not available children sometimes use empty shelves for this purpose.

We know that these cozy places sometimes represent an area of safety from a threatening world. One little boy, Art, came from a rural Spanish-speaking environment and had trouble adjusting to the preschool group. In the following account we see him using a protected position as a means of participating in the group at the same time that he is separated from it, thus giving himself the chance to water down the impact of this new culture to the point where he can master it.

Millie crawled into one of the boxes and sat down. Art watched her and laughed. He said, "I'm going next door." He crawled into the other box and began to take animals from the shelf, piling them up in front of him. "This is a dog, this is a pig." The other children had left and he remained by himself, playing with the animals and talking to himself. He stood up and looked over the top of the box at the other boys who lined up blocks in a straight line. He called out to them, "You've got a train, you've got a little train." Don returned with Millie, and Art sat down inside his box again. The teacher passed by and he said to her, "You are a little pussycat." The teacher asked why, and he just smiled. Then he took out all the animals and lined them up very carefully and pushed them under the steps. He then leaned back against the steps in a relaxed way and watched some children playing. The teacher came over and asked him to sing "Yankee Doodle." He began to sing very quietly. She asked him to sing louder. He said, "You heard me. Yes, you did." Teacher, "I'll ask Don to sing." He said, "No," and sang the song louder and smiled in a satisfied but shy way. He piled the blocks up, working quickly. Millie came over and tried to take the steps away. He ran after her and got them back. He and Millie had a short conversation. He got a block and offered it to her as if to make up. He carefully made a hollow structure with blocks high on the two long sides, then placed some boards across the top. Frank asked Art what he was making and he said, "A house." Cal came over and tried to break it down. Art said, "No," and defended his structure. He continued building the roof on his house. . . . "Look what I made," he said to Millie. She pushed him as she went by and he said, "You made me fall." He did not sound belligerent. He started to take the house down, placing the blocks carefully on the shelves where they belonged. When he finished he went over to Bobby and Frank and sat down on a small block. They began to sing, "Art is a little boy." He smiled and Bobby told him to get another block so that he'd be taller. They all sang "Happy Birthday." The teacher came over and said it was time to put everything away. Art got up and placed the toy back on the shelf, then ran over to the big boxes and climbed into one and lay down. The teacher came over and said, "I bet I can beat you into the bathroom." He got up and ran into the bathroom.

Not all children use block structures and associated materials for solitary retreat. Sometimes several will crawl behind a wall or into a box together, in that way asserting the solidarity of their small group against the rest. Since these youngsters are usually rather advanced in their social development, this may be a definite step in the direction of greater social maturity. For we know that between the ages of approximately five and seven, children are beginning to grow toward the gangs, cliques, and clubs that are so common among eight- to twelve-year-olds.

We have observed also that children who are at once fearful and aggressive find that enclosures and block walls are well adapted for enabling them to express hostile impulses without enduring their consequences. Again they have a "safety" value but it is quite a different thing from using them for comfortable relaxation—as the following record shows:

Hal is talking rapidly, shouting directions as he pushes the blocks about. He climbs into the structure and ducks down. He pops up and is attracted by a boy pushing a big red box. He shouts and the box is brought over. His face is full of tense excitement as he pushes his way out of the blocks. With much lifting, hauling, and racing around, the box is gotten up onto the blocks. Hal and three companions climb in—Hal first. They all crouch; there is a lot of laughter and chatter. Christie is on the floor. She is on her stomach propelling herself about in a modified breast stroke and frog kick. Hal peers over the edge of the box. He is very excited and when he sees Christie, he yells jeeringly, "Oh, look fiss." All come up quickly, yell, "Fiss," and duck down. Hal peers again, and in what seems pretended fear, dances up and down shouting, "Fiss."

It is important to note that hiding and withdrawing were not limited to the obviously fearful and timid children. In fact, many youngsters would alternate between attack and withdrawal. Some, indeed, could not express their need for tenderness, the longing for their lost babyhood, except by seeking refuge behind the ramparts of the block corner. In particular, the boys more often withdrew into boxes or behind walls, while the girls would make beds and litters for their own use. Very young children, from two to three and one half years old tended to use blocks in relation to their own bodies, sitting or lying on them, sucking them, or carrying them about. Among older children this seemed to indicate a desire for more care and fewer demands. For example, the following report was made on a little girl with impaired hearing who found it very hard to be separated from her mother.

It was a frequent sight to see Patsy curled up in an improvised bed of blocks or on the floor covered with scraps of material, sucking her thumb and twirling her hair. She was also fond of using the shelves and the little seats in the doll corner for playing "going to bed." . . . In the last two months her block building has improved greatly. She can spend a lot of time on one project and make fairly elaborate structures decorated with cubes, though, of course, these are not nearly as complicated and functional as those of the older children. She still likes to get into direct physical contact with her buildings, to sit on them, stand on them, or lie on them.

Neat, safe structures—floors, beds, platforms—were found to have a decided appeal to children who tended to be socially withdrawn or inhibited in their use of "messy" materials. Occasionally youngsters who seemed to be self-reliant and mature would give evidence of an incomplete acceptance of their state by a persistent use of blocks for beds or bottles. A conference on one such child brought to light the fact that she was the youngest of three children, that her mother worked during the day and had little time to devote to her in the evening, and that at four years of age she still used a bottle to help her fall asleep at night.

Enclosures also have a variety of other possible meanings. When constructed only occasionally they have no deep significance, but when a child concentrates on them repeatedly, they may indicate a desire for control, since things put inside them are "under the thumb" of the block builder—or they may spell safety to the child who is not yet ready to leave his crib, his carriage, or his mother's arms. We cannot emphasize too often that the specific meanings of any given structure—when they have a meaning—can be elicited only in the light of other aspects of the child's behavior. The child, who builds platforms because they are "neat" will hesitate to use clay and finger-paints—the child who is attracted by their "safety" value will be hesitant about climbing to the top of the Jungle Gym or tend to remain on the fringe of the group or withdraw into a corner by himself.

Children who use blocks as barriers or for hiding valuable objects frequently have reason to resent or fear the world in which they live. Below we present a condensed record of a three-and-one-half-year-old boy who, in his short life, had been subjected to three major pressures: the indifferent care of a succession of maids, the birth of a baby in the family, and the loss of his father by divorce. His mother was much too busy with her own affairs to concern herself about him. He was ordinarily destructive in a defiant and diffuse way, and obviously suffered from guilt. It may be that for this disturbed and guilt-ridden child being shut away from the world was the only opportunity for peace, especially after the retaliation of his group mates.

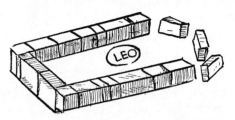

LEO'S CORRAL

Leo half kneels in the middle of a corral-shaped fence of blocks. He puts in eight long blocks, then lays two long, flat, thin boards over them, creating a small cubbyhole underneath. During this time he is quite alone, his back to the classroom and his crouched position seems to be almost a hiding posture.

He now puts a large cow and pig into one corner and pushes a warship in under his cubbyhole structure.

LEO'S SMALL WORLD

Cort, an impish child, runs over and pushes Leo, as much from momentum as intention. He falls back, stumbles, and the two scatter the end of the corral structure with their scuffling feet. Leo lets out a loud scream, a crescendo cry, more rage than hurt. The teacher comes over immediately and says to Cort, "Don't knock down Leo's road, dear." Leo's large eyes lose their flash. Mollified, he turns back to his blocks, climbs over the far side to pick up four long blue automobiles, which he arranges carefully in a close compact row. He turns his back on the scattered ends of his structure, but soon notices two boys playing with his blocks. He turns, and says in a plaintive, whining tone, "That my roe" (apparently meaning "road"). The teacher is again on hand, and Leo watches her repair the fence. She asks if this is the way he had it before, and he watches, says a laconic "yep" to each move she makes and to each question.

When the repairing is finished, Leo smiles timidly and starts to play. Bobby chooses this moment to assume an air of exaggerated casualness, but in a split second he kicks the row of automobiles viciously, his small face alight with a kind of savage glee. Leo sinks back on his heels, almost as if the kicks were directed at him. The teacher, in a mild tone, calls Bobby off. Leo just sits and stares after him, his large eyes round and sad, as if on the verge of tears. Roy, a bigger boy, runs up and with clenched teeth jumps into the center of the corral and quite methodically and deliberately kicks every block he can see that is standing at all. The result is a complete shambles. Leo now sits on the floor, a completely beaten look on his face. Finally he grasps his knees with his small hands and looks at the mess, stunned, sighing softly, "My roe—my roe." Suddenly he gets up, goes over to some blocks about six feet away that have been left in the form of a circle by some other child. He first makes an opening, goes inside apparently more relaxed— talks and giggles with Donald, rearranges them to form a long swooping curve, fitting them precisely together. Having fixed this to suit him, he climbs over to sit inside, now facing the class.

Symbol and Fantasy

It should be clear by this time that the use of blocks is anything but literal. Very frequently blocks have a symbolic value which is expressed at times in dramatic play, at times in the forms which the child creates, at times in the functions these structures perform. We have already mentioned their use as food, nursing bottles, and guns, as well as their value in building symbols of power and safety such as cars and busses. Here we would like to draw attention to some striking parallels which seem to prove that blocks may represent things of great importance in the child's particular situation.

Four-year-old Maisie is taller, stouter, and more ungainly than any other child in her group. During periods when her awkwardness is most pronounced, she starts off her block building with a remarkably high and solid structure, then leaves it standing and joins her friends in some coopera- tive project. . . . Play appears to reflect home environment as Larry, a young apartment dweller of three and one half years, arranges his blocks to form small roomlike enclosures filled with toys and figures. The parallel seems to break down when he puts a man on one of the walls as if super- vising those inside—for there is no man in his immediate

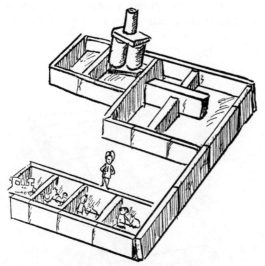

LARRY'S BLOCK BUILDING

family. However, further inquiry reveals that a male relative of Larry's mother has recently come to take care of him. . . . Amy, a little older, also has adult figures overlooking enclosures—but the figures are male and female and the enclosures are usually empty. Investigation shows that her apartment is larger and less cluttered than Larry's—and that life in it is a constant battle between her parents and herself. . . . Hal, on the other hand, puts his figures of a man and a woman inside, and shields his building from invasion. This four-year-old, we find, is the only child of overprotective and overrestrictive parents and is quite unable to express open rebellion even against the adults at school. Here is a portion of his record.

Hal has joined other boys in building with small blocks. His construction is very symmetrical and tall. He balances each block carefully. Occasionally he stops to look at Lenny's bridge and watches him run trains and cars under and over it. Hal gets two painted wooden figures, a man and a woman, and by opening the foundation, places them inside, then shuts it up again. . . .

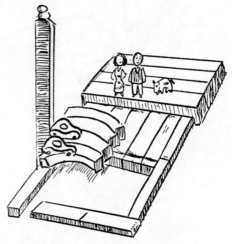

AMY'S BLOCK BUILDING

Michael comes over to Hal's house and removes the bottom block. Hal immediately calls, "Teacher, Michael opened my building." Michael answers in an apologetic tone that he just wanted to see what was inside it. Hal goes over to Michael's house and threatens with his foot to kick over the blocks. The teacher interferes. Hal runs and shields his own building protectively with his arms, complaining, "Teacher, teacher, Michael is going—." But he did not finish the statement because at that point he realized that Michael was busy building.

It is difficult to separate the symbolic aspects of blocks from their use in the expression of fantasies. In dramatic play we find them not only serving singly as symbolic accessories, becoming food, skis, trains, crutches, guns, nursing bottles, pocketbooks, cakes of ice, and valises—but in combination they are transformed into an endless variety of structures. Sometimes, too, we observe a movement from relatively barren and simple uses to rich and complex expressions in the

course of a child's growth. But since we have already illustrated these points in Chapter II, we shall confine ourselves
to some specific ways in which blocks help the child express
his fantasies. First, however, we must repeat that it is not
easy for an observer to understand their full meaning for a
child without hearing what he says about them and without
knowing something of his background, his basic problems,
and the way he functions with other materials. We should
like to illustrate this point by citing an excerpt from a record
of Bud, whom we have encountered earlier.

Bud builds a road along the shelves: "See, Rex, how I do
it." Rex looks. Bud: "This train is going to go to San Fran-
cisco. Long subway, its going to be so long that you're going
to say 'Holy Mackerel.' Now watch. (Rex is not looking. Bud
is rather talking to himself.) The train's going to start from
here, hoooo, hoooo. Watch out, the train is going to go. I'm
going to make it this long. . . . (Goes on building.) I'm going
to make it longer. The express is going to go to Coney Island
for the whole night, and you're going to miss me, and you're
never going to see me again. . . . I want to keep on a long
subway. See how long it is. Hoo, Hoo." He pushes the subway train slowly, singing part of "Jingle Bells."

At first glance Bud seems to be playing train in much the
same way as other little boys the world over. Only when we
hear him talking about his train do we suspect that it is both
a weapon and a means of escape. And when we learn that
he has suggested during a puppet show that the little boy
puppet could punish his parents by going away and never
coming back, our insight into the meaning of Bud's block-play
grows more definite.

Interestingly enough, many of the fantasies externalized
through blocks are concerned with doom and destruction.
It may be that because blocks are so solid and indestructible
the child feels safe in playing out both his fears of disaster
from without and his destructive impulses from within.

Moreover, in projecting these feelings on something so concrete and real, the child is able to rob them of their power and their threat. In the following records we are not aware of all the implications of Rex's persistent resort to magic and his dramatic fantasies of violence and catastrophe, but we can be sure that a large component of anxiety underlies them, and that he is trying to master it by proving to himself that no matter what happens, he can control the situation and keep himself safe. The first brief excerpt was quoted in Chapter III, when we were studying Donnie's dramatic play.

Next they all pile blocks on the car and pretend they are burning it up. Rex is the leader in this play. He announces, "I'm going in the fire," and lies down over the blocks and Jackie follows suit. . . . Donnie helps to pile blocks on Rex to "burn him up," as Rex tells them to do. The other children excitedly drop bricks on Rex.

When Allan wanted a gun to shoot over the walls, Rex said mysteriously, "I know where a gun is," and danced off on tiptoe, peeking back at the group, weaving his body, and making many gestures. He went a few feet away, and made gestures in the air, and said, "Abacadabra." Then he came back. "Now we've got a gun," he said and held out an imaginary gun to Allan. . . . Allan, Rex, and Jackie began to say "Bang, bang," and knocked the blocks off in their excitement. Then they ran around and put the blocks up again. Rex tired of this in a few moments, and said over and over, "Let's have this a post office." No one seemed to pay any attention, so he stood up and said to Eric, who had just come back, "Where are your wings?" "You have to have wings." Eric said, "Where are yours?" Rex replied, "You can't see mine. They are magical."

Later, after building a "big, big boat" and an airplane of blocks Rex said to Donnie, "I can blow you up, huh, cause I've got bullet, bullet, bullet [pointing to parts of his plane], and bullet. And bullet, bullet bullet." Donnie said, "But this is a machine." Rex: "You can't crash. I can't crash into you because you'd blow up and I'd blow up."

Then Rex built a bigger plane. "My airplane's better, huh. You better watch out. [He talked to himself very low.] Yah, yah, open gates. Come on. Open gates," and he pushed Donnie's blocks. . . . Rex said, "My plane is moving this way," and ran it into a chair. It fell to pieces and he said, "Oh, a bomb fell and it all fell apart." He dropped some blocks on Donnie's plane. Donnie, with a set expression, threw a little block past Rex and then looked at him. Rex began to rebuild and built partly on Donnie's plane. He seemed quieter and more relaxed.

We cannot leave this discussion of destructive impulses without reminding the reader that children also advance their growth through more beneficent types of dramatic play with blocks. Henry, an anxious and infantile youngster, had difficulty with everything he attempted in the preschool program and spent most of his time running around in apparently aimless fashion. His block-play, however, is rich and mature for a three-year-old and he assigns himself roles of leadership and strength. It may be long before Henry is able to sustain similar roles in reality, but these block fantasies are very probably a first step in that direction.

Record 1. Henry helped Max and Freddie build a large tower. Henry: "Let's build a garage for the car." They brought more blocks and piled them near the tower. Henry stopped and climbed up the ladder saying, "I'm the fireman. I'm putting out the fire." He pulled the wagon about, shouting, "Hey, I'm the fireman, get out of the way." He stopped suddenly at the tower, sat in the wagon and watched Max and Freddie build the garage.

Record 2. Henry made a bus out of large blocks, high in the front for the steering wheel. He looked at the observer and said, "I made a bus, I'm going to drive the children on a trip." Several children sat in the bus, making noises like a car.

Whether beneficent or destructive in quality, we know that the dramatic play which blocks help to implement serves to "fill out" the personality of the child. It is an external expression of inner feelings, confusions, and gropings which helps him master in concrete form what was before only shadowy and mutely sensed.

Blocks as an Aid to Social Integration

We begin with a picture of Lonnie. For two of his three and one half years this little boy had been living with his mother, a younger sister, and a succession of maids. Neither child was wanted by the parents. Lonnie did not understand why his father, whom he saw occasionally, had left home, nor why his mother let the maid take him to and from the bus every day and was rarely in when he returned. Little wonder, that his school day often begins with "I break . . . "—which he then proceeds to do. His favorite occupations are smashing jars of paint, running away into the street, the office, or the kitchen (his appetite is insatiable), and smearing paint, food, or anything at all. Clay is especially attractive since it can be rubbed into one's hair, bitten, put in one's ears or up one's nose. Crayons have no appeal. but the paper does, since it can be ripped up in tiny pieces and flung around the room. When confronted with situations he cannot handle, Lonnie shrieks and throws things about. He crawls more frequently than he walks and sometimes urinates in the room. He rarely speaks, except to say "no." But if his teacher should happen to say "I like you," his immediate reply is, "No you don't, damn you!" He never wants to go home. When the group is indoors, most of his time is spent in the director's office to save the other children and equipment from his depredations. This is Lonnie. Now let us look at him in the block corner.

Lonnie is sitting on the window sill in the housekeeping corner, his feet firmly planted on the top of the stove which stands directly below. The thumb of his right hand is held tightly in his mouth (no sucking movements). In his left hand he holds a toy broom which is dangling loosely in mid-air. He has a serious, somber expression on his face. Dave wants to use the stove for cooking, and he cautiously pushes Lonnie's feet to one side. Lonnie quickly and rather forcefully replaces his feet right in the center of the stove. Dave looks pleadingly in the teacher's direction, and says in a soft, plaintive voice, "I want to cook." The teacher walks across the room to Lonnie. "Now dear, let Dave cook. You put your feet on this half of the stove and Dave will use this half for cooking." She gently pushes Lonnie's feet to the right side of the stove. He makes a quick half-turn and plants his feet firmly in the center of the stove again, a defiant expression on his face.

The teacher walks to the block shelf. She busies herself with the long blocks, lifting them high up so that Lonnie, who watches her movements very cautiously, can see them. "Anyone care to build?" she asks, and places the blocks on the floor near the shelf. Lonnie relaxes, slides down from the window sill to the stove, and from the stove to the floor using the broom for support. Once on the floor he flings the broom carelessly across the room—his attention rivetted on the teacher. She says in an encouraging tone, "Lonnie is going to build something for us." Lonnie removes his thumb from his mouth. Charlie follows him, quickly gets down on his knees and pulls the long blocks from the bottom shelf to the floor. Lonnie's expression changes to one of anticipation and a happy smile lights up his pale little face. He squats down on the floor next to Charlie, picks up a long block and props it up on the floor, long end up. "Sit up, block," he says happily. He laughs loudly and sings, "Happy birthday to you," to the block. Charlie rests one side of the long block on the shelf and the other side on the floor, then adds others to build an incline. Lonnie moves over on his knees, and tries to place his block in line with the others. The block slips. Charlie picks it up and deftly places it in line with the others. Lonnie does not seem to mind. Charlie stands up, picks a small green car from the top of the shelf, stoops over and slides it down the incline. Both boys laugh loudly. "Do it again?" he asks Lonnie. Lonnie happily answers, "Yep." They send car after car down the ramp and out into the room. Both boys are now laughing so loudly that they are bending over clasping their stomachs. Then they begin to shriek. The teacher, attracted to the scene, picks up one of the long blocks and places it on the floor about twelve inches from the incline, apparently to stop the cars at that point. "Want to put it there so that the cars do not go too far?" Lonnie shouts. He does not remove it. . . . Now he tries to see how the blocks fit in under the incline. "Very funny," he mutters to himself and giggles (such a contrast to his former sour, apprehensive, challenging mood). As he tries to push still another block in, he realizes that there is no more room, and with a disappointed note in his voice he calls out to Charlie, "No more room there." Charlie goes over and succeeds in getting three more under. Now they both stand up and proudly survey their building structure.

What is there about blocks that can tame a young hellion like Lonnie? Can it be that they are the only part of his environment which he can control? Are they the only materials that do not evoke memories of punishment, of painful and confused feelings? Notice how he personalizes the blocks, talking to them as if they were human, making them do what he wants. Perhaps they represent the people of his little world who won't "sit up" when he tells them, but on the contrary force him to sit or stand or move as they desire. One thing we know: Lonnie is happy when he is with the blocks—and when he is happy he can play pleasantly and constructively and even gaily with another little child.

The magical power of blocks is quite as evident in the case of Wallace, an only child of five years whose father had also left the household. He lives alone with his mother and a maid and visits his father occasionally, always returning in a fighting mood. In school his behavior is hostile and disorganized. He spits at adults, throws paint and other things into the toilet and out of the office window, smears anything that will smear, and brings matches to "burn up the school." The other children resent his constant abuse and frequently shout, "Take him out! Punish him!" Yet, strangely enough, even this disturbed youngster can play with blocks—and only with blocks. What is more, his buildings are extraordinarily mature and ingenious and he can play with other children for long periods.

Wallace opens a book, looks into it anxiously, skips a few pages, scans a few more—and he's off at a gallop to the block corner. He notices Van (of the first grade) building. "Can I play with you, Van?" he asks politely. "You may, but don't break anything." Wallace: "Let's play garage." "Well . . . O.K." Van bends down to arrange some blocks against the wall. Wallace runs to another corner and brings back some cars, busses, and trucks. "Here," says Wallace, "put them in here," pointing to a space between two blocks. "Wait, I'll make a stable for you." "I can fit them in here," insists Wallace, placing them in the empty space. Van doesn't like Wallace's aggressiveness and says, "Look here, I'm boss." Wallace does not budge. They push each other around a bit. "You'll leave me now," demands Van. "No I won't, we're partners," answers Wallace. "You leave, you bad boy." "No, I won't." "I'll go somewhere else," says the gentlemanly Van. Wallace sees that he is victorious and says, "O.K. Look, weren't you here first? You be the boss, I'll be your partner." They begin working together but the blocks don't fit well. Another child comes over and asks why the garage isn't finished. Van stumbles for something to say, but Wallace diplomatically takes the situation in hand: "He built it first; it got too messy, we had to break it down. We started over again, but he's still the first boss and I'm the second boss." They return to their work. John, building nearby, gets up angrily and comes over to Wallace's and Van's combined project, and pushes over a block. "Why do you do that?" Wallace asks in a fatherly fashion, not angered in the least. "Because he almost broke mine." (He points to Van). "But," answers Wallace, "He broke *ours.*" (He said this as if to mean—He broke his own which he likes, he certainly didn't mean you any harm.) John nudges Van and they begin to argue. Wallace returns to his blocks and cars; he is not interested in their argument. He runs his cars over his blocks and fits cars, trucks, and busses into their stalls. Suddenly he runs to get two jeeps, puts them on the floor and says, as if delivering a lecture, "Busses must go with busses, trucks must park with trucks, cars must park with cars, and jeeps must park with jeeps." Van: "Wait till we finish." He is trying to enlarge the garage by adding blocks to it. "I'm a boss, too," he adds implying that Wallace is the real boss, which is quite true. The teacher comes by and says, "Clean-up time." Van and John are ready to break up their masterpieces. Wallace is at first reluctant to do so. But he delights in breaking it up. Then when his garage is in pieces he exclaims enthusiastically, "Let's make something else."

Somehow blocks seem to mean order and peace to Wallace. In playing with them his hostile feelings are subdued, his emotional tangles forgotten, and his intelligence comes to the fore. Over and over again we find these aggressive and solitary children making positive contacts in the block corner and maintaining them with flexibility, ingenuity, and an amazing mastery of social techniques. But again—why *blocks*? We have already given several reasons for their "magical powers," but more possibilities suggest themselves at this point. First, they are generally the most familiar kind of play material the preschool program offers, and since they are associated with home and mother as much as they are with school, they may supply a comforting link between the two. Secondly, they are extremely permissive. In the block corner a child may build completely alone, in parallel fashion, or in active cooperation as he wishes, since others are also relaxed and absorbed in creative activity. Moreover, when children who comprise the "ingroup" are having a good time, the newcomer and the isolate are tempted to join them and are likely to be accepted. Thirdly, the more complicated block projects lend themselves readily to group participation in which leaders may put aside personal demands and the unskilled or unwanted may find a place for themselves. Time and again we find a spirit of camaraderie that is rarely duplicated in any other type of play. In view of these considerations, it is not hard to see why the block corner contributes so materially to the social growth of many a child.

Brigands of the Block Corner

Block-play has frequently been extolled because it does not require a teacher's supervision—thereby freeing her for other activities, and enabling the child who does not quite trust adults to be himself. However, it is important to recognize that the lack of supervision may actually prevent some children from getting the full benefit of the activity. These are usually the timid youngsters who readily fall prey to the aggressors of the block corner and ironically they are often the ones whose inner pressures block all other channels of expression. We believe that if teachers understood fully the extraordinary service which play with blocks can perform for such children, they would make every effort to protect them from attack. For documentary evidence of what frequently happens to such children when teacher awareness is lacking, we now present an episode from the record of Billie, an intelligent five-year-old who seemed to be completely isolated from the others in his group.

Billie has been running up and down the room shouting "Bang, Bang," with some other boys—not quite with them, but among them. He is quiet now, watching three boys build a fenced-in fort, then staring into space. He suddenly joins the group and goes to work immediately making the joints more neat. He looks happy and absorbed. Suddenly, as if with a purpose in mind, he gets up and goes across the room to get the wooden block dolls, and he smiles as the children look approvingly at his addition to the game. The others begin to put the dolls in a row on one end of the fence. Billie wants to put one on top of the other and stand them up double height. The nearest boy takes them apart and puts them side by side. He tries again with the next pair of dolls, but the other children protest. Then he firmly begins to take over—lining them up more accurately, shoulder to shoulder. At this point Sammy almost leaps into the fort center, knocks all the dolls down with his foot, and shouts, "Dead! Dead!" Then he runs off. Billie frowns, quietly picks up the dolls, and starts to rebuild them. But Sammy comes back and knocks them down. Billie goes to the pile of blocks about four feet away, sits down, and starts to do his own building. He will add to the fence gateway. Sammy stands up immediately, pushes it away with vehemence, almost yells that he does not want it done that way. Billie looks up with a tightening of the lips, but does not protest. He simply pushes backward on the floor and picks up different blocks and begins to play entirely alone. He makes an arch out of curved blocks and balances other pieces on top—until Sammy reappears and deliberately kicks and steps on his structure. Billie is sad faced, almost weeping, but says nothing even when Sammy says he is using his blocks.

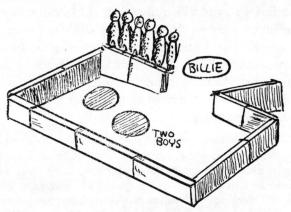

BILLIE'S BLOCK BUILDING

Billie quietly moves back another few feet, starts to build with smaller blocks, but Sammy again follows him, this time leaping on Billie's structure with full force. Billie picks up two blocks and holds them; he is now partly angry and partly fear-

ful. Sammy turns and tries to pull them from him. Billie
holds tight and they tug: "You're taking most of them, you
tramp!" But it is a losing battle since Sammy is bigger and
stronger and is standing up. Billie suddenly changes tactics,
drops his anger, begins to plead, "But these are the only blocks
I need." He smiles a tremulous smile, tries to placate further,
saying, "Please!" When this doesn't work, he gets up and
sits down even further away, where there are only very small
blocks scattered. When Sammy comes over and takes the
blocks away, Billie just looks, his face tense and sad. Finally
he picks up two small arch forms nearby and carries them over
to Sammy and asks if he would like to use them. With a
slightly surprised look, Sammy accepts them, puts another arch
over his now lengthening railway. Billie squats down nearby
and attempts to make quiet suggestions. He tries another arch
himself, putting it over the railway. Sammy just as carefully
takes it off, but without vehemence. Billie looks at him,
frowns—then giving up completely, he abruptly trots over to
the teacher.

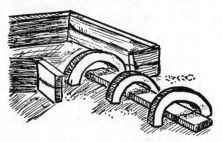

BILLIE'S AND SAMMY'S COOPERATIVE EFFORT

Many other instances of such laissez-faire treatment can be
found in our records. Sometimes a child who is already confused and badgered by life will be completely abandoned to
the persistent persecution of a playmate at a time when he
is manifestly unable to take care of his own defenses. It is
not uncommon to find such a child literally driven to take
shelter behind his block rampart. In our discussion of dramatic play, we showed how Donnie was a frequent victim of

Bud and Jackie, and we reproduced an especially poignant incident in which he was prevented from using his "car" to develop a compensatory fantasy. Precisely because blocks have such a unique value for inhibited or timid or disorganized children, and for those who can find no comfort in people, it is essential that the block corner be maintained as a place of refuge and that interference and persecution be prevented.

What Can the Teacher Do?

At this point many a reader will be thinking, "Well, granted that all you say about the importance of block-play is true, just what can the teacher do about it? How can she help the child derive all possible benefit from it?" Since a direct question deserves a direct response, and since space is limited, we shall offer our suggestions in summary form. In general we feel that the answer lies in providing an abundance of four things: space, materials, permissiveness, and teachers' alertness.

MANAGING SPACE AND MATERIALS

Since a large floor area is needed for free block-play, movable screens or sets of shelves may be used to mark it off and to protect both builders and buildings. Another way of providing plenty of space is to allow indoor blocks to be used out-of-doors—particularly by timid youngsters who find it hard to work through their problems with the more overwhelming outdoor blocks and accessories. The teacher might well try this experiment either when the child shies away from outdoor construction or rushes about incessantly from one part of the outdoor play area to the other.

Several block areas and storage places are better than one, both to attract children to other activities such as household play and to prevent some of the depredations that occur when many youngsters are concentrated in one spot. The teacher might enclose a space for the timid child without limiting his freedom of movement. This can be done most easily when blocks are stored on movable shelves in the corners of the room.

Since there is no limit to the number of block units a group of children can use, we suggest that provision be made in the budget for building up the supply. This would also make it possible to keep a few buildings standing, since some children are more interested in the product than the process. When this poses a space problem, a table or a corner in the office might be provided for the more permanent buildings. Teachers report that these structures are often used day after day for rich and varied dramatic play. Moreover, some of the "destructive" behavior we have observed may stem from resentment over breaking up the buildings at clean-up time.

As a matter of fact, cleaning up calls for more consideration than the average teacher gives it. Instead of merely issuing a general order to put things away, she might use the occasion to show appreciation of her children's feelings about their handiwork. To give her time to move from group to group making comments she might start the clean up a little earlier. Warning the children ahead of time also has its merits, not only in getting a readier response but also in stimulating more effective play during the last few minutes. The teacher might well take a cue from particularly obedient or particularly uncooperative behavior at this time. The rebellious child may need more satisfactory block-building opportunities, and the conformist might profit from more emphasis on active and creative play, since he has probably been subjected to excessive pressure toward cleanliness and tidiness at home.

GUIDING THE PLAY

The alert teacher will be on the watch for ways of luring the withdrawn child into activity. When he hangs around a group, he is showing signs of interest which she can encourage by bringing him materials and by suggesting that he play in an area somewhat apart from the others or with a group of the gentler and more passive youngsters. She might also suggest a role which would be acceptable to the other children, such as bringing them blocks or building a structure that would fit into their plans.

No general statement can be made about the amount or kind of teacher help in block-corner play, but here are some guides that might prove useful: be sure to understand the child's own intentions so that you may implement them; hold back until you make certain that he cannot solve the difficulty himself; if he asks for help get him to tell you just what he wants. This approach will minimize the risk of interfering with his private expressions of fantasy and of stifling his creativity or his sense of mastering things without help. Sometimes very slight assistance pays very large dividends. One teacher of a group of three-year-olds thought that her new children were slow in approaching the block corner. By simply laying some blocks on the floor she succeeded in arousing their curiosity and from there on it was not hard to lead them to handle the blocks themselves. She then encouraged them by showing an interest in what they were doing, and as they gained satisfaction from their achievements, she was able to leave them to develop the play on their own.

We cannot overemphasize the danger of setting patterns in block work. It has the same disadvantage as making models to be copied in clay or pictures to be reproduced in poster paint. We know definitely that teacher-initiated activity is unsuccessful unless it is an extension of the child's own wishes. Some children betray an excessive desire to please adults by imitating the teacher; others feel hampered if she even looks at them, as if their block-play were expressing something too private to be scrutinized by others. It is well to keep an eye on the behavior of such children, but it should be done from a distance.

PERMISSIVENESS

We have already spoken of the value of permitting blocks to be used in other than the accepted constructive fashion. We realize that teachers are frequently apprehensive about behavior that smacks of aggression, but we believe it will be possible to keep aggressive activities within manageable limits by making it clear that blocks are not to be used as missiles against people. Instead of making children feel guilty about their destructive impulses, the teacher might do them a great service by arranging a "throwing corner," with a piece of heavy wallboard to receive the blows. If she feels that her presence is necessary for the protection of possible victims, she might say, "Call me when you feel like throwing blocks because we don't throw them unless a teacher is nearby, and we don't throw them at other people."

Summary

Blocks offer a great variety of play values. They are used to satisfy needs for "adventure and risk," for "formless explosions" and substitute objects of hostility, for safety and passivity, for both privacy and social contact, for expressing fantasies and exploring reality. They are perhaps the least threatening of the materials available in the preschool program and from some points of view the most productive of behavioral cues which the teacher can use in assessing the child's development and her own role in relation to further growth. But to understand what the child is saying, she must be on the spot while the play is going on, she must listen as well as look, and she must relate what he does in the block corner to his behavior with different materials and with different people. If we can retain this orientation to personal meanings, and at the same time note the learning that takes place regarding spatial relationships, designing, and construction, then our observation of the child as he plays with the blocks is bound to be rich in results.

CHAPTER V

The Benefits of Water-Play

ANYONE who has watched a three-year-old zestfully wash and rinse and squeeze a pair of doll socks cannot doubt the irresistible attraction that water holds for the very young. The child's utter absorption in this rhythmic activity and the almost hypnotic effect it has upon him inevitably calls to mind the fascination of a waterfall or of waves rising and falling on a beach.

In view of this fascination, one would expect that water would be given a conspicuous place in programs designed for preschool and kindergarten children. It certainly is easily obtainable and little expense is involved. It is one of the few basic substances still easily available for exploration by urban children. It lends itself to a variety of activities and offers a wide range of manipulation and learning. But it has not merely learning values to recommend it; it has something even more valuable—the absorbed delight and joyous enthusiasm of the children as they play with it. Yet, in spite of the fact that contemporary psychology tends to accept the child himself as the best indicator of his needs and regards need fulfillment as a necessary precursor to healthful advances in development, strangely enough, the child's apparent urge for free and uninterrupted experimentation and exploration with water seems to have been almost completely overlooked.

When water *is* included in the nursery program it generally seems to be accepted in a rather grudging and half-hearted fashion by those who administer the activities. Of twelve teachers interviewed casually concerning the materials available in their groups, only two spoke of water as something which had a place in its own right. It was very rarely mentioned spontaneously, and when pointed questions were asked, it was merely conceded a place as an accessory material, subsidiary to such activities as washing dishes, cleaning shelves, or other household play. Quite frequently teachers did not even understand what we meant by the term "water-play."

Our first suggestions concerning the possibility of using water as a basic material met with considerable resistance. The objections were varied. Some teachers feared that the children would be "confused" if they were permitted to play with water in the group and not at home—forgetting that the same argument might be used against any material in the program except perhaps crayons and blocks, and that group experience is designed to supplement the home. Others feared that they would use the water "wildly," and that their exuberance would brook no bounds. Still others professed willingness to use water more freely but insisted that the parents of the children would object to their getting wet. In view of all this hesitation, it would appear that the teachers themselves have considerable resistance to the free use of water in the program.

The effect of this resistance is also indicated in statements made by teachers who were evaluating different materials. One teacher stated flatly that she thought water had the greatest therapeutic effect, that just having his face washed soothed a troubled child; yet in her own group, water-play was largely restricted to washing doll's clothes on rainy days. The following statement might explain this restriction to some extent, "John and Jane were washing the floor one day; I felt that it was all right but I was afraid of what the parents would say. They feel it isn't the thing for their children to do outside of the home, because of the stigma attached to people of their means doing menial work." Another said, "The children love water, but still feel inhibited in their use of it as they are afraid to get wet because of what their mothers will say." A third remarked, "This is the most popular activity in my group. The children seem to get the most relaxation from using water. One can learn quite a bit about the children from watching them using water." She added, however, "We only bring the large tub out for them on rainy days." A fourth teacher, ordinarily rather conservative in her approach, testified that she found water a source of release. She said, "The most disturbed children would sit at it for the longest time, whereas with other materials they couldn't settle down at all. They would pour water from one cup to another. I would get it for them, and during bad weather when we had to stay indoors, I would see that they had a good period of water-play." Yet the same teacher indicated a less than complete acceptance of water by adding, "In the case of children who followed their own needs with other equipment, I would only get the water when it was asked for."

The teachers' resistance to water-play probably has many sources. As children they may have suffered the strictures against playing with dirt and water which operate in most middle-class households. The resulting tensions may be revived when water-play is considered for their groups—particularly since their training courses have never given it the acceptable status of blocks, clay, and paints. On another level, we can readily understand their reluctance in view of the cleaning up required. However, it is easy enough to make the cleaning-up process part of the ongoing play with water. (Indeed, one of the reasons that children are so willing to clean up after using clay and finger-paints is that the cleanup involves the use of water.) Anyone who has witnessed the repeated and delighted scrubbing of shelves, chairs, chests, and floor in the doll corner cannot doubt that spreading water over surfaces has a fascination of its own.

A third explanation of the resistance might lie in the teacher's lack of familiarity with the procedures involved. This, however, should disappear with a clear description of the way water-play can be set up. Indeed, this is exactly what happened in several situations where water had never before been used except as a minor accessory to household play or as a substitute for paint in outdoor play.

As used in this study, the term water-play refers to the free and unhindered use of water during which the child immerses various articles, pours, blows bubbles, or simply splashes or agitates it to produce movement. A large metal washtub serves these purposes well, but washbowls or small basins may also be used. If fairly small vessels have to be used, it is best to provide enough for each child to have his own, in order to avoid interference. Soap, bubble bath, and other foam-producing agents are valuable accessories for enriching the play. Other useful equipment includes containers for pouring the water, absorbent materials such as sponges and cloths, and objects which can float. Funnels and strainers might be added for learning purposes and small rubber dolls, unbreakable dishes, doll clothes, straws, bubble pipes, small cakes of soap and utensils from the housekeeping corner also serve to increase its possibilities.

It is obviously desirable to keep the atmosphere as free as possible so that the children may develop the play in accordance with their own concepts and needs. If limits must be established, they should be set down at the beginning to avoid confusion. However, real thought should be given to these restrictions. It was found during the course of this project that many of those originally proposed could be eliminated once the teachers were able to accept the activity as part of the group program. They discovered that mopping up was just as much fun as splashing, and all that was needed was some foresight in choosing a waterproof spot for the play. They found, too, that the children themselves can be easily protected by poncholike garments and even footgear of plastic material. However, since most nursery groups require that a complete change of clothing be available in the child's locker at all times, there is little ground for worry about chilling even if the protective garments are not completely effective.

It might be appropriate at this point to consider the contributions of water-play to child development from a more theoretical point of view. Most children in the preschool age range have not yet completed the adjustment tasks set by society in relation to the control of body processes—oral, anal, and urethral. Although their experience is still largely in terms of sensation, their urge to explore is constantly being curbed. Food is to be eaten, not played with, and feces and urine, which have a very intimate connection with their self-hood, are never to be handled at all. In the child's view, body products are as legitimate as any other substance, and his desire to learn about them is particularly urgent since they have been part of himself. To deny him this right is, in a sense, to alienate him from part of his being. Now, we know from recognized studies in genetic psychology that children are able to accept substitutes for activities that are denied them, and often seek them in proportion to the degree of deprivation. We know, too, that they frequently equate water with urine. In view of all these related facts, it therefore seems logical to assume that free access to water will give children an opportunity to satisfy in substitute fashion legitimate needs which our child-rearing practices usually frustrate.

Basic Sense Experience

It is generally accepted that sensory experiences precede and form the basis for later abilities to comprehend and manipulate abstract symbols. Indeed, the whole concept of the activity program—learning by doing—is based on this axiom. In view of the wide recognition of this fundamental psychological theory, opportunity for free exploration and direct sense experience should be offered every boy and girl. This is particularly important at the preschool level where the child tends to learn through his body and to sense and feel rather than think his way through experiences. This suggests another essential function of water-play. It helps the child build up the basic mass of intimate organic experience on which his cognitive life will later depend. It stimulates a multisensory investigation of the physical world that no other substance can quite duplicate.

In the following description of a boy at play with bubbles, not only can we see this multidimensional quality, but we can also sense the extraordinary vividness and pleasure the experience affords. This is all the more striking because the situation is set up in a comparatively restricted manner, the accessories involved suggesting only one kind of play.

The teacher began gathering together the necessary equipment to blow bubbles and asked Bud to help her, which he was quite ready to do. He trips after her, chirping happily to himself. "Bubble, bubble pipe, bubble, bubble pipe," over and over. Miss K joins in and chants softly, "Bubbles, bubbles, bubbles." When she lifts the pitcher off the shelf, he laughs with joy, throwing his head back. He proffers his cup to Miss K so the water can be measured. He snatches the cup back to put his nose into it and makes a noise. Cocking his head, he listens to the echo and laughs. Miss K shakes some soap flakes into the pitcher. Bud puts his hand on the box to help, leaning close over the pitcher; his face is radiant, his lips are parted in a half-smile. He wriggles his nose and looks up into the teacher's face. "Soap flakes go right up my nose," he remarks gaily, his voice rising. The teacher turns on the water and Bud, carefully holding his cup in two hands, fills it and empties it into the pitcher—once, twice, three times—each time peering into it. He thrusts his hand into it and swishes the water around vigorously, loudly sing-songing "Bubbles, bubbles, bubbles." Miss K picks up the pitcher and with a nod of her head indicates the table where the bubbles are to be blown. Bud scurries over to the table and with tentative, busy little motions helps Miss C put down the paper. Miss K has begun to pour water into the cups of the children already sitting at the table. Quickly Bud whirls around, pushes his cup closer to Miss K and urgently rasps out, "Me first!" As Miss K fills his cup, he maneuvers around the edge of the table, still holding on to his cup, and squirms into a seat with a grunt of satisfaction. Miss K sings a little impromptu song, "Bubbles for sale!" as she dispenses the sudsy water. Bud begins a song of his own, softly at first, "Bubbles, bubbles, bubbles, bubbles," becoming louder and then softer again. He grabs for a straw as Miss C calmly passes them out. Hunched over the table he blows bubbles until the surface of the water in his cup is covered. He leans back in his chair and looks at them with a pleased expression and a suggestion of a smile on his face and a gleam in his eye. With the palm of his hand he touches the top of the bubbles, ever so gently. Then he breaks some of them with his hands. He feels some of the soapy, sudsy water between the tips of his fingers. He seems to be utterly detached from the others at the table. Leaning down to the cup, Bud blows across the top of the bubbles; he seems intrigued that some pop and others do not. He takes a deep breath and blows more forcefully, breaking them all. An expression of disappointed surprise flits across his face. "Awm, aw," he laments in a low, sad voice. Recovering his spirits, he says in a jaunty, singing way to no one in particular, "Bubbles are done-y. . . ." He reaches for a straw which Miss C hands to him. He settles down in his chair and puts his face close to the mug, blowing the bubbles until they are heaped high over the top. Leaning down he puts his chin into the bubbles. He chortles. Putting the tip of his tongue into the bubbles he carefully tastes them. He laughs to himself. He drinks some of the water and makes a wry face but it seems not to be entirely unpleasant. In a very businesslike manner he goes briskly to the bathroom to refill his cup. In the act of getting settled at his place again Bud sees that Rod's bubbles have spilt onto the table. Reaching across the table he spreads the soapy water over the table with gross, sweeping motions, wildly, with great excitement. His face is flushed. . . . He lifts up a handful of bubbles, squeezes his hands together and feels the soapy water of the broken bubbles. His expression is thoughtful. He seems to be enjoying the sensory experience of feeling the soapy water in his hand as he slowly rubs his fingers against his palm. . . .

Bud picks up the cup which still has a little water left in it, holds it over Eric's head, smiles, and says teasingly, in a low voice: "Pour it on your head." Eric ducks, his elbow raised to ward off Bud, and smiles but yells "Waaa." Moving the cup over his own head, Bud says decidedly and firmly with the suggestion of banter in his voice, "Pour it on my head. . . ." He sticks his nose into the suds and, sniffing, says to Rod and Eric, "It tickles." He blows himself a moustache and laughs. When Eric blows himself a moustache Bud laughs harder. In a sudden movement Bud buries his chin in the soap bubbles, looks up, and exclaims gleefully, smiling brightly: "Whiskers, aah, hey look!" Miss K suggests that they look in the mirror. Echoing Miss K, they both bolt out of their chairs. . . . Bud stands up and remarks, "It goes in my eyes." He reaches across the table and with the palm of his hand bursts Eric's bubbles, saying matter-of-factly, "Bubble pipe, bubble pipe." His face is calm. Eric snarls, "Hey," and reaches across to get at Bud's cup. Bud sits down quickly, grabs up his cup and turns away, snarling back, "Hey!" They look at each other angrily, and then all at once the anger is dissipated and they both laugh and return to blowing bubbles. . . . Standing up, Bud picks up the cup and straw, dips the straw in the soap suds, and holding it over the cup, blows the bubbles into the air. "Way ray," he exclaims happily, watching the bubbles as they float off and pop. "I did this. Ray, wheee." he exults.

In most urban environments the child's sensory experiences are extraordinarily restricted. This is especially true when he comes from a middle- or upper-class home. He has no direct contact with mud; a layer of concrete insulates him from the earth. There are innumerable things which he may not explore by touching, and yet he is constantly faced with a tempting multiplicity of forms and textures. What better function for the preschool group than to provide an opportunity for exploration denied him elsewhere? And what better material is there than water to meet this need? It is so universally at hand, so completely shared as an experience by all the children, that it seems inconceivable that its potentialities have not been more widely recognized.

The Feeling of Mastery

In addition to the wealth of sensory pleasures and learning experiences offered by water, it is a basic material through which a child can early experience the satisfactions of mastery and achievement. For some youngsters, particularly those with few adjustment problems, the primary gratification found in water-play seems to be connected with the control of a fluid medium. As an example of this interest we offer the following excerpt from the record of a well-adjusted three-year-old.

A child runs by saying something about a tea party. Carl jumps over the railing into the housekeeping corner: "Teacher, where is the tea party?" She says they will get some water and have one, so she takes a pail and proceeds with Carl to the bathroom. She allows him to carry the pail back, which he does with a smile on his face. He pours it into a pot without spilling any. Martha asks him whether she can have some coffee. Carl emphatically says, "No." He pours the water back into the pail. There are four cups on the table where he is standing; he pours water into them with a moderate amount of spilling. He sees some cups on another table and pours water into them and back into the pot.

Carl spies a muffin tin near the kitchen stove, and says, "I'm going to make a pie." Ellie attempts to take the pan away. He holds on to it firmly, absorbed in pouring water into it. He appears to be interested in how the water pours into this type of pan, then pours it back into the pot. He finds this difficult and loses quite a bit of water, spilling some on the floor. The teacher notices it and asks Carl if he knows where the mop is and he replies, "Yes." Because Ellie has appeared interested in obtaining some water from him, Carl asks certain conditions of the teacher before going to get the mop. He says to her, "Mind my water, teacher, that little girl wants some." . . . . He pours some in a cup. Ellie takes the frying pan from him. He shouts, "Teacher, I'm gonna beat her up." He proceeds to the stove with his cup of water, and pours the water into another cup. Then he pours from one to the other three times, but there is only a very small amount of water, so he says to the teacher, "My water all fall out." She gives him a pitcher and permission to get more water, cautioning him against filling the pitcher too full. He walks to the bathroom and brings the pitcher back half full, walking slowly and grinning (in exalted fashion). Allan asks him for some water and Carl says, "I ain't gonna give you no water." He fills the cream pitcher with water. Nearby is a cup with a funnel; he removes the funnel and pours from the cream pitcher to the cup.

For uncertain children who are generally constricted in movement and show little or no initiative in attempting new activities, blowing soap bubbles seems to offer tremendous opportunities for ego building. Children not only are avid for the activity and participate for long periods at a time, but also talk about it with unmistakable satisfaction—as the following report of two such youngsters indicates. One of the pair, Timmy, was more backward than the other, and just before engaging in his water-play had attempted a puzzle in the following characteristic manner.

The teacher helps Timmy (four and one half years old) take his puzzle apart. After it is spread out, he stands up, one knee on the chair, and looks at it. The teacher says, "Where does this belong?" She starts to piece together the puzzle. Timmy watches her, fascinated, his hand twisting in his hair and his mouth open. "Why don't you try it now?" she asks him. "Look, try it in each place and see if it won't fit." Meanwhile she is doing it for him. Timmy turns to Sheila. "I'm all finished," he says to her, as he picks up one of the last pieces and tries to fit it in its place. He tries awfully hard, but try as he will, it won't fit. "I can't put it in, it won't go in," he cries in exasperation. He does not really concentrate on the task because his eyes are constantly darting first toward Sheila and then toward the teacher, asking partly for help and partly for attention. Sheila started to walk away and Timmy became a bit panicky. He shouted, "I can't finish it, I can't finish it," about six times before Sheila turned around. The teacher helped him fit the last piece of the puzzle together.

Now contrast the frustration and dependence produced by the puzzle with the satisfaction and self-esteem Timmy derives from water-play.

Timmy is saying, "Let's go into the bathroom where we can have soap bubbles." He and Sheila follow Miss C and she ties aprons on them. He rubs the soap on his hands and says to Sheila, "I give you some soap." He turns to look at the basin. "The fishes can't go in there," he says to no one in particular. "My hands are clean." He continues rubbing soap on them. "Me can't make bubbles like you, me have to blow, blow." He blows on the water. Sheila spits into the water. He looks at her and smiles and then stamps his right foot and says, "Don't spit, that's dirty—me got some soap." Miss C comes back at this point with some long reeds to be used as pipes. They each grab one eagerly and set them in the water and blow vigorously through them making a lot of noise and few bubbles. Sheila says, "Me make no bubbles." Timmy says, "No bubbles." Miss C leaves and returns with more soap which they put into the water. They both return to blowing vigorously into the water. He bends over the bowl and blows. They both laugh

and giggle, looking at one another and still blowing. He holds
the pipe in his right hand and rubs it furiously in the basin
creating big splashes of water. Then he goes on blowing, looking at Sheila from time to time. Suddenly he says, "This won't
go for me," and goes back to blowing. Sheila says to Miss C,
"Timmy's won't go." Timmy to Miss C, "Mine won't go."
Miss C takes his pipe and leaves. She returns soon and hands
it back to him saying, "If you wouldn't bite so hard on it, it
wouldn't close up." Timmy returns to blowing, saying to Sheila,
"Me have two soaps." He is now getting a fine froth of bubbles
and he notices it. He lifts the pipe out of the water in his
left hand, holding it high in the air, and crows gleefully,
"Look what me done." He repeats it about four times and
Miss C comes to look. His face upturned to hers, he goes on
gleefully, "They won't know what we are doing when they
come back." He goes back to blowing in the water and really
works up a mountain of bubbles. He stops suddenly, removes
the pipe from the water, then, holding it in his right hand,
puts is horizontally into the water and swishes around with it,
his arms in froth up to his elbows. Sheila says to Miss C, "I
want some more water." Timmy stops what he is doing, raises
his head, and repeats Sheila's words, "I want some more water
too." Miss C turns the tap on for a second for each one and
then leaves the room. Some of the children have now returned
from their walk. They enter the bathroom and walk over to
see the goings-on. Each one says, "I want to blow bubbles too."
Timmy looks at them timidly but with a pleased smile on his
face. He raises the pipe to his mouth with his right hand and
blows into the air for a second. He says, "Me blowing bubbles,"
and blows again. He stops and laughs aloud—his head thrown
back and his hands still in the water. "Mine blows," he says.
He laughs again and stamps his feet this time. Then he throws
both hands into the air.

Satisfactions for the Immature

In many ways water appeared to be the royal road to the
hearts of children who were behind others in social development, attention span, and initiative. They seemed most avid

for all kinds of play with water, concentrated much longer on it than on any other activity, and seemed to derive the keenest pleasure from handling it as they wished. For these youngsters—whatever their actual age—it seemed to minister to two general types of needs: oral and tactile pleasure and the expression of aggressive impulses. It was therefore especially important to include such accessories as bottles and nipples, small cups, soft cloths, and sponges. Their play was usually extremely simple, repetitive, and organized around one theme, but the expressions of delight, the jealousy with which they guarded the implements, and the tenacity with which they returned to the activity in spite of interruptions and distractions testified to its importance for them. The following records illustrate these points very vividly. The first shows oral and aggressive outlets of a three-year-old boy who is described as hostile and disorganized.

Two children are washing an easel. They have a basin of water on the floor beside them. Bud comes over and kicks the basin and the water splashes all over the feet of another child. Bud laughs and kicks it again, harder. The other child is furious and yells, "You stinkin' bitch," and runs after him. Bud runs out of his way and calls back, "*You* stinkin' bitch." He is laughing and he repeats this phrase three times. Now he runs back to the basin and kicks it over and all the water goes on the floor. . . . Bud picks up a dirty rag which was in the basin and soaks it in the water, then he puts it in his mouth sucking the water from it. The teacher sees him doing this and leads him into the bathroom where he starts to play in one of the sinks. . . . He leans over the sink, turns on the tap, and drinks from it. He keeps his bubble gum in one side of his mouth while he drinks from the tap. Now he holds a little boat which was in the sink under the tap, fills it with water and drinks from it, holding it up with his left hand. He takes the gum out of his mouth putting it on the edge of the sink, and chews the little boat while he gazes around the room at the other children.

In the next record note how persistently the little girl of three pursues water-play, in spite of the "extremely short attention span and lack of organization" shown in her usual play activities.

The twins, Karen and Harvey, were playing together when the observer came to give Karen a chance to play with the miniature toy set, which included a bottle full of water. She immediately gets the bottle and drinks out of it, showing it to Miss K. Although they usually played in the corner by the cots, this time she goes to the doll corner and, sitting down in a chair, gives a doll the bottle. She says to the observer, "Take the nipple off. I want to drink." The observer does so and she starts to drink at once. Karen says, "My mommie is coming now." Then she asks the observer, "Is your mommie coming now, too?" Again she drinks out of the bottle. The observer suggests that they play with more of the toys. Karen takes out the high-chair and taking the pipe-cleaner father doll remarks, "Here he got shoes. Put him in the water. Let him have a bath. . . . MMmmm" (humming to herself). . . . She takes out a car and asks, "What is this?" When the observer considers the question, she herself answers, "A wagon." She rolls it for a second, then drinks again. She throws the car back into the box, takes the bottle in her hands and drinks from it, a dreamy expression on her face. She says, "Mommie says no more water." She gets up and goes to the bathroom and fills the bottle, splashing violently. While she walks back to the corner, she drinks out of the bottle, then cleans the shelf with Kleenex, drips some water from the bottle on it, and cleans some more. She gives the doll the bottle. . . . Karen gives Harvey the bottle and says to him, "Drink, baby." He drinks. She says, "He baby. Come on baby." She sits down and says to him, "Now come over here on my lap, honey." He runs away, saying, "Let me go outside." She goes to the bookshelf to get some books. She takes the bottle, sits down in a chair, and looks at a book, *The House that Jack Built*. She takes another book from the observer and recites to herself, "This boy is hiding behind a tree. . . ." Then she takes a big doll and tries to pour some water from the bottle in the area of the doll's anus so that it will wet. She says, "He gets a stomach, too." After putting the doll down, she falls down and the bottle spills. Taking a cloth she wipes the floor. She gets the bottle and drinks, then wipes the floor; she slips on the floor and smiles happily. She starts to wipe the adjacent shelves, pours water on a cloth, and wipes the portable screen. Then she washes the couch. She takes the baby's crib. She says, "There is soap in; nice and clean." Then she climbs up and cleans the window, wiping regularly, and asking, "How is that clean window?" The observer asks, "Shall we go outside now and put our toys away?" Karen answers, "No, I want to play with them." Taking the miniature bureau out of the box, she says, "Piano." Then she drops it and says, "I have to clean the window." She starts to go to the other shelves, also, and finds the scissors. "I wash these," she says, and takes out all the scissors and cleans them. Then she puts them all back and cleans the floor once more with water from the bottle.

Outlet for Aggression

In addition to the pleasure it affords, water-play offers inviting channels through which aggressive impulses can be released. But we generally need running comments of the children themselves to prove that they are covertly expressing sentiments they dare not express more openly—sentiments such as resentment, defiance, and hostility. In the next record note the revealing hints given by an extremely aggressive three-year-old girl who insisted on turning all her miniature-toy sessions into water-play.

One day while playing in the water with the miniature toys, she squirted water from the bottle into the toy bathtub. She said, "I make squirt go in my face — watch." She squirted it in her face; then she picked up the miniature baby doll and turned it over in the bathinette, face down. She said, "See the little hole in there. That's where the water comes out, right in my face." Again she squirted water into her face from the nipple of the bottle. During another session, after pouring water from the bottle into the miniature bathinette and into a small car, she simply turned the bottle upside down and let the water cascade onto the floor. Then she did the same with the water she had already poured into the car and looked at the observer apprehensively. During a later session she made no pretense of pouring from the bottle into other vessels, but simply picked up the bottle and poured water directly onto the floor; afterwards she rubbed another toy into it, spreading it further. Next, after replenishing the water in the bottle, she got down on her knees and took out the miniature toilet. She poured water into that spilling some on the floor, then rubbed and scraped the toilet in the water. Finally, during the dramatic play with an adult, while taking the part of a baby, she sucked and drank from a baby bottle and then spilled water all over the floor, saying to the adult who was supposed to be taking the part of the mother, "The baby spilling. See, I'm spilling. You must scold me." When the adult obligingly followed her directions, she continued, "I'm spilling some more." This little episode subsequently led to more direct expression of hostility towards her mother than had previously been encountered in more than a year's observation of this child.

Another instance of the close connection between water and very primitive hostile impulses is found in the behavior of Bud. A study of his play also illustrates the necessity of making numerous observations before the full intent or meaning can be discovered. For, in his case, we first noticed only indiscriminate delight in playing with water, but as we continued our observations we began to understand that water meant much more to him. For example, in his first session with miniature life toys he splashed some water on the floor and explained that the toy horse he was playing with had urinated. And another time, he used water to obliterate a male figure which he had molded of clay during a series of hostile fantasies.

Numerous teachers have testified to the value of water-play in freeing impulses. One very observant group teacher contributed the following comments: "James uses materials in the same way he has always, but he can get rid of hostilities better now, for example, he has been pouring water out of containers 'by mistake' and has gotten rid of some hostility that way. Jacqueline went through a period when she would dump water in the doll carriage and then insist on having me clean up the baby for her. I was the only one she would ask to clean up the mess." In addition, so-called "violent" water-play has been observed to be one of the first signs of dramatic behavior changes—usually among children who have been extremely inhibited and are moving in the direction of greater freedom.

Relaxation and Absorption

In contrast to some of the statements cited above, other teachers emphasized the soothing and absorbing qualities of water for children ordinarily rather scattered and explosive in their play. For example, one teacher of very young children in a guidance nursery said, "Water is a relaxing kind of thing; it is good in that very few aggressive feelings are expressed there. A very disturbed child, Beth, would be happy at water and retreat to it and play for a long time. We have used water-play to relax a child when he was disturbed. When the kids were hectic and wild we would take a group to the water, especially on rainy days. We could accommodate about seven children at a time. Outside we used water for painting and for scrubbing with soap. The children had a lot of tea parties, pouring the water; they used water in the sandbox, too. This would make a noticeable difference in them."

In another center the head teacher testified, "Water has been an outlet for many children. For instance, Jennifer, a very aggressive child, loves it. She becomes absorbed in it. After using it she seems to tone down for the rest of the day. She can stick at it for a couple of hours at a time. She does not stay at anything else very long. She enjoys the easel but she leaves it quickly, saying she wants to wash her hands. The same thing with clay."

It would be a mistake, therefore, to believe that ministering to oral and aggressive needs is the only advantage of water-play. It seems outstandingly fruitful in these directions for the very young or very immature children. But for older children and for other kinds of children it seems to offer additional benefits. Many aggressive children are definitely soothed, relaxed, and quieted by a chance to play freely with water while other children, who are ordinarily extremely inhibited, become stimulated, gay, and free, even inviting social contacts that they cannot ordinarily undertake.

The peculiarly soothing influence of water-play on children who are ordinarily overactive and aggressive is brought out most clearly by comparison with their behavior at other times. The subject of the next two records is a four-year-old child who was extremely hard to handle—as you can see by the following report of his yard-play.

Record 1. Jake climbs up on a plank—runs down it and straight across the yard and back again—runs off and across and back again—runs over to some children and then over to a teacher who picks up his falling pants. He wants to take off his jacket, but the teacher says, "No, it is not warm enough." He runs off and around and around the yard; he stops to comfort a boy who fell and is crying. He strokes the boy's head and finds out who pushed him over, then yells, "Come on, come on," and runs off with Eddie. Jake punches the boy but then runs over the boxes after Eddie. Then Eddie hits another child and Jake sits on this child. Jake goes over to the sand-box and starts to throw sand at the boy there. The boy throws the sand back and they continue in this manner. Jake picks up a rock to throw but is stopped by a teacher. He starts to get on a bicycle, but Eddie runs over with a rope and they tie each other together and run off. Then they untie and chase each other.

The contrast with Jake's water-play speaks for itself.

Record 2. Jake goes into the play kitchen, takes a basin, puts all the play dishes in it, carries it over to the teacher, and asks her if he may wash them. She says, "yes," and he goes into the bathroom. He fills the basin with water and gets a rag to wash with. Engrossed in his work, he then fills each dish and cup with water and stands them all around the edge of the sink. He works slowly and carefully to prevent spilling, and pays no attention to the others around him. He goes into the play kitchen and takes a pot off the shelf and goes back to sink. He fills the pot with water by emptying the previously filled cups into it. Another child comes in to fill a pan. Jake stretches out his hand and says, "I'll get some water for you." The boy gives him the pan and Jake fills it. . . . He takes a damp mop and starts to mop the floor and says, "I'm helping to clean up." He mops all around the room using short and long strokes. The teacher sends him to where the floor is wet and he mops it. Then he continues to mop in the play kitchen. When some wooden milk bottles fall out of the icebox, he pretends to mop up the spilled milk at the direction of another child. He puts the mop away and takes a towel offered by the teacher to help dry the dishes. He is helping another little girl and says to her, "I'm doing a good job, aren't I?" They work together. He dries the dishes and puts them on the shelf. Both dry a big basin together and put it away and then Jake helps to put away the remaining dishes.

Liberating Effects

Teachers who recognize the release and stimulation derived from water-play are often particularly impressed with its catalytic effect on youngsters who are ordinarily solitary and lost. Not only do they mingle with other children during the activity, but afterwards they freely approach materials which they had been hesitant to use. An uninterrupted session with water will often prove the open sesame to activities with clay, finger-paints, or the easel.

In the following description, note the evidence of progressive freedom of action as well as the gradual crescendo in the expression of pleasure. The child's approach to all other materials was exceedingly tentative, and no other activity seemed to offer as stimulating and as completely unthreatening an avenue to enjoyment as water.

The teachers discover that it is raining so the children must stay downstairs. They plan to have water-play. Teacher: "Do you want to play with water, Marion?" Marion (three and one half years old) shakes her head "yes" and puts her fingers in her mouth. The teacher puts an apron on her. Betty and Arlene are with her. She takes a pot out of the water and empties it. She looks about as a child splashes water on her. She shrugs her shoulders. She reaches for a boat, gets two, moves a cup around in the water, fills the cup, and then empties it. She swishes her hands around underwater finding things. She swishes the toys about, gets more forceful, pushes dishes around underwater, splashes accidentally, and picks up things and puts them back. Turning, she watches the teacher. She takes two pans, puts them together, and swishes them about. She swishes the boat back and forth under the water and splashés. Girl: "Marion, stop splashing." Arlene goes to the teacher and tells her. Teacher: "That's all right if Marion splashes." Marion swishes her hands violently back and forth and splashes. Smiling she takes the suds and squishes them in her hands. She pours soapsuds into Arlene's hand. Marion takes a handful of suds and wipes them on the side of the pan. Sensuously she opens and closes her hands and rubs one finger. Suddenly she claps them on Johnnie's arms. She smiles at Johnnie. She laughs and spanks her hands on the water. All do this, laughing. Marion looks at the water spilled on the floor beside her. All are roaring. Marion roars while holding the cup. The teacher comes with the mop.

Because children are freer in every way while engaged in water-play, it can be useful in furthering the social contacts of a withdrawn child. Toby, the four-and-one-half-year-old boy under observation in the next record had very few friends in the group and was beginning to annoy the only other child he played with, a little girl. To help him build his social relationships—and to relieve the little girl—the teacher asked another boy to join him in water-play. Although he displays no startling social techniques, at least he is able to make some positive contact with this boy.

While washing his hands in the bathroom, Toby starts to play with water. The teacher comes and says, "No playing in the bathroom." He and Arthur come out and the teacher gives them a tub of water to play with. There are two dishes and one coffeepot in the tub. Toby gives one dish to Arthur, "Here, Arthur." He tries to fill the coffeepot by scooping water with the dish, then pours the water from the coffepot onto the dish. He says, "Look what I made. I said medita, I said medita. Doopedapee. Doopedapee." He and Arthur then both fill the coffeepot with their saucers, Toby holding it. . . . Now Arthur has the coffeepot. Toby says, "No, I had it first." He whimpers. He plays with the dishes. The teacher comes over and Toby says, "I had that first." Arthur relinquishes the coffeepot. Toby keeps filling it up and emptying it. He says, "Give me some soap." To Arthur, "Why are you washing with me—because you like me?" He puts his hands in the coffeepot and says, "I'm washing it." He turns to Arthur and says, "We're going outside, Arthur. We're going outside. Arthur, get it." He gives the coffeepot to Arthur, then puts water in it. The teacher comes along and tells them they'll have to stop and go outside.

Finally, to illustrate the initiative and concentration which some children show only in water play, we should like to present a report on a four-and-one-half-year-old named Rodney. First we offer the following fragment to indicate the detached and desultory character of his usual behavior.

The children are busy at various activities—painting, playing with clay, block building, and doll-play. Rodney stands in the middle of the room trying to fix the buttons on his overalls. He keeps at it in an absent-minded manner, looking around the room as he does so, but not settling on one particular activity. He walks over to the bulletin board, still trying to button his overalls, and smiles as the teacher talks about the pictures. Now he turns and looks at the buttons and succeeds in fixing the overalls. He takes the miniature man doll and bangs it down on the floor, leaves it, and sits down at a table—alone. The teacher suggests that he build with some blocks. "I can't," he says. She makes another suggestion and points out what Rosa has built. Rodney does not go. He sits fingering the light battery which is on the table. He turns the light on and off with his left hand in a very mechanical manner as he watches Mary at the clay table.

In dramatic contrast to this disorganized behavior, it was observed that Rodney would spend as much as forty-five minutes at lively water-play. The fact that only a limited type of activity was offered makes the following record especially noteworthy.

Rodney walks over to the table where the teacher is bringing out basins with soap flakes and water in them. He watches her with interest. "Teacher, can I do that?" Phyllis to Rodney: "Baby, come here." Rodney ignores her and watches two children stirring soapy water with wooden spoons. He blows out a soap bubble and listens to their talk. He hums. The teacher brings him a basin with soap and water. He sits and does not use the water until the teacher brings him a wooden spoon. He stirs round and round, looking at what he is doing. He stands up and stirs, saying to the two other children, "Making supper. . . ." He sits on the chair and plays hide-and-seek with Melvin, bending his head below the table. He goes back to stirring as Phyllis puts her head on his lap. She lifts her head, but Rodney says, "Get down." She complies and he continues stirring. He chants with the other children in good rhythm, "All I want for Christmas is my new front teeth." He continues stirring. He picks up a spoon and says to Cathy, "Look at my bubbles." The teacher comes over and Rodney, pointing to the egg beater, asks her belligerently, "Why don't you give me that?" The teacher gives him one. He turns it quickly.

The other children are still chanting, but Rodney stops, concentrating on the egg beater. He tilts the basin to stir the water. Only he and Melvin are left at the table. Paul comes back, and then Melvin carries a jar of red paint over and pours a little into his basin. Rodney watches the water turn pink. His mouth opens and his eyes light up, but he says nothing. He continues beating his own soap and water vigorously, banging the sides of the basin. The teacher comes over and tells him that it is time to stop. He goes on beating. He gets up and brings over green paint, pours a great deal of it into his basin, using it all up. He smiles as the teacher asks him, "What shall we use for the easel now?" Phyllis says to Rodney, "Look at my blue." Rodney gets up and gets the pink paint. The teacher tilts his basin so that he can beat more easily. She goes away and he continues to beat. He calls out to her, "I want red, too. Can you give me some red, Paul?" (Paul has red in his basin.) The teacher calls out, "Time to clean up." Rodney outwardly ignores this. He beats his water and splashes some into his eyes. He starts to pick up his basin, puts it down, runs over to get the red paint, and pours a great deal in. The teacher takes it away. Rodney continues beating and stirring but his interest seems less intent, as he looks around. . . . He goes over to the table and sits with the others who are reading books.

The liberating effect of water frequently brings greater spontaneity to the use of other materials. Some children who had turned their backs on miniature life toys, entered into elaborate and absorbed play when water was a part of the activity. Likewise, teachers attribute the unusually tender and realistic handling of "Didee" dolls to the inclusion of water in the play.

The Versatility of Water

Viewed in perspective, the observations of teachers and special observers present a challenge on theoretical grounds. Why should this simple substance have such varied effects? No other material, not even clay or finger-paint, has its protean quality to the same degree. For one thing, the repetitious and somewhat monotonous nature of water-play, together with the soft and yielding quality of the material, may account for its relaxing effect on tense and overactive children. The fact that it demands no special skills and involves no achievement goals may explain why it neither threatens nor thwarts the anxious child who cannot take the pressure of social contacts or the adult-directed use of other materials. Again, its mild yet pleasurable sensory qualities afford withdrawn, constricted youngsters stimulation without excitement. Likewise, the chance to pour and splash and mess offers these children, as well as more active and outgoing ones, not only a means of expressing aggression but also a way of escaping the pressures of growing up and of regaining the privileges of infancy. Moreover, clinical reports on inhibited children often reveal that they have responded to parental prohibitions by a generalized lack of interest and venturesomeness. They retreat into safe and "good" behavior—but free play with water gives them a chance to explore and experiment with a medium that has been denied to them. Time and again we have seen water-play lift the burden of anxiety and release hidden resources of interest and vitality.

But what of the possibility of arousing guilt reactions which might block any benefits that water-play could hold for the child? We can only report that not one of the hundred and more children we observed seemed to suffer sufficient anxiety to interfere with enjoyment. In only two cases was some tension reported. In one, the child simply refused to play with the water at first, but after a period of observation came to accept it fully. In the other, a three-year-old was reported to need reassurance after pouring water over miniature life furniture. Close contact with the teacher and assurance that it was all right to play with water at a special time and with special toys were enough to relieve this child's mind.

The neutral quality of water is another reason for its enormous flexibility and varied effects. Because it offers so little resistance and makes so few demands on the child, yet lends itself to so many satisfactions, the range of its appeal is unlimited. As we have pointed out, the very young child finds in it a substance that he can manipulate and master more easily than any other—provided adults do not interfere. He can transform it into almost anything and use it to experiment with his own powers and with the qualities of other materials. The following description of a three-year-old girl playing with sand and water suggests this multiplicity of function.

Riva is now playing with sand and water, a ladle, and two vessels. She puts sand into one of the dishes, mixes it with water, and ladles the mixture from one vessel to the other. She seems quite happy and secure just now. No one is challenging her and she talks to herself. "Making coffee. This is water. Make a pie." She pours the water and sand onto the floor and then goes back to ladling. "This is a sand-pie. Make a tea. So-oh." She puts her finger into the water and says, "A crab done it." The observer asks "What did the crab do?" Riva replies, "He did bite, see the crabs?" She continues to be very absorbed in what she is doing, pouring sand and water from one dish to the other.

Children frequently use water as a strand on which to thread an immense variety of play forms. Even comparatively restricted water-play can lend itself to elaborate and complex patterns. The following record suggests the flexibility of this single simple substance and the ease with which the play changes and new meanings are projected.

Dan and Joan were busily washing toy dishes in the large tub. Mischievous Dan shouted, "Here, have some whip' cream," and he smeared some soap foam on Joan's face. She began to whimper. He scooped more foam in his hand and started to blow it at her, but just then he spied an old piece of wood which someone had brought in from the playground. Forgetting

Joan, he quickly ran over to get it, and thrust it into the water: "Clean it off! Clean it off!" He scrubbed steadily for two minutes, then suddenly had an idea: "Make sump'n," said he. "Get me some blocks," he ordered, and Joan brought three or four small ones. Floating the board in the tub, he put two blocks on top in precarious balance, and Joan said in admiration, "It's a boat!" "Yeah, it's the Queen Mary, and this is the ocean. She's going to Africa." "Toot! Toot!" said Joan, "Look! We made a boat!" Hearing this, Ronnie, one of the older boys, came running over, "That's no good, it hasn't got a smokestack." "It's the Queen Mary," repeated Joan proudly. Ron rushed to get a peg from the pegboard, but Dan wouldn't let him put it on his boat, "It's my boat, *I* do it." Some wrangling followed, then Ronnie let him have it. After several tries Dan managed to perch the peg on top of his boat and Ronnie started to push it. "I'm the captain," Dan reminded him. "No, I am," said Joan, " 'cause it's a lady boat. . . ."

Teachers' Approaches to Water-Play

A desire to play with water is frequently indicated in the way other materials are handled. When the children are permitted to prepare their own clay or finger-paint, for example, they may persistently add more water than is appropriate for ordinary use—even after the teacher has explained and demonstrated the proper consistency of the material. It is well to have the materials for water-play ready for use as the children show their need for it.

Almost any activity involving cleaning or wetting may be the start of water-play. It is necessary, however, to foresee a spontaneous development in the play and to provide for broader and more complex activity as it goes on. It is important also for the teacher to realize that her intentions may not be those of the child and that his motivation may differ completely from her own. She may want to have the shelves washed or the dolls cleaned, but he may be motivated by a need to mess and splash. The wise and sensitive teacher will discern his needs from the manner in which the child washes the same dish over and over again, bathes one doll for a full half hour, or extends his cleaning activities from shelf to table to wall to floor. She may then be sure he is expressing an inner need for water-play rather than evincing a lack of judgment.

Simply permitting youngsters to play with water, however, does not automatically confer on them the multiple benefits suggested by our observations. The activity is often surrounded by so many restrictions that it is robbed of any salutary effect it might otherwise have had. The very presence of the water tempts the children to an indulgence which the restrictions frustrate, and as a result they almost inevitably become irritable, uncooperative, and aggressive. To mention one common example, children are usually fascinated by egg beaters, but the need to keep the water within the limits of the pan and the separation between child and water act as limiting factors. While egg beaters may have their value as accessories, it is a mistake to think that this type of equipment gives the child access to all the values of water-play.

Sometimes the children have to steal a chance at the sheer sensory pleasure that water holds for them. It is not unusual to find them lingering over routine washing, or snatching odd moments during other activities involving the use of water. The record cited below is fairly representative of what can be seen in almost every nursery program where the adult's drive for achievement controls the activity and the child's own desires are ignored. Just before the report was taken, Warren, an anxious four-and-one-half-year-old, had offered to wash some sticks that had been used in pasting.

Warren goes right to the sink, dumps out the sticks and fills the jar with cold water and shakes it. He watches the teacher wash the sticks, then fills the jar with hot and cold water alternately. The teacher says, "That's all nice and clean," and starts to take it away. Warren says, "No, no," and goes on washing, "it's not clean yet." He puts the jar under the tap, saying, "Gotta take the paper off," and starts to scrape it. He gets a piece off and hands it to the teacher. She points to the wastebasket and tells him to put it there. He scrapes a little more off, then puts a bar of soap in the jar. The teacher takes the jar away saying that it is as clean as it will get and leaves him to wash his hands. Warren calls "Tupid, you big tupid," to a child coming in to use the toilet. He stands soaping his hands singing, "lululululu." He looks up at the children entering the washroom, then bends to drink from the tap. The teacher points out that he still has paint on his hands. He puts his hand under the tap, rubs it, then drinks again. She gives him a cup of water. He drinks some and pours some into the sink, then drinks the rest.

Careful reading of the above report will reveal the cross purposes of teacher and child. For the teacher, apparently, the major object was the end result of getting the jar clean and the child away. She interpreted his behavior in matter-of-fact terms without any apparent recognition of the pleasure-seeking element in it. When he bent to drink from the tap she handed him a cup of water; she treated his insistence that the jar was not clean as bad judgment instead of a request for further contact with water. How easily this need could have been met! Merely supplying him with a cloth to be soaked and soaped and squeezed would have been ample.

Unfortunately children are rarely permitted to play with water to the point of complete satisfaction, but when it does happen, there is nothing to equal the absorption, exuberance, and joy they display. The excerpts given below are only a sampling of a record taken of a little girl less than three years old during a single half hour. Trina was considered an aggressive child.

Trina was crying when the observer came in, but she brightened up when the teacher told her she had some bubble bath she could play with, and went happily with her to the bathroom. Paul was invited to go along and was also very enthusiastic. As soon as the teacher moved away, Trina dipped her left hand into the bubbles delightedly and extending it toward observer, said, "Look, bubbles." She plunged both hands into the bubbles and withdrew them, shaking them off in Paul's direction saying, "Look it." She repeated this, giggling, and then a third time thrust both hands into the water, splashing quite a bit on herself and on the floor. Giggling she said, "Look me splash." With no protest from Trina, Paul put his hands in the water too and began to splash. Holding her two hands like a cup, Trina dripped out some bubbles and threw them at the mirror above the basin. She repeated this several times exercising considerable concentration, her tongue between her teeth. Thrusting her hand almost into Paul's face, Trina said imperiously, "Here." He blew the bubbles away and she giggled happily. . . . The teacher led Trina over to the tub on the floor. She filled her cupped hands with bubbles and, walking a few steps toward the observer, held out her hands and said, "Look," with almost a crow of delight. She began to jig up and down, first on one foot, and then on the other, throwing the soapsuds over the floor and giggling.

Meanwhile Judy, Bonnie, and Alice had come into the bathroom. Trina went back to the tub, leaned over and scooped up a double handful of bubbles and threw them on Alice, who fled from the room shrieking. Trina got to her feet, both hands filled with bubbles, and stamping her feet in a marching rhythm went out of the room, with Paul, Bonnie, and Judy following and imitating her. The teacher called to them to stay in the bathroom and Trina turned around and came back, continuing her stamping rhythm. . . . Trina returned to the tub and the teacher gave her a paper cup to play with. Holding the cup in her right hand, she scooped up the bubbles with her left and then tried with fair success to get them into the cup. Then she stood up and, transferring the cup filled with bubbles to her left hand, held it up triumphantly, in a Statue of Liberty pose. Taking a few steps toward the observer, she threw the bubbles in the cup toward her, barely missing her. She returned to the tub and repeated the whole action, just missing the observer again and giggling mischievously. She returned to the tub and got interested in patting the bubbles into the cup with her right hand, the cup held in her left, in a much more careful way than the slap-dash method she had been using. . . .

Judy was playing with a tin pan which she had heaped up with Bubbles. Trina said in a teasing voice, "I want all that, Judy." Judy got up and with the pan in her hands ran out into the hallway. Trina chased after, both hands cupped and full of bubbles. As she ran she chanted, "Bubble, bubble. . . ." Trina took a pan from Bonnie, went to Miss F, and held it out to her saying, "Got bub." Miss F touched them and said they were nice. Trina said, "take some," and Miss F scooped some out.

The occasional conflicts described in the above record are not unusual, since water tends to release aggressive impulses in some children. Actually they were not particularly destructive and occupied relatively little of the total time. More important, perhaps, is the striking change in mood brought about by the water-play.

In the following record, where the teacher is both sensitive and permissive, the fascination of water, used in combination with a variety of other things, lasts throughout the day.

Laura (three years old) joined a group of children playing with small table blocks. She didn't remain very long and somehow, somewhere, got hold of a small paste brush. She took this to the sink saying, "I want to paint something." I gave her a tin can which happened to have some dried clay at the bottom of it. She took this to an empty table and for several minutes went back and forth wetting the brush and painting the outside of the can. I filled a small soap dish about one quarter full of water and placed it on the table near her. She seemed pleased with this arrangement and painted away gradually soaking the clay and making a thick paste, which was now spread over her hands and shirt. She squeezed her hands together tightly and opened them quickly. She did this several times, laughing and staring at her hands. Suddenly, she said, "I gotta clean my hands off." She jumped out of her chair, pushing it over, and ran to the sink. In no time at all she was washing her hands and was back at the table. "My hands are clean." She held out her clean hands for the observer to see. She proceeded to paint again. The clay was now a rich, thick mixture and it seemed to give her a great deal of satisfaction as she spread it thickly on can, soap dish, and hands. She seemed very intent on what she was doing. She used a great deal of pressure to get the clinging clay off the sides of the dish. She suddenly ran to the sink, washed her hands, came back, then poured the water from the can to the dish and carried the full dish to the sink (spilling some), and washed the brush and the soap dish. She fills the can full and holds it up high, allowing the water to pour into the basin. This pleases her and she repeats it several times. At this point the light goes on signalling that lunch is ready. Laura turns around protesting, "I wanna play some more." The observer tells her that she can. . . .

After lunch, she notices the pouring-can again; however, half of her attention is on the group of children listening to a story. She stirs the water into the can with a spoon and sips from the spoon. She paints her hand with the brush then with the spoon. She fills the can very full and lifts it. It is heavy and she exclaims, "Ooooh!" She paints the wall. . . . She remains at the sink until every other child is on his bed with his shoes off and fairly quiet. The observer tells her that she can play a few more minutes and then it will be resting time. . . .

As soon as Laura awakens she whispers, "Give me the paint and brush," pointing to the top of the cubby where it was put. "And now I could play water." Laura whispers since there are some children still asleep in the room, "Hey, teacher, I want clay, I want clay in here." She holds out the empty can. I put a small lump of clay in the can. Laura plays for a while. Afterward, she puts the paint brush in the water and sucks on it. She sees the observer moisten the paste for Rick. Laura, "What's Rick gonna do?" Teacher, "He's pasting." She goes back to wetting and sucking the paint brush, then suddenly says, "I wanna draw."

At this point it will be relevant to quote from two reports of the reception accorded free water-play. The first was written by a teacher who was in charge of a fairly large group of very young children, ranging in age from two to three and one half years old.

I intended to borrow Mrs. F's tub, but as they were using it, I filled three sinks in the bathroom with warm soapy water. I put a good number of pots and pans on the sides of the sinks and some small boats into the water. The children were busy in the room at the time with clay, crayons, paints, pegs, and all the other room equipment. Nobody was taken to the bathroom, but it was left to chance as to who would come along. Janice was the first. This was her fourth day in school. She walked right over to the sink and began to put all the pots in, pouring water from one to the other. Within a few moments she was so engrossed that she did not turn around or notice other children coming over to play near her. Gradually she began to abandon pots and boats, just splashing in the water and hitting it with her flat hands, laughing as it splashed. She stayed at it for twenty minutes. She did not say anything during the whole period.

Bud beamed when he saw the water and equipment, looked at me questioningly. I said only, 'Would you like to wash our pots and pans?' This was the signal to begin. He filled all the pans to the brim, carefully placing them on the edge of the sink. Then he emptied them into the water. He repeated this performance several times. He held the boats down under the surface and laughed loudly as they rose to the top when he released them.

Max was so anxious to get started that he hardly gave me a chance to put the apron on him. He began very carefully, too, but his movements are not well coordinated on the whole so that he kept spilling a good bit as he poured the water from one pan to another. He kept saying, "Boats, boats," laughed and looked at Brad and Roy for ideas. This was probably the first time he was allowed to play with water in his life.

Roy and Brad had a good deal of conversation as they were playing. They put the boats into the pots, then turned the pots upside down dropping the boats into the water from the distance of their arms' reach, and laughed as they splashed into the water. They put boats on edges, pushing them very carefully and slowly until they fell in. Most of the conversation was confined to, "Watch me." Max was the first of the three to tire, and he took his apron off, announcing that he was finished after about three minutes. He had stayed at it longer than at any other activity ever, except bicycle or block building with others on the roof. He had come in rather scrappy this morning, not knowing what to do with himself. After water-play he seemed more relaxed, went to crayons for a while, then to beads and music.

Jock came over to go to the toilet. He was so fascinated by what he saw that he began to urinate on the floor, not even noticing it. I asked him whether he wanted to play and he nodded with a big smile. He stood at the sink looking at what Roy was doing and at me for reassurance. He did not say one word, but played intensively for about ten minutes . . .

The first group was very interesting to observe because there were three distinct age levels and stages of development: Janice, two and one half years old, was completely absorbed in the manipulation of water, unconcerned about her surroundings; Max, between three and four, who imitated Brad's and Roy's play; and finally Roy and Brad who held conversations, made plans about how to use the pots, and showed typical three-year-old behavior.

The second teacher was in charge of an older group, ranging in age from three and one half to five years. She wrote:

It was the first time we had used this type of play, although we have always used water in play. By that I mean that the children have had opportunities to wash doll's clothes, to paint with water on the roof, to sail little boats in the bathroom sinks, to play in the shower and large tub filled with water on the roof in hot weather.

The day Miss T. was with us, it started to rain about 10:30—half the group were on the roof, the other half returning to the roof after music. Such a time is generally confusing, and the children are upset by the sudden change in routine.

The large galvanized tub had arrived over the week-end so the children had not even seen it. As soon as all outdoor clothing was removed, we put a large piece of oilcloth on the floor, placed the tub in the center of it, and poured some Lux flakes into it. Next we took five of the oilcloth aprons, and there was a lively scramble for them. Miss N filled the tub, using the large watering can—which was great fun. We had to explain over and over that we would try to give each one a turn as almost every child was anxious and eager, and there just was no more room at present.

At first they merely washed their hands and squeezed the suds through their fingers and fists. Then they wanted pots and pans from the doll corner—they filled them and emptied them; poured from one to the other; washed them. Each additional five did about the same things. The only child who actually resisted and refused to participate was Liza. However, she was one of the chief painters with water on the roof, and the first each day to get to that activity. Rocco resisted the first time only.

All the children seemed to get great pleasure out of the experience. We have had many requests each day for the activity and have repeated it.

We have not discussed the contribution of water-play to a sense of participation in the adult world. Cleaning up offers an opportunity for identification with grownups. Unfortunately, however, some teachers regard water-play as largely a girl's activity and limit it almost completely to cleaning dishes, bathing dolls, or washing doll's clothes. But in centers where water is freely used as a substitute for paint (water-painting), as well as for washing surfaces such as tables and walls, for blowing masses of bubbles and pouring from vessel to vessel, boys are just as eager to participate and frequently remain at the activity longer than girls do. It may very well be that in the cleaning-up function boys can find an accepttable channel for identification with a mother figure which they need at the preschool level, but cannot find in other activities because of cultural taboos against male interest in "women's work."

Conclusion

To sum up, water-play has many values and can be used for many purposes in the preschool and kindergarten program. To the development of sensation and feeling it offers more varied experience and a keener pleasure than any other material except finger-paint; to intellectual development it contributes its great flexibility and vast opportunities for experimentation and exploration. It stimulates the inhibited child and soothes the explosive. Scattered, disorganized youngsters are able to concentrate on it for long periods of time. Those who are uncertain of themselves gain a sense of achievement and find in it a channel for expressing emotions not condoned in their primitive forms. Many children who have had trouble in the group situation begin their adjustment through water-play. Others who are tense, fearful, withdrawn, and inhibited indicate a general loosening up and growth in spontaneity by their acceptance of water as a medium and by their increased freedom in using it.

It should be possible to realize the values of water-play in almost any group program. All that is needed is a minimum of adult supervision, a variety of accessory materials, a setup that minimizes interference between children, and long uninterrupted periods for play. Time after time our records depict children making promising advances in absorption and spontaneity, only to find their activities interrupted by the teacher in charge. This was never done out of malice, but on the other hand there was often a lack of appreciation of the children's experience and no recognition of what was being done to them. Sometimes, of course, these interruptions are unavoidable, but when they are, it should be possible to arrange for a continuation of the play at some other time. In some cases, too, the child might be permitted to continue while his group mates are busy with routine matters like cleaning up. The critical factor here as always is the teacher's awareness of the meaning of the play, her sensitivity to the implications of its development and her willingness to manipulate schedule details in the interest of the individual child.

A few words of caution seem appropriate here. Because of the striking and varied advantages of water-play, there has been a tendency among some educators to expect it to be a universal panacea. This we must guard against. We have no evidence that it is effective in every kind of developmental problem or personality difficulty. Our evidence simply indicates that it is particularly valuable where there is a question of overactivity or constriction of interest or movement. We have reason to suggest, too, that the child who "gets stuck" with water-play and who uses it repetitively in the same patterns or around the same theme needs special help in finding other avenues of expression and special encouragement to grow beyond the joys of infancy.

CHAPTER VI

What Clay Can Do for the Child

IN RECENT YEARS clay has had two distinct functions among those concerned with very young children. For teachers of preschool groups it serves as a raw material out of which things may be made, an approach that is appropriate within an educational framework that emphasizes the imparting of skills, manual and verbal. For clinicians, it serves with apparent success as a projective tool, since it supplies a means of communicating inner difficulties for young children who cannot express themselves verbally. One of the objectives of the present chapter is to bring about a rapprochement between these two functions, since each of them can be of enormous benefit to the child in the nursery or kindergarten group.

The variety of meanings which a plastic material may have for children and for those who observe them is well expressed in an article by Bender and Woltmann.[1] The following quotations summarize fairly completely the observations of those who have worked with clay in a clinical setting.

The child's treatment of the material is . . . an investigation of the external world by rhythmic activity out of which patterns are built. . . . An accidentally gained form or shape might be called a "man," a "tree," a "mother," a "baby," and so on. It is not necessary that there exist a resemblance between the object and the interpretation given to it as long as the object can carry out the role it has been given by the child. These creations, unintentionally made, therefore become carriers of a meaning. . . . It is the story the child has to tell which completes his work.

Further, these investigators found that a group of mentally retarded, emotionally blocked, or otherwise handicapped nursery children would "examine the Plasticine by looking at it, smelling it, poking and hitting it, by putting it into their mouths, trying to chew and swallow it." By accident these children may mold it into a flat shape and exclaim, "Look what I made. I made a cake." When this occurs, others follow suit and, "since all the children work in groups, all the inherent benefits of group therapy also apply to our group work in clay class." However, the other children "modify the original creation according to their mental and motility development and their emotional needs." The plastic figure that results may be merely played with or it may "talk and act." It may also help the child "solve problems such as body composition, body posture, and curiosity towards anal and genital regions," as well as to express difficulties having to do with his family and surrounding society. Thus "the child is given a chance to 'create' his conception of the world in a real, visible, and tangible form. Consequently, all these activities constitute a great emotional release," and "the child can be easily brought to an insight of his self-created symbols thereby gaining access to the social reality."

In an attempt to see how far this experience of clinicians could be applied in nursery schools, and to bridge the gap between the teacher's and the therapist's use of clay, we had special observers record the play activities of 78 children ranging in age from 2.6 to 5.6 years. Although the 112 records that resulted vary in quality because of differences in training, background, personality, and skill among the observers, taken together they shed considerable light on the objectives we had in mind. These were roughly as follows: first, to explore the differences between the teachers' aims

and practices in the use of clay and the meaning of the
material to the children; second, to investigate its values
(a) as an aid in assimilating social demands, (b) as a channel
for the expression of fantasy, (c) as an agent for evaluating
emotional and developmental status; third, to discover its
unique values for different children, that is, values which are
not characteristic of other materials, and values it might
hold for children showing specific kinds of behavior patterns,
such as overaggressiveness or inhibition.

In addition to the records of children in action, we also had
access to a group of educational consultants serving as super-
visory personnel for approximately 91 nursery centers in New
York city, and to 35 teachers who were interviewed directly.
The teachers gave us their opinions concerning the general
value of clay and its relation to behavior changes in specific
children under observation by the personnel of the project.

The information contributed by the educational consultants
can be summarized briefly. They had frequently found it
difficult to persuade teachers that clay should be included
in the preschool program, since it involved more cleaning
up than "clean materials" like blocks and crayons. (A deeper
reason came to light in workshops held by the consultants,
namely, the teachers' own inhibitions concerning the enjoyment of "messy" things.) Teachers who were convinced that
clay might be a desirable material tended to regard it as a
socially accepted method of messing, "but they did not yet
seem to understand why a child should have a chance to
mess." In other words, they were using it because it had
been recommended very strongly, not because they were
aware of its educational value or its meaning to the children.
There was little or no recognition of a need for spontaneous
exploration in the child's early learning and development.

Since there was no common conviction about the value of
clay, its use was based on expediency rather than educational

policy. It is not surprising, therefore, that wide variation was found in the accessibility of the material and the manner of its presentation, ranging from its occasional use on rainy days or when more favored activities were not available, through specific scheduling as a group activity dominated by the teacher, to constant availability of the clay crock and accessories. A great many teachers seemed to expect the children to use clay to create representations of objects from the first, and expressed disappointment when they "just messed with it." This approach was constantly reinforced by asking, "What are you making?" or "What have you made?" and by referring to the products as "worms" or "snakes." Many of them made models to be copied, such as snow men or simple animals.

The interviews with teachers revealed notable differences. One commented, "A lot of aggression comes out at clay time. It is evident in the way the children handle the clay; they chop it or pummel it. We restrict pounding to each child's board so that there should be no throwing. . . . The clay is brought out only on occasions. Clay period is always a group activity. They are always interested. With children as young as these are (two to four years) there are so few things that they can do in a group, and clay is one thing that could be used in group activity. When you are short staffed it is hard to give clay to a two-year-old and not sit with him. At that age they are still messy with it and it goes all over everything. . . . Plasticine isn't as good as clay, I think."

Another, on the other hand, spoke only of the children's "liking" for clay, and the imagination and leader-follower characteristics shown in their use of it. She controlled the amount rather rigidly—for example, because they liked to take the products home, she gave them small quantities to work with.

A third teacher insisted that for the most part her children (ages two to three and one half) shunned clay and added that when they did use it they did not make anything, but just pounded it. Another spoke of it almost entirely in terms of individual children. She had noticed that one of her very inhibited little girls could sit and play with it for a half hour at a time; and that an exceedingly overactive and anxious little boy used it a great deal, squeezing it and tearing it up. She seemed to have no realization of its meaning to this child. Several, however, mentioned that when very withdrawn or inhibited children had achieved better social relations and more freedom in self-assertion, they derived greater enjoyment in the use of clay. On the other hand, one anxious child used it less as she came to verbalize more freely about her anxieties and her difficulties at home.

By and large, teachers seemed to be more aware of the effect of water-play and finger-painting than of clay. This may be because those activities require more supervision and the awareness of their impact is increased. It seems all the more important, therefore, to bring to notice the potentialities of clay through the medium of records which give a detailed picture of children at work.

We begin with a striking use of clay that was not mentioned by many teachers. For inhibited or anxious children who are insecure about their status, it can serve as a means of contact or a protective shield behind which to lurk and study the group. Engaged in manipulating a lump of clay, they are given a right to group membership without being subjected to the direct pressures of the doll corner or the yard. At the same time, the sharing of a common activity, the freedom to talk, and the ease with which the clay is picked up and handled give them an opportunity for making or inviting advances. The following excerpt clearly illustrates this use of the clay period.

When this observation began, John (four years and six
months,) had a large glob of clay in front of him. He gave
it several lusty smacks, then pulled off a small segment and
pounded it flat. The teacher told the other children at the
table that John had made some nice things with clay the
other day. Whereupon he proudly explained, "I made a sidewalk yesterday." He thought for a moment (still pounding
the clay) and then said, "I guess I'll make a sidewalk today."
Thereupon he pulled off several segments from the mound and
proceeded to thoroughly flatten them into a creditable appearing sidewalk. Then he yelled out three times, "I made a sidewalk." He looked at the teacher and said, "Teach, I'm finished."
In the meantime Martin was grabbing up all the tongue depressors. John sighted him and indignantly shouted out, "Martin
takes all the sticks. Teach, he is taking all of them." The
teacher prevented Martin from usurping the whole lot, and
John was able to procure one. This he used to cut thin
grooves with little depth into his sidewalk. While thus engaged
Vi handed the teacher a flattened oval hunk of clay and said,
"Here is a birthday cake." The teacher thanked her and in
less than a second John called out to the teacher, "Teach,
here is my birthday cake." When the teacher come over she
asked what was the matter with his sidewalk. He answered,
"My sidewalk is broken." Then he called over to Phil (who
had brought a little toy cement mixer), "Cement mixer man,
my sidewalk is broken." Phil came over and John watched
him go through the motions of mixing the cement and repairing the sidewalk. Then he spoke up, "Teacher, look, I've
got a fixed street. Cement mixer fixed it." Then he proceeded
to cut another long thin groove and yelled out, "Cement mixer
my street is broken." Phil came over and went through his
activity under the close scrutiny of John. As soon as Phil left,
John hastened to cut some more grooves and again called
out, "My street is broken, cement mixer."

The almost magical tongue-loosening quality of clay stands
in vivid contrast to the general impression that it is hard to
get children to talk about things that bother them. To those
who have the time and will to notice, the flow of talk and

the references to significant figures in their private worlds can be exceedingly revealing. In the next record Alice, four and one half years old, chatters constantly as she manipulates her Plasticine and clay. Notice that she initiates reference to members of her friend's family, hence to her own, and that her pounding and her remark about being mean immediately follow the talk about her mother's name. Later she discloses her feelings about her mother more directly.

Vinnie to Alice: "Are you my friend?" "No, I know your sister. I know your mother, too." Vinnie: "What my mother's name? Want me to tell you?" Alice starts to sing to herself. She pounds the Plasticine hard and says, "We're mean, aren't we? 'Cause we're their masters"—pointing to Kurt and Jack. . . . She makes ridges in her Plasticine. Vinnie: "What are you making? A cake?" "No, cold buns." Alice to Jack: "We're friends, aren't we?" "No, you're not my friend." "Then you're not mine, if I'm not yours." She makes a lot of little balls and squeezes them all together. To herself: "Here's my snake. [Gruff voice.] A snake! A snake!". . .

(Later, the same day.) Alice to Sonny: "When you close your eye [holding the basket over it] it's dark." Alice gets up, goes to Kathy, gives her the basket, "It has something in it, but you can't see it." Then to Vinnie, "I'm not going to sleep all night." Sonny: "Come back and finish your clay, 'cause soon you'll have your juice." She comes back, makes a flat cake, and uses two tongue depressors to make a design on it. To Vinnie: "I'll stay here nights and days and nights and days until I want to go home. And even mammy dies I'll be here. Huh?" She wants to flatten a large clay ball. She gets up in order to put her full weight on it.

The record of Carl (three years and nine months) cited below reveals an emotion similar to that of Alice above, in his case focused on his father. His reference to a "pony daddy" corresponds to the silly behavior many children indulge in after secret feelings have slipped out. We do not know, of course, whether the clay is still the "daddy" when Carl is stamping on it and calling it a "pie."

Carl takes another piece of clay from the round mass and rolls it out very thin. He looks up and notices Miss K nearby and says to her, "You don't know my daddy's name—it's Carl." He pauses and then says, "I know my mommy's name, but I won't tell you." He looks up at her and grins, "Her name is Bette." Miss K says to him, "I know your sister's name—it's Chris." Carl is pounding the clay during this. He says, "No, it isn't. Her name is Carla." He takes the clay and makes a fairly round flat piece, takes another piece and molds it into a coil, which he places around the first piece. He says to Miss K, "Teacher, look at the man I made." "Good," Miss K says, "Where are his arms and legs? I'm gonna make them." He makes large holes with his index finger (approximately where eyes would be if the mass were considered a man) and says, "Eyes are gonna show." He takes the clay and mashes it with his right hand holding it up above the board and smiles. He says, "I'm mashing my daddy up." Miss K asks, "Why?" "Cause I'm gonna make me a good daddy,"—he pauses—"a pony daddy." He places the mashed clay back on the board. He looks up at Miss K and says, "I wanna make something," although she is too far away to hear him. With his fist he begins to pound the whole mass of clay in rhythm. He pulls a moderate size piece from the mass, places it on the floor, and pounds it vigorously with his right foot a few times, and then with his left. This is accompanied by a chantlike grunting and he looks about the room and smiles. (The smile appears to be a kind of mischievous one, as if he is enjoying what he knows is the wrong thing to do.) He says to Miss T, "Look at my pie, I stomp on it." "Let's pick it up and put it aside," says Miss T.

STAGES IN THE USE OF CLAY

Four stages in the use of clay can be readily distinguished in our records. First and foremost, it is something to explore and experiment with. The children seem to approach it in a "What is it?" frame of mind. For youngsters this is tantamount to the question "What do you do with it?" and the clay becomes something to examine and have direct contact with—they eat it, smell it, paste it on their faces, or stuff it up their noses; they pat it, pound it, cut it with sticks, bang it with blocks, throw it on the floor, and stamp on it. The following record illustrates this phase.

Ben, three years old, sits down at a table where Tillie and Pete are playing with clay. The teacher tries to soften the clay; Ben waits patiently, watching intently. He takes a small piece from the larger piece and rolls it on a board, first with one hand and then with the other, sometimes with both. He breaks off small pieces and some drop; he looks at his soiled hand and then picks up the dropped pieces. He rolls them into a ball and puts small scraps on top of it—then pats it down very hard with his whole hand. He stands up and walks around rubbing some in his hands. The teacher wets the clay for him. He goes to the teacher, shows her the clay he has in his hand, and says "More water." The teacher moves a chair over and sits next to Ben. He takes up a big piece, shows it to the teacher, and says "hard." Then he watches Roy, who is pushing a table around the room. The teacher makes an object out of clay; Roy picks it up, smiles, and shows it to the observer. He walks around the room with the clay in his hand, goes to the table where Valerie is playing with a hammer set. He puts the clay down on the table, bangs it with his hand, picks it up from the table, walks around the room with it, then puts it on the floor and steps on it. The teacher asks him to put it on a board on the table. He picks it up off the floor and throws it. The teacher asks if he is finished and he shakes his head "yes."

In the second stage, clay is a material with certain characteristic and unique qualities which the child has already discovered. His attention is still focused on manipulation without any intention to create an object. The mass of clay is a medium for immediate sense experience rather than a raw material, as indicated in the first record that follows. But even more prominent is the satisfaction derived from making a positive impression on it by rolling, tearing, or hitting it. This sense of achievement is often expressed by such comments as "Ahunk! Ahunk!" or "See!" which are found in Record 2 below.

Record 1. Lou (four years and four months) goes to the clay table where Ernie and Ann are sitting. Lou asks Ernie, "What are you doing?" She sits down, pounds the clay with the palm of her hand, and looks at Ernie. She puts her finger in the center and pushes tentatively. She pushes the clay on all sides gently with her hands. She stops and watches the two boys at the table. She puts a hand shape on the clay and pushes its upper surface gently with her fingers. She pounds hard with the flat of her hand, picks it up, and turns it over. She tickles it with her fingers in a back and forward motion. One of the boys is watching her. She scratches the clay and frowns. She pounds it hard with her hand, takes the piece in both hands, and breaks it in two. She bends the pieces into a semi.curve and stands them side by side. Then she gets up and leaves.

Record 2. Miss K wets the clay and Pat (of the two-year-old group) picks up a big piece and begins to break small pieces from it, rolling the small pieces on the board. He hits the clay with the fist of his right hand, pressing it with a block, saying, "Ahunk! Ahunk!" All the children at the table begin to say this. He breaks more small pieces from the big piece (the clay is not as soft as it should be), and slaps it gently. He hands his clay to the teacher saying, "Break it! Break it!" She breaks it as Pat waits with both hands up and fingers stretched tense. She puts it on the board and he pats it gently. Dan is using a block with clay. Pat turns to the observer and says, "I want block." The observer says to go and get one. He gets a block and brings it back and hits the clay with it, using both hands; he looks at the clay, says something about a man, pats the board again, holds the clay up to the observer, saying, "See." The observer tells him it is very good and then says, "What is it?" Pat says, "Clay," and shows it to the teacher. Dan calls his clay "duck." Pat immediately shows the observer his clay and says "duck, duck." He puts it down and hits it with a block—rocking the block back and forth on the clay.

In the third stage, clay is approached as a raw material to be made into something else, usually but not always with intention. The child may start with manipulation, create an accidental form, and give it a name. We might call this the product-process phase, in view of the double source of satisfaction. The product, however, is dealt with as an entity in itself, not as a representation of something else. For example, when the child makes a ball of clay he proceeds to play with it as if it were a real ball; and when he produces what he calls a piece of candy, he is likely to nibble it. We illustrate this phase in the following account.

Liza (three years and two months) rolls a small piece and eats a bit. Now she takes a large wad and pounds it flat . . . takes off a small piece and rolls it between her hands . . . eats some more. Miss N takes the clay away and Liza calls to have it back. When told she could have it if she wouldn't eat any more, it is returned to her. She breaks off a small piece, pounds it, and says, "I made a candy." She holds it up to show to the little girl beside her. She rolls a large wad in her hand, now flattens it out then crunches it together, pounds it on the table, and again rolls it into a ball. She sings, "I made a bally," and continues to work the clay. She gets up to retrieve her ping-pong racket from a small girl, then sits down holding the racket in one hand, the clay ball in the other. She slaps down the racket on the clay then places the racket beside her. Taking a small bit she pastes it on her face near her mouth. She throws the clay ball into the air and catches it.

The fourth stage is the one most teachers assume from the beginning. Here the children indicate an intention to make something of the clay, and realize it is not the object itself but only a representation of it. Bender points out that the product may result from "motor impulse," from copying things seen, from the child's own body image, or from fantasy and personal problems. The following record of a four-year-old group illustrates this stage of representation. The selection of objects probably reflects the private fantasies or problems of the individual children.

Jean to observer: "We're making pancakes. Eat the pancakes." Elia: "I'm making a knife." Paddy then joins Elia, "Here, look, a garage." Bob: "Look, I'm making a snake. I have two snakes. . . . Now I made the snake flat. Did you ever see a snake with a wing?" Elia: "They only have snakes with wings in the country." Bob: "I'm going to make a very very big snake." Elia and Bud then decide to make a cake. Elia: "After I get the dough fixed, I will put the cake in the oven." Bob: "Look at my cake. Look how my cake came out, isn't it beautiful?" Elia: "I have to make a very special cake for my little girl." Bob: "I'm going to make a candle." "So am I." They put candles on their cakes. Elia: "My little girl is six years old." Bob: "So is mine." "Let's make the cake bigger." "No." "Well, I am." They continue patting the clay. Bob: "Look at my birthday cake with cherries all around it." To the observer: "Do you want a piece of cake?" He then goes over to show his cake to Miss O. He runs back to the table and decides to make another cake and says, "I'm not going to put candles on the cake. I'm going to make an ordinary cake. . . ." Later Bob says, "After the cake gets dry, I'm going to paint it and then I'm going to take it home."

Unfortunately some teachers overlook the fact that there are different phases of clay work, and treat a child as if he had attained a later stage when he is still in an earlier one. The bewilderment that results shows up quite clearly in the following record of Tony, a boy of three years and nine months.

The teacher asked Tony, "Would you like to paint your snakes and worms?" (She is referring to clay products made previously.) He nods and seats himself at a table nearby. Miss A brings a board with a few dried-up pieces of clay on them and by this time Sandra is also seated opposite him with a board full of clay objects in front of her. Miss A brings a jar of red paint for Sandra and a jar of green paint for Tony. He promptly overturns his. Sandra calls to Miss A, "Look what Tony done." She receives no reply and turns to painting her clay objects. Tony picks up what looks like a dog bone in his right hand and a brush in his left and daubs the bone with green paint. Seeing Miss A, he says, "I'm finished." She replies, "Tony, you have a worm there too, haven't you?" He looks down and picks up the clay "worm" and daubs at it in a desultory fashion. He says, "I made a worm." Sandra says, "Me show mine to my mommy." Tony looks around, "Where Bud gone?" (Bud had been sitting next to him.) Then he rubs the brush into the board in front of him, "I made this, this, this, this," he chants as he rubs. Then he picks up a piece with his free hand and throws it at Sandra. She dodges, picks up a small piece of clay from her own board, and says, "Did me make this?" Then she picks up a larger lump and paints it, saying, "This is my snow man, my wow wow." Tony watches her, his head a little bent, chin on chest, looking at her from under his lashes. She says, "That's you no man." He says, "I made a peanut." The teacher passes by, and he says to her, "Look at me, I'm painting my snow man. . . . What is me painting?" He turns to Sandra for corroboration.

The age limits characterizing each stage mentioned above are extremely fluid. In some cases the second stage of manipulation extends through the fourth year. In others the beginnings of fantasy can be seen before the third year. Since most of the children had been exposed both to the teacher's insistence on a meaningful product and to influences of other children who were producing specific named forms, it is impossible to conclude what the spontaneously developed limits would be. However, judging from the records, it seems that most children who have had some group experience with clay will have arrived at the object stage by the fourth year.

A process which might be described as moving from primitive satisfaction in manipulation, to an accidental product, then to purposeful activity can be recognized in several of the records. These processes frequently follow each other even in the short space of one session, as indicated by the record below.

Violet (three years and ten months) sits down very quietly opposite Clem and waits for the clay. When it is there, she first puts one finger in it, and rubs a bit of clay on it. Then she takes the stick and splits the clay straight through (using both hands) into two unequal pieces. She looks one second at them and puts them together again. Then she makes two parts once more and turns a little ball between her hands, lets it go from one hand to the other, repeats the process, not looking at the clay, and says to the assistant, "I made a big sailboat." She puts the little ball down and pats it firmly until it gets flatter, and then announces: "I make a cake." She takes another piece and rolls it lengthwise making it very short and puts it on the cake. She says, "This is a cake." "What cake?" the teacher asks. "A happy birthday cake," Violet answers, and puts three or four more candles of different sizes on it. She is satisfied and gives it to the assistant. At once she starts to split the rest again and takes one piece, rolls it lengthwise between her hands, then makes a ring out of it. She makes it long again and repeats that twice. "I make a basket," she says to the assistant. She looks at Clem while making a new roll between her hands. Making the rolls into rings, she puts one over the other, five in all. Then she tears little pieces from the remaining clay and pushes them into the openings of the rings. She is twice as active as any of the others and says, "I make a big basket," but then she starts to pat it together harder and harder, so that the end result is just one big mess.

Individual Reactions to Clay

The satisfactions derived from clay vary with each individual child, but for the most part are quite clearly congruent with their behavior in other areas. Youngsters who tend to be rather freely aggressive will pound, punch, dig holes, pinch, and mess with the water. Those who seem rather gentle or even inhibited in their approach to other children and materials are usually content with gentle patting, rolling, scratching, and scraping. The following records represent this wider range of behavior. The first shows a "gentle, somewhat withdrawn" girl of four years and five months.

Sandra sits for a while, looking around her. Then she stands making designs with her index finger in the dried-up clay on the board. Miss K comes over to the table and Sandra says, "Give me my clay now. Give me mine." When Miss K gives it to her she smiles. She now has two chunks of clay, each about the size of a teacup. She takes a small piece, rolls it to make it look like a snake and puts it on Max's piece of clay. She sings, "Happy birthday to you." Miss K comes over and pours some water into a depression in each of Sandra's two pieces of clay. Sandra takes a piece of clay and rolls it in her hands and then in the water on the board, using two fingers. She squishes it around in her hands, rolling it some more. When the girl next to her takes a little piece, she says, "Stop it. Don't." She puts the clay back on her own board. She takes one of her lumps of clay and pats the whole thing consistently, flattening it out, a serious expression on her face. She sticks the index finger of her right hand into the clay about two dozen times. She takes a small piece, rolls it, and puts it in one of the holes. She says "Happy birthday." She makes more holes. She takes another bigger piece, rolls it snake fashion, breaks it in two, and puts one half in another hole. She repeats this, filling up the holes systematically. . . .

The next record depicts a boy of less than three who was described as bewildered and inhibited in the group. When playing with clay, his behavior is integrated and his inhibitions are at least partially overcome.

Bert sits at an angle in his chair. He hits the clay with the board. He picks up another piece and gives it to boy next to him. Again he hits the clay with the board, takes another piece and puts it on top of his clay ball and hits it with the board. He takes a small cookie cutter and lines the top of the clay. He hits the clay with the board while staring at the observer. Putting the board down, he picks up the clay and hits the underside. Taking it in his left hand, he spanks it with his right. His mouth is open. He picks up half of the flattened clay and shakes his head. He stares at the child sitting across from him. He puts the clay pieces together. He takes the cookie cutter and marks the top piece of clay. He picks up the board and hits the clay. Taking another piece that has been left at an empty space, he puts it on top of the other pieces. He sits and hits it with a board. He gets up, takes the large cookie cutter from the floor, sits down, and marks the top of the clay. He gets up and walks away pulling down his sleeves.

The following episode deals with a child of two who is described as vigorous and outgoing.

Bernie pounds his clay with his clay board. He lifts it up—"Look what I made. See?" (He is speaking to no particular person.) Using the end of the clay board he makes ridges in the clay, then rolls it up again. He breaks off several pieces, puts them on top of the large piece, and pounds them down with the board. He repeats this several times, laughing—"I'll do it some more!" He makes holes with his thumb. He takes two blue plates and places them close to his clay board, breaks off a piece of clay, rolls it in the palms of his hands, and puts it on one of the plates. He repeats this, putting the second piece of clay on the other plate. He makes holes with his thumb. "Teacher, look." Teacher: "What are you making?" He breaks two small pieces from the large piece, puts them on one of the blue plates, then puts them back on the large piece and pounds with the clay board. He repeats this process with several pieces of clay, smiling as he works.

Emotional Values of Clay

The emotional implications of the use of clay depend upon the needs brought to it. It seems to offer the best outlet for aggressive impulses that we have been able to discover among the creative materials available for very young children. It is also an outlet for forbidden interests having to do with sex parts and body functions. It adapts itself well to a variety of fantasy expressions and is used for this purpose both by troubled children and by those whose development seems to be proceeding smoothly. It seems to be valuable, too, in helping boys and girls achieve a sense of mastery over their world. Delight in molding something, in leaving an impression of one's self, can be perceived in records of children under three as well as over four. It offers, in a word, an unexcelled medium both for destruction without guilt and for construction with satisfaction.

Clay affords an outlet for aggressive impulses to youngsters of many age levels. The younger children gain satisfaction from primitive pounding and stamping activities, while those who are older can integrate it into dramatic fantasies. The record of Bud, below, is a vivid example of the more complex kind of expression. Here we see a development from general objects frequently suggested by teachers to a more and more explicit description of a male figure involving more and more direct and outspoken hostility. The excerpt takes on more meaning when one knows that in other activities Bud had used trains as weapons and had identified water with urine. His father was exceedingly abusive to him, and he was terrorized of the "boogey man," who, he was convinced, lived in the basement of his tenement. These activities and experiences suggest that even the conventional objects

—snow men, balls, and birthday cakes—may be highly compressed symbols with idiomatic meanings for this child and for others as well.

Bud, age four years, literally tears into the clay, saying, "I know what I'm doing, I don't need an apron." His fat chunky little fingers dig and he mutters, "Monkeys go like that. . . . Squeeze him and squeeze him and tear a hole and stand him up." As he says this he fiercely pounds the clay into small pieces, using his whole body to press on it, and gets red in the face. Then he takes one piece and rolls it into a ball, "A snowball, ha, ha, ha! Look what I made, going to make a big snowball. . . ." His very expressive fingers keep pressing holes into a new mass and he mumbles, "Deep holes. Going to dig a deeper one. Going to put a piece of clay into it." He looks up at the observer and says, as he molds long strips, "Make a long piece, a candle burning, going to have a party. Don't you know that? Two snow mans are coming to the party." He is very intense again and explains his every move. "There, the funny snow man." He tries to stick the "candle" into the mass of clay—"Candle burning." He pushes more holes into the clay, "Look what I made!" He takes a flat thick piece and says, "I'm going to cover the party up." Then he puts everything together and bangs the mass on the table. "Going to make a deep tricky hole." Violently he pulls pieces off and then makes a long strip. "A train"—he mutters to himself. "Wee, the choo-choo." He continues to roll out more strips. "A big train is coming to town." He connects the long pieces. Now he is more relaxed and calmer as he rolls out long pieces. He says, "Clay it up." The teacher says it's time to stop. Bud says, "First can I make the legs on the conductor? He has a broken leg, that's why it comes off. It comes off because it's broken. Must have long legs—ooh [as 'leg' comes off clay which is supposed to be the conductor]; it's the broken leg—lands in a hospital." Here Bud gets quite excited again and his eyes are fiery now. He makes two new long strips for the legs and says, "Look at my conductor. Woo, look at the head." He pushes a hole into his mass of clay and says, "A boogey-man, he's scared, the boogey-man." With this he pounds another hole into the mass, goes to the water can and pours water into the hole. Water spills over the block of stone and Bud squashes the clay back and forth over the wet. Here he is interrupted by the teacher.

We have observed many other indirect ways of expressing hostility and aggression through the use of clay. Jill, a child of four years and nine months, had been extremely inhibited, timid, and asocial. Recently, however, she had begun to play with other youngsters, and the record below shows her at the clay table with her "best friend" in the group. Notice how she resorts to teasing as a means of expressing hostility to this newly won friend without running the risk of losing her.

Vickie, Sally, and Jill are giggling together at the first feel of the clay. As they dig in, Jill repeats what one of the others is saying, "What's that?" She brings a small portion back to the table and starts to roll it into a ball. She then flattens it and pounds it. Her fingers are extremely deft and sure. The group of three all pound and giggle. Jill's giggle seems to come from way down inside and is rather throaty and her whole body moves with it. She makes four holes for eyes, nose, and mouth and says, giggling, to Vickie, "This is you. . . . Yes it is." She takes it over to the teacher and repeats, "This is Vickie." Then she starts to make something else and when the observer asks her what she is making now, she replies, "A basket." Then she flattens and pounds some more, giggling a deep "Hee, hee." She makes a flat piece with three balls in it and puts a handle over it. She says to Vickie, "What is it?" Then she says, "Cooking a face." They both giggle and Jill says, "Well, you started it." She makes a round flat mound with a thick handle (her usual creation), and Vickie whispers something into her ear. They both giggle at this. Jill makes another mound about 1½ inches around and in it she puts eight tiny round balls, saying that they are candy. She is talking with Vickie; other children come over and mess up some of Vickie's work. Jill takes a piece of her own clay and says consolingly, "I'll roll it for you," and she rolls out a long strip for her friend.

Another child, described as extremely aggressive, presented quite a different picture. Her intense interest in tearing down and breaking up was characteristic also of her approach to other children and other areas of living.

Tina, four years and nine months, is the only one at the table. Some pieces of clay are scattered about. She begins with a dynamic, workmanlike attitude, does not bother even to sit, but remains standing for a while. First she gathers up all the thin sticks lying about, then puts them down and picks up a large lump of clay, places it on a board, and pounds on it. She works intensely but is not overly interested in it and does not sing or murmur to herself as is her usual custom. She stops her pounding and stares at the clay, disinterestedly playing with a small piece with agile fingers. Seeming to make up her mind, she takes a rather large piece of clay from the bottle and picks smaller pieces from it, then places them back in the bottle. She takes out the rest of the large lumps of clay from the bottle and spreads them out, continues to break them down into small bits, and returns them to the bottle. Her fingers are continually clawing and picking. Once or twice she is distracted and looks toward different parts of the room. But even while she is looking elsewhere, Tina does not stop tearing the clay apart.

Of another child, a three-year-old, her teacher reports, "One day at clay time last week I observed her closely and these aggressive outbursts were quite evident. She transformed clay into cakes, chopped meat, etc., as she does sand, water, and snow on the playground. She worked away, cutting up meat, her tongue curled around her upper lip. Suddenly she began to look abstracted and then began to scream, 'Oh, oh, oh,' and pound the clay violently. This pattern was repeated several times."

Explicit references to family figures are not infrequent. In the record of Alice reproduced earlier in this chapter, the little girl said she would stay at the school nights and days "and even mammy dies," and then proceeded to flatten the clay with her full weight. And in another record, also in this same chapter, we found Carl "mashing my daddy up" to "make me a good daddy."

The record of Jack, given below, points quite clearly to a basic difficulty in the area of sexual identification and sex play. The fact that the observer was a male may have been important, since the boy tended to hide his sex play activities from his teacher, who was a woman. In this brief episode we find references to a male sex organ, to "not seeing" something, to squeezing, to the emergence of a substance like orange juice, to its metamorphosis into something as large as an elephant and its trunk.

Jack (four years and two months) is seated at a table working with water, clay, and spatula. He leans over to watch the observer write, and says, "Look what I'm makin'. A coal truck —a big one. A piece came off—it's a man." He laughs. "Isn't he funny? Look at his mouth and his nose and his eyes and his face. Now watch." He breaks off small pieces—"See?" He shapes a small pointed piece and laughs. "Look at the pee-pee." Alternately he watches and smiles in a friendly manner at the observer and works with the clay. "See the man. His eyes—he can't see, can he?" He squeezes the clay hard. "See how tight it is? I'm squeezin' orange juice. I'll make an elephant—want to see?" He forms a long trunk and attaches it to the large mass. He laughs. "That's his trunk." He looks at the observer questioningly. The observer suggests making peanuts. He forms small lumps and places them before the "elephant." He laughs, "He's eatin' peanuts."

It is unfortunate that the observer did not encourage this child to continue to develop his own themes instead of intruding adult suggestions. For Jack may have been leading up to a crucial remark or question which would have been helpful in understanding the specific confusions responsible for his difficulties, which manifested themselves in unwillingness to confine defecation to the toilet, persistent sex play involving self-exhibition and masturbatory activities with little girls, inability to defend himself effectively against aggression, and failure to make a place for himself among the boys of his group.

The following observation also indicates fantasy involving body products:

Rollo (four years and five months) begins to roll clay, using more energy with each roll. He breaks off a piece and rolls it hard, and then breaks off another. Now he tries hard, using up much energy in his effort to put the pieces together again and makes one ball out of them. . . . Jasper comes over and points to a small piece of clay which Rollo broke from his rather large ball and asks, "Do you need this?" "Yes," retorted Rollo as if that piece meant his life. Jasper walks away disappointed. Then Rollo smiles and oddly enough gives his clay to the teacher as she passes. Clumsily he gets up and begins to walk around the room, characteristically scratching his buttocks and pulling up his pants. Soon he spies a piece of clay (brown) on the floor, makes a grab for it, dashes into the toilet room, throws it into nearest toilet, and quickly flushes it down. He then glances around quickly, and seeing that the coast is clear he walks out of the toilet like a little angel—then goes back to see a job well done (the clay had been flushed away). He turns around, smiles broadly, walks back slowly to his own room, and sees Tita playing with brown clay. "That's not chocolate," he laughingly says, rubbing his face with his hands and squirming. "That's not chocolate," he repeats three times, each time getting louder. (He seems to derive much pleasure out of saying this or from mocking Tita.)

Here, too, an alert teacher might have obtained valuable information by following up a child's remarks. When Rollo said, "That's not chocolate," she might have responded smilingly (to match his mood). "No, Rollo? Then what is it?"

The interest in sex parts and feces was, however, encountered comparatively rarely in the group under observation and the manner of expressing it was likely to be rather indirect or at least nonverbal. One of the children, a four-year-old boy who had been referred for study because of extreme aggressiveness, used the snow man, a favorite object in his group, as a basis for expressing this interest. He did not say anything specifically about sex parts but made a figure composed of five slightly flattened balls of clay piled on top of each other with a long symmetrical form extending from about the middle. He described it this way: "I made a snow man. I put on his hat. This is the daddy one."

It may be significant that in the few records where discernible references to specific anatomy or toilet functions did appear (only in 5 out of 112), each of the children had been referred because of difficulties in adjustment, although the histories and the characteristic patterns of behavior varied widely. It may be that the presence of an observer inhibited some youngsters who might otherwise have expressed "forbidden" interests. However, since Bender and Woltmann apparently found similar interests frequently manifested by disturbed children, it may be that such expressions should be used as a sign that a child is experiencing special anxieties and needs clarification in this area.

A number of the boys and girls seemed to gain particular pleasure from mixing water with their clay, but no explanatory comments accompanied this behavior. However, judging from the records of several who identified water with urine during other kinds of play, it would not seem too far fetched a suggestion that the water-clay type of play bears some relation to interest in body products. It may also be significant that children for whom water-play and wet clay had the greatest appeal were among those considered "immature." The less satisfactory their infancy period, the less warm and tender their mothers, the more zest the children seemed to display for this kind of play.

Because clay also involves water, and may be used to smear as well as to mold, the watchful teacher may sense a child's need for other materials through his approach. In the following record of a four-year-old we see clearly that although clay itself does not yet offer the child a medium of expression he can use or enjoy, the way it is handled indicates that he would profit by an opportunity to play freely with water, finger-paints, or mud.

Mrs. H asks Rudy to bring the water which she needs to soften the clay. He brings it over and pours all of it into the clay pot and goes to get more. As he does this, he drinks from the pail of water first. At Mrs. H's suggestion, he gets a paper cup from the closet and goes to get a drink. When he comes back, he throws the top of the garbage pail on the floor and jumps up and down on it, laughing as he does so. Mrs. H gives him a sponge to wipe off the clay boards. He does so willingly, squeezing the sponge with obvious delight. He squeezes the sponge more than he wipes the boards. In due time he wipes off the four boards. When he is through, he sits and fingers the sponge and rolls a small ball of clay around in his hand. He watches Mrs. H talking and playing with Glenna, while he squeezes the sponge and makes faces by puckering his lips.

The variety of fantasy expressed through clay is not limited to unpleasant or forbidden areas. For instance, one of the younger girls announced happily that she had made "Wheaties with butterscotch sauce." Frequently children confine their clay products to one type, although the products may differ widely in form. These may all be objects which could be used to hurt or to frighten, such as guns, snakes, crocodiles—or "happy" things such as cookies, pies, birthday cakes, candy—or impersonal articles like chairs, sidewalks, ferryboats. The meaning of these persistently recurrent objects cannot be completely understood without an intimate knowledge of each child, but it may be significant that food

objects appear with relative frequency in the work of apparently happy children while aggressive objects such as guns
and crocodiles appear more frequently in the work of those
who are belligerent and troubled.

The joy and self-assurance which seem to be connected
with creative activity frequently characterize manipulation of
this material. Below we have the record of a spontaneous
little girl of three years and ten months.

Angela to Ellen: "I'll roll it and roll it." She does so in
rhythm to her words. She punches a thumb hole in the ball
and rolls some more. "Around and around and around we go,
around and AROUND and AROUND we go [rising pitch on each
'around,' voice drops at 'we go'] this *early* in the *mor*-ning—
[again rolling clay with her right hand in rhythm with her
voice]." She pushes a depressor through the middle of the ball,
peering to see it come out of the other side, pulls it out, and
rolls the ball again. Ellen pushes the depressors into the clay
in the can. Angela: "Don't take it out. Leave it there. Don't
take it out. Now you can stick another stick in, then you take
them out, don't you. When you need them you take them out."
(She means that it is a convenient way to keep sticks, instead
of loose in the can.) "These are the same as the doctor's—
these sticks are the same." She puts a little piece of clay in her
mouth, takes it out, rubs it off on the board, looking at the
observer. To Hilda, "I put a piece of clay in my mouth, and
took it out again. He-he-he-he [laughing]." She walks away,
shows her big ball with the thumb hole to Ray and Steve, "I
make a key hole—a big double key hole." She walks away
singing to herself.

The following record illustrates the same thing in a minor
key. It is significant that it mirrors the behavior of a boy who
was described variously as a "vegetable," and an "amoeba."

Tony (three years and seven months) sits down and watches
Sandra who is poking a finger into a ball of clay. The teacher
comes and puts some clay in front of him. He looks at it and
then at the teacher. His eyes follow her as she walks to the

bathroom for water. A boy sitting opposite Tony pats his clay, lifting his hand high. Tony does the same, lifting his right hand up and down, not quite so vigorously as the other boy, but evidently enjoying it because he smiles and laughs to himself, looking down at the clay. The boy now does the same thing with both hands and Tony follows suit, then rubs his hands together. The teacher brings water and pours it into a hole in the clay. Tony starts to massage the water into the clay. The teacher says, "I will show you how to do this." She kneads the clay and water into a soft, homogeneous mass. She leaves. Tony slaps the clay, then pokes a finger into it, looking at Sandra meantime. Then he tries to pull the whole mass off the board with both hands, but can't do it. Finally he holds onto the board with the left hand and pulls with his right. The clay comes away and, still holding it in his right, he slaps it with his left. Then he holds it in both hands and looks around. He slaps it and says to Sandra, "I can't hear it." To the teacher who is passing by, "I am making a hat." He pauses, "It's a pancake now." The boy opposite says, "I am making a boat." Tony: "I'll smash it. I'll smash it. I'll smash it." (This is a very unusual utterance for Tony.)

The particular need served by clay frequently depends on its place in the day's activity. It can offer a calming and integrating experience as well as a release for hostility and aggression. The observation of Violet, reproduced earlier in this chapter, was made after the child, an ordinarily aggressive three-year-old, had had a very satisfying and intense experience with easel painting. The controlled and constructive quality of her play was rather unexpected, judging both from our knowledge of the child and from our experience with other children who seemed to be of a similar temperament. The observer who made this record believed that she had gained so much release from her previous activity that she was ready to settle down to constructive work when she came to the clay.

Conclusions and Recommendations

It should be clear from the foregoing discussion that clay can render several valuable services to both teachers and children. It is spontaneously sought and vigorously used by aggressive children who often create the teacher's most difficult problems of group management. Therefore, if it is readily accessible, it will be used to drain off some of the energies which otherwise find expression against group mates and largely vitiate the benefits of group life for many of the other children. For the inhibited child, work with clay in a group offers an opportunity for learning about his playmates and for experiencing feelings of kinship with them, without the necessity of responding to direct social impacts which he may not yet be able to manage.

Because clay lends itself so easily to use in a group without necessitating constant care and direct supervision by the teacher it offers her an opportunity to observe her children in many ways. It may, indeed, give her some helpful indications of what to expect, if it is offered early in the term before she has had a chance to get to know them. The child's manner of approaching and manipulating the clay seem to be characteristic of his whole approach to life. As we noted before, there is a striking difference between aggressive and well-adjusted children on this score. Generally the well-adjusted children make a more direct approach, using tools and molds much less frequently, and they handle the clay in a vigorous and forthright manner. They tend to poke, pound, and pinch instead of gently slapping, patting, or scratching. More actual molding is found among well-adjusted children than among either the aggressive or the inhibited children, but by and large the aggressive children tend to create and name more products than does any other group.

For some children, of course, the messiness of clay seems to be a threat, and they tend to withdraw from it with expressions of disgust. Such an attitude in itself is a sure indicator of some difficulty in adjustment. Fortunately, there are many substitute materials which resemble clay to some extent but which are more acceptable to such children. Dough made with equal parts of flour and salt has similar properties. It looks cleaner than clay and it has the virtue of resembling something familiar if the children come from homes where they can observe baking. Papier-mâché is another substitute, and Plasticine might be used as an introductory plastic material for a child who seems unable to accept clay, since it is somewhat less messy and adhesive. Finally, the best material so far found has been snow. Almost without exception, children who had shown inhibitions with respect to clay seemed to lose them after a severe snowstorm had given them some zestful experience with molding and wielding snow. In reports of teachers about behavior changes in individual children we find numerous references to "the big snow."

Without exception, youngsters who seem well adjusted in other areas turn to clay with enormous enthusiasm and express a good deal of satisfaction either with the creative process or with their products. Extremely bright children tend to talk more about what they are doing and express more grandiose intentions about creating things than their less gifted peers. They are also more fluid and flexible, swinging with great ease from one concept to another.

Some anxious children find clay an ideal material for projecting their private worlds. For these it would be well if some arrangement could be made so that playing with clay need not always be a group activity, since they sometimes refuse to participate with the others. However, at other times a child may ask for clay, and it is not advisable to let considerations of routine interfere with such requests because they often mean that the child has something vital to express and cannot or will not do it while others are present. It may be that the teacher herself cannot understand what he is trying to communicate, but it is well to note what happens for the sake of a fuller understanding later on or for reference to a worker trained in the interpretation of projective materials. In at least one instance, that of Bud, cited earlier in this chapter, a record of the clay session led to questions about the child's background which eventually clarified the basis for some of his difficulties. The records of Jill and John (also reported earlier in this chapter), contain material which could be similarly fruitful.

It may be helpful to remember also that when children offer the teacher bits of information about themselves or their families they are often trying to establish closer contact with her and may be on the verge of really talking about things of great moment to them. The manner in which she receives their confidences will determine how far they will go. When Carl (whose record appears earlier in this chapter) started to talk about his mother's name, his teacher might have said simply and invitingly, "Yes?"—and waited for him to continue. Instead she volunteered his sister's name. Similarly when he announced that his product was a man, she might have said something like, "I see. . . . What kind of man?" rather than ask where his arms and legs were. The object of such noncommittal remarks as these is to assure the child of his teacher's attention and interest and to encourage him to communicate what he may wish to say without imposing her own ideas. As we see from Carl's report, a suggestion from the teacher which does not correspond to his own intentions is ignored by him—but in a less assured child it might have interfered with a stream of expression, either turning it or damming it.

Perhaps the greatest source of interference with the potential usefulness of clay as a medium of self-discovery lies in the teacher's lack of recognition of its meaning to children. Her overemphasis on named products frequently bewilders and frustrates the young child, since he cannot understand what she is talking about and she obviously does not understand what he is experiencing. Instead of speaking about what the child is *making*, it might be helpful if the teacher commented on what he is *doing*. "We're having lots of fun, aren't we?" will strike a more responsive chord than "What are you making?"

Offering models for the children to copy or showing them what to do with the clay can often have a stultifying effect and in some cases a devastating one. In the record below, notice how the imposition of too high a standard produces a reaction of disgust and unprovoked hostility.

Ronald (four years and four months) went to the clay table from the block corner. He is pale and coughs a great deal. He rolled a piece of clay in his hand, saying, "I'm making a dog," then rolled another piece and fastened it to the first. "I can't make a dog. . . ." There is a new little boy in the group today, and his mother sat beside him at the opposite end of the table from Ronald, and made some clay animals skillfully. He rolled some more and fastened it to a black piece of clay, then made small balls and flattened them. Arnold and Eddie joined the group. Ronald made a man with pieces of clay and made white clay rolls for arms which he curled around the body. The other children were asking the mother how she made the cats with curly tails. . . . The mother is getting the others, especially Arnold, to follow her example in each step of rolling the pieces for the animals. Ronald made a roll of black clay and put a small roll of white clay on top of it and two rolls of white clay under it, looking at the animals the mother had made. He mashed it all up together with a disgusted expression. Erwin joined the group. "I'm making Santa and his deer," Ronald told him. Ronald said to Eddie, "I can beat you, Eddie." "No, you can't. Can he, Arnold?" Ronald: "I can stick a needle into you. It would hurt you."

The endless snow men and birthday cakes that follow a teacher's example undoubtedly constitute a barrier to further exploration. Even a well-intentioned compliment about something a child has made may prevent his moving on to other things for a considerable period of time. It seems wiser to express appreciation of what he is experiencing than to admire a product which may only be an accident and which holds little meaning until the teacher weights it for him by her comments.

Sometimes youngsters need long uninterrupted periods of time with clay really to get going. Rigidly scheduled sessions which are arbitrarily terminated to maintain a preplanned routine would obviously interfere with the fullest use of the material by such children. They might be permitted to continue, if they wish, while those who are finished with the clay go on to other things. If the teacher would regard the clay period as not just busywork or an activity to keep the children from getting into mischief, but as a legitimate channel for exploration, expression, and self-assertion, having unique meanings for each child engaged in it, we feel sure she would make possible this extra opportunity.

CHAPTER VII

The Use of Graphic Materials

CO-AUTHOR OF THIS CHAPTER: MRS. ELLEN SCHINDEL

POSTER PAINTS, easels, brushes, paint jars, crayons, newsprint, and drawing paper are almost routinely included in the budget for every preschool group. The reasons for their inclusion and the best approach to their use, are, however, not so commonly recognized. Despite a widely expanded interest in the possibilities offered by these graphic materials in recent years, a great many misconceptions and groundless assumptions still surround them. Probably the most persistent and most damaging of these is the notion that whenever a child paints he must be copying something in the outside world. The first question in the mind of many adults is, "What are you painting?"—as if to imply that whenever a child wields a brush he is trying to become an artist—and a limited, literal-minded one at that. Such an approach effectively blocks, confines, and angers the child, as the following observations indicate:

Record 1. Erica (four years old) paints with careless and easy strokes, not too precisely. Holding the brush in one hand while the other hangs down, she covers one side of the paper with a mass of brown paint. The brush strokes are vaguely like concentric circles. No specific form has yet come out of the painting. Erica is, for the most part, quiet, but she calls to the teacher, telling her that she is painting. The teacher comes over and watches her paint. She asks what she is painting, but Erica does not answer (possibly out of shyness). The teacher leaves and

Erica returns to her painting. The question, however, seems to have made her self-conscious, for now she leaves the aimless solid mass and starts to paint lines on the other side of the paper, with slow and careful movements. The color brown has been used exclusively throughout. Some of the lines painted are curved, some circular, and others end in curlicues. Stopping, Erica puts down the brush and looks critically at her work. She does not seem satisfied, for, picking up the brush once more, she quickly adds some dots on the top of the paper. Putting down the brush, she runs to the same teacher and enthusiastically tells her that she has finished her painting. The teacher returns with her and again asks what the picture represents. Erica smiles hopelessly but does not answer. Following is a sketch of this painting.

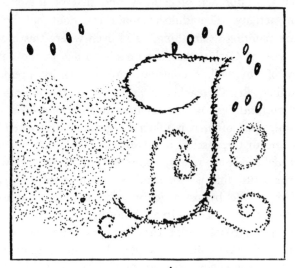

SKETCH OF ERICA'S PAINTING

Record 2. Carlos (four years and ten months) grabs a purple pencil and draws while Oliver watches. Oliver: "Water?" Carlos: "No, boat. This is the chimney." Oliver: "Make me one, Carlos." "Can't you make one yourself?" He proceeds to show Oliver how to make one. "There (puts his picture before Oliver)—you look at that and see how it goes." Oliver draws a fluttering line across his paper. Carlos slaps Oliver's hand. "No, a straight line—that's right. Now make the house." Carlos inspects it, takes the crayon from Oliver and draws in portholes. Adult watching: "What is this, Carlos?" "This is a car." Adult: "But isn't this a boat?" Carlos: "Yes, but the car is underneath. . . ." He turns and shows the picture to the admiring teacher. Adult: "What's that?" "Oh, that's the sun shining." The teacher asks, "That is the moon isn't it, Carlos?" Carlos: "Yeah." Adult: "What's that?" Carlos: "That's a lil' conductor house." Adult: "What's that?" Jessie: "Mind your own business." Carlos: "Yeah, mind your own business." Carlos scrawls over the book again, as does Oliver.

These records leave no doubt that there is a yawning gap between the approach of children and that of adults to the painting activity. The adults assume throughout that the children are painting "something," and even where this is so, as in the case of Carlos, they are unable to accept the natural fluidity of the child's concepts. Moreover, by premature questioning, Erica's teacher interferes with the child's own expression, and destroys her unabashed absorption in spreading paint. Too often it is taken for granted that when children come to the easel they do so with deliberate intention, clearly defined and readily expressed in words. How far from the truth this is, we shall see even more fully from statements made by psychologists who have worked extensively in the field of children's painting.

The most striking point that emerges from the writings of such specialists as Bland, Despert, Liss, and Alschuler and Hattwick, is the general agreement that young children have no intention of representing objects when they paint. Instead of painting things, they paint feelings—instead of expressing ideas they are trying to say what they feel and how they feel. However, not all observers agree that the emotions themselves are the starting point. Some point out that painting is first of all a motor activity and an extension of the child's movements. However, it seems to us that in mirroring movements the paintings may also be expressing what the child is feeling, since his body is still his primary vehicle of expression.

All this means that to understand these products we must forget the traditional approach to painting as an art form, as something that "holds a mirror up to nature," and regard it as a reflection of the emotions and attitudes of the individual child. This point of view fits in well with the objectives of the present study. Our aims here, as with the other media, are to discover the meanings that painting and drawing have for children, what they do for them, and what help they offer the adult in understanding and guiding them. We shall refer occasionally to the many explorations of painting as a means of assessing developmental status and discovering diagnostic clues for screening and therapeutic purposes, but by and large we believe they are of limited use to the teacher. On the other hand, we shall not regard painting and drawing as skills to be perfected for achievement purposes. We shall approach them, rather, as positive instruments for healthy growth. The fact that they seem to be so intimately related to inner states of feeling makes this approach a promising one.

First Approaches to Painting; Exploration and Experimentation

We begin with an aspect of the painting experience that has rarely been mentioned in the discussions to date. When a young child is first confronted with the materials, he does not see them as a means to something else—even to the expression of feelings—but rather as a challenge to investigation and a source of immediate experience. He therefore brings them into contact with his organs for exploration, his eyes, skin, nose, and mouth. Until he has fully satisfied himself about their intrinsic qualities, he is not ready to venture further.

Again and again our records show a blocking in the conventional use of painting materials because this primary exploration has not been completed.

The second step in the child's approach is still exploratory, but focuses on objects outside himself. He finds no special significance in putting the paint on a piece of paper—he would like to see how it spreads over everything, and he cannot see why he should not put it on tables, chairs, walls, etc. At this stage he is still not interested in producing anything resembling a picture. But he is now achieving a satisfaction beyond the discovery of sensory qualities; he is making a lasting impression on things around him and in a small way changing the world itself. To this extent he has created something, but it is not yet a planned and purposeful creation. In fact, the effects he produces are likely to be a complete surprise to him since he has trouble making the brush go where he wants it to go. Yet, no matter how far the results are from any intentions he might have, we do know that they arouse his interest and suggest further possibilities for action.

To illustrate these early stages in the painting process, we should like to offer several records of very young children, ranging in age from two and one half to three years. In the first record, Terry, a two-and-one-half-year-old girl, shows more interest in putting paint on herself than in what she can produce on the paper. She is clearly experimenting not only with the paint but with her own movement patterns.

In a purposeful way Terry took the brush in her left hand, dipped it in the pot of red paint, and with the brush dripping wet made several quick, long, vertical strokes on the left side of the paper. Then dipping it again and grasping it in both hands she reached up and tried to cover the top of the paper with color, still using vertical strokes, however. She then went back to making horizontal strokes on the left side. After a few strokes with her right hand Terry shifted the brush back to her left and, more aimless and relaxed, began to get it very wet and hit it against the paper. Her attention was on the resulting drips which seemed to please her greatly. Turning toward Ron, for the first time, she began to paint his fingers (with his complete cooperation). Then wordlessly she handed the brush to him and held out both her hands. Very quickly then they handed the brush back and forth daubing at each others' fingers and giggling. Ron finally got up to show the teacher his hands and she drew him into a group for a story. Terry looked intently at her hands for a moment and then very purposefully began to paint the nails of her right hand, doing a remarkably skillful job of getting a blob of paint on each tiny nail. Then she tried to paint the nails of her left hand with the brush in her right but was not so skillful and was obviously not quite satisfied. She ended by painting each finger on her left hand, not just the nails. Terry then went back to painting on the paper, then she stood up and literally pounded the brush on the paper, spattering herself and me. She did this quite solemnly and intently.

The following record of a three-year-old is typical of a spontaneous young child's approach to easel painting. Notice that his major preoccupation seems to be with making an impression—on the paper, on the walls, on the woodwork, on another child's painting. In the second excerpt, when he says, "I'm painting right here," he makes it quite clear that paint means the sheer activity of spreading the paint, and not producing something he needs to name or explain.

Excerpt 1. Barry (age three) puts the brush in his right hand and dips into the red paint. He changes the brush from right to left using large up and down strokes, and plenty of paint. When the paper is completely covered he goes to the teacher and says, "Finished." With brush in hand he goes to a picture on the wall and paints. The teacher asks him to put the brush back in the jar; on the way to the easel he paints the woodwork. The teacher wants to take his smock off, but he pulls away and points to the easel. She gives him fresh paper. He draws a line down the paper with one stroke and plenty of paint, then makes a large circle next to it. With brush in hand, he goes over to look at the picture on the next easel, and begins to paint on it. He goes to the woodwork again and paints, but for only one minute; then he goes back to the other easel, picks up the brush in the yellow jar and paints.

Excerpt 2. Barry starts to paint again while his smock is being buttoned. He begins to use two brushes at once, one in each hand, dipping into the green paint. Then he concentrates on using brown paint and one brush, alternating hands, and he completely covers the paper with paint. He starts another paper with large round strokes with his left hand, using brown paint. He paints slowly, jerking the brush over the area. He mumbles and hums, then sings "Fairy Boat, fairy boat go round," over and over again. He goes over, looks at Pat's painting, and smiles. Pat comes over to see Barry's painting and Barry says, "I'm painting right here." Then he goes over to Pat's paper and paints on his picture.

After a child has learned to confine his efforts within the edges of the paper, he still works in a direct and uncontemplative way. His paintings are almost fortuitous results of feeling and movement with perhaps some elementary appreciation of spatial relations and color qualities. The record reproduced below presents a child who has reached the stage of recognizing his product as a separate thing from the process of making it. However, his painting is still an experience to be enjoyed in itself, not as a symbolic representation of something else. Here again it is apparent that the questioning of an adult is an embarrassment, although the boy tries hard to find a reply that will be satisfactory. It would certainly seem that an insistence on questions to which the child can make no valid response gives him at least a mild push in the direction of hypocrisy.

Carl (age three and one half) looks at the drawing board and without any hesitation takes the yellow paint and starts to paint the corner of the paper. He makes large firm strokes, all straight lines. He appears to be intensely absorbed and to be enjoying himself. He takes the next colors, green, blue, and red, in the order that they are lined up and repeats the same type of strokes in each color. The teacher asks him what he is drawing. He does not answer, so she repeats the question. He states, "This is your pic-cher." She removes the painting and he starts a new design. He starts to make larger strokes using all the various colors. He paints the clips holding the drawing paper and states to the teacher nearby, "I'm painting this." The teacher explains that we don't do that. He paints the clip for just one last stroke, and seems to get a great deal of fun from this. Now he makes broader, more energetic strokes, and starts to fill the entire paper. His tongue is out as he works. When one hand gets paint on it he places the brush in the other hand and continues painting while cleaning the dirty hand on the smock. When the hand is clean he resumes painting with that one. The teacher passes so he looks up and states very proudly and confidently, "This is my picher." The teacher asks him what he is painting. He repeats after her, "What is it?" Then he says, "It's an airplane." He starts to paint with blue paint, using both hands. The teacher asks him, "Is that the way we hold the brush?" He does not answer but removes his left hand. He takes two brushes and paints simultaneously with both hands, chuckles, and seems to get a mischievous delight from this. He watches the paint drip down in complete fascination. He makes splashes of green and springs back a step so as not to be splashed. He repeats this about six times jumping back in perfect rhythm and coordination so that it almost approaches a dance. The teacher asks him if he has finished. Carl emphatically says, "No!" Asked about his picture he says, "It's A and P." Asked if he would like finger-painting, he says, "Yes."

Painting as Expression

When we move beyond the child's first approach to painting, two major functions become apparent: first, the expression of inner impulses not at all understood by the child, and second, the release of emotional pressures. Alschuler and Hattwick[1] suggest that "children can use paints and crayons to express absorbing experiences and preoccupations which they are not yet able to express in words." Moreover, when they begin to make drawings of human beings, it is suggested that their representations reflect themselves—not as they look but as they feel themselves to be.

Bland also emphasizes the use of drawing and painting as a form of communication. She points out that it is as natural for children to draw and paint as it is for them to talk and that these media provide a more basic kind of language than speaking or writing because they are more direct and immediate. That is, through color, line, and shape it is possible to project emotions and feelings without the intervention of words. This is reason enough for encouraging a child to express himself in his own way, and we may be sure that if he is satisfied with his efforts, they are adequate for his own purposes.

Because painting so often expresses the inner life of the child, it can furnish revealing clues to aspects of the world that are important and challenging to him. This is particularly the case during the preschool years when children function more impulsively, more freely and spontaneously than at any other stage in their development. When we look at a painting from this point of view, as a substitute for or a precursor of language, we see once more how inappropriate it is to ask a child *what* he is painting. Such a question demands that he put into words what he only senses in a vague and formless way, and what he must express through painting precisely because he cannot put it into words. Later in this chapter we shall consider paintings as a source of clues to the child's emotional life; at the moment we shall examine only their expressive qualities.

The joy that children experience when they are able to express themselves through painting is clearly evidenced by their rhythmical body movements, by singing, dancing, smiling, by their absorption and their unusual warmth toward others and generosity in giving away their products. Notice in the following record of four-year-old girls, the evidences of absorption, relaxation, and pleasure, both in the process of spreading paint and in the final product. The association of Christmas and birthdays with the painting activity is also an indication that it is a happy time for them.

Wanda (four years old) put the brush in the blue paint and tried to make a circle. She was apparently concentrating hard, her tongue sticking out. Then she took green paint and made a line down the middle. Next she took yellow and put it on in blotches, then dabbed on brown, rhythmically, making noises with her mouth in time with the movement of her brush. "Oh, how pretty I made it!" she repeated over and over. She dabbed on green, saying, "More and more and more," then used blue, named the color out loud, and began to dance and sing. "Teacher, isn't this a pretty picture I made? Isn't this a cute picture?" She almost sings this out, smiling very happily. "I'm going to make another picture, a cute picture." She started to sing, "Here comes Rosa walking down the street." She worked quietly on a new picture, using green, "Christmas tree this time. A little girl Christmas." To the tune of "Happy Birthday" she sang the words, "Make him happy to you. Make him happy to you." Then she sang, "Good night, Carl, la, la la. . . ." Carl was painting on the other side of the easel. She took her painting off the board and called the teacher.

Even very active children will become absorbed in a painting experience. Eldon, almost five, was a rather blundering, poorly coordinated lad who seemed to find most of his pleasure in large muscle activity. However, at the easel he gave every evidence of pleasure and produced apparently aimless patterns with the appearance of being engaged in a very meaningful task.

"I want to paint." Eldon goes and gets himself an apron and mixes all the paints with each brush. He takes the brush, holds it in the middle and, with his mouth open, paints a wavy red line across the paper. Then he takes the next brush and with heavier red paint makes a thick curved line. He takes the next brush and color, and with both hands firmly holding the brush he rushes to rub paint over the thin red line he made first. He takes the blue brush and makes a circle, then goes over it with red paint. He makes an orange circle, then a heavy green circle and a heavy green line extending from it. He turns and tips his head to follow the curved line as he paints it. Singing, he takes a brush with green and then takes orange, and across the green line he paints orange. He stamps his feet. Taking the brown, he makes a line straight down. He makes a red line down and then a brown line across, a heavier red line, and another red on the top of the page. Calling the teacher, he says, "Mrs. S for you." She writes his name. "Is that you?" Teacher: "It's Eldon because you painted it." Eldon looks pleased.

For some children, indeed, painting offers a means of expression not offered by any other medium. Sally, Eldon's sister, was such a child. Ordinarily shy, quiet, and mousy, her vivid paintings foreshadowed the attractive, alert little person she grew into.

Sally (age three) puts red paint at either end of the two easels which she and the teacher are setting up and pink at the upper end of one. She gets some red paint on her hands, drops everything, and runs to the teacher excitedly, "I got red on my hands!" The teacher suggests that she wipe it off, showing no concern. Sally does this and returns to the easels. She places blue next to the pink, then picks up a big yellow jar. "And yellow!" she says animatedly. The paint spills and she stares at it intently for a second, then runs to the teacher. Teacher: "Get a spoon from Mrs. S." She runs right off on this errand, calling, "Mrs. S, give me a spoon." "Orange paint spilled," she says as she returns with the spoon. Sally wipes with a rag. She catches her breath. "Some paint on the floor!" she exclaims. She wipes vigorously, then stands back to observe. "Still painty!" she comments, and wipes some more. "Now you can paint," says the teacher. Sally jumps up and down in excitement. "Me want red." "You've got red," says the teacher. "Yellow now. Yellow," says Sally quickly. She skips over to the easel. "Me going to sit down on chair," she announces. A smile of interest plays over her face as she settles down to paint. She dips her brush in the red and makes the painting sketched here.

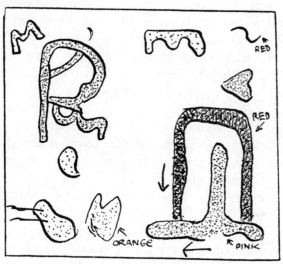

SKETCH OF SALLY'S PAINTING

Within the preschool period, the years between two and four seem to be especially appropriate for the use of painting as a purely expressive medium. These are the years when it is least representational and most directly the fluid derivative of the child's approach to the materials. It is also the time when a channel for immediate expression is most needed because of the intensity of feelings and the difficulties encountered in putting them into words. And it is interesting that this is the time when the children themselves seem to be most attracted to this activity. But it is the active process of painting rather than the product that is significant. It appears, therefore, that the period when easel painting has its greatest significance occurs when its products have their least apparent meaning.

Painting for Release

All authorities interested in the use of painting for promoting mental health agree that it offers an opportunity for emotional release that is not readily available in many other media. Its particular virtue seems to be that the individual can achieve this release without necessarily telling someone about his difficulties or the nature of his feelings. Liss[2] echoes the sentiments of many other workers when he says, "Firstly the activity is an emotional release, a cathartic phenomenon which may have a temporary and not particularly purposeful element other than a safety valve to repressed energy, or it may be a step in a process which subsequently becomes objectively more purposeful." He also points out that ". . . abatement of anxiety and the attainment of satisfaction are important by-products of the finished art form."

Other workers have made more specific statements about the significance of painting for different kinds of children. Alschuler and Hattwick enumerate the following indicators of release: freer behavior during the painting situation than during other activities, more personal verbalizing, more social interaction, more laughter and other expressions of pleasure, and more indications of feelings such as demonstrations of affection or hostility. They suggest that it offers genuine therapeutic value since it lends itself to symbolic expression and may be used for sublimating feelings and anxieties that can not be expressed in more direct and overt ways. As a result of their intensive research in the field of painting and personality, they suggest a simple description of the kinds of children who most frequently seek out easel painting and for whom it serves as an outlet for impulsive or emotional drives. These children, they say, tend (1) to be among the youngest and least mature in the nursery group; (2) to come from homes which have exerted too much control over them; (3) to be involved in strong emotional conflicts and to be more preoccupied with resolving these conflicts than with reacting objectively or wholeheartedly to people and situations. They also point out that children whose emotional life is still largely unchanneled and undefined seem to find easel painting a particularly satisfying medium for expression.

Despert observes that drawing is a good outlet for active children because it provides a means for pure motor expression. In this connection, Bland also is convinced that art can be a safety valve for the explosive child, who paints and splashes out feelings of aggressiveness and hostility that would be far more dangerous if expressed in other ways.

For the withdrawn or constricted child, it is agreed that painting can also have a stimulating and wholesome effect. Because there are no rules about how to say what you need to say through painting, the timid child need not be afraid to approach this medium. Those who have been made afraid of dirt and mess can find in it an outlet that does not violate their established controls. Through this medium, many of these children make their first step toward free expression without feeling a sense of guilt.

For the child who is withdrawn because he is preoccupied with inner problems and confusions, painting can be a great relief and a bridge to reality. Once his pressing but nebulous feelings have been given tangible form, the child finds it easier to talk about his troubles and accept the help he needs.

Older children can use their paintings and drawings as symbols of their conflicts and as a means of telling their stories in safely disguised form. Bender and Rappaport point out that deeply troubled children tend to use animal figures for symbolic representation of parents or of feared qualities in their parents. However, all workers in this field unite in the warning that the meanings cannot be understood without a good deal of verbalization on the part of the children. Even then understanding is not easy and frequently requires the highly developed techniques of the depth psychologist.

From our own observations it is apparent that painting serves four different "release functions." Each of these will be described and illustrated in the sections that follow.

1. Painting and Messing

Because painting permits "messing" in a controlled form, it provides overly inhibited children with a release from their need to suppress an unspoken desire to mess. When they use a brush, they do not have to get dirty. Also since paints may be mixed to produce colors resembling body products, they offer an excellent substitute for direct investigation and manipulation.

The following record was taken in a therapeutic nursery center where finger-painting was purposely avoided because it was felt that it might overexcite the children. Note that the subject, Rose, seems to come alive only after she has cast her brush aside and come into direct bodily contact with the paints.

Rose (three years old) dips her brush in the yellow paint with her right hand and with her other hand picks her nose; she has a dreamy far-off look on her face. She makes three downward brush strokes, stops and looks around, then continues dabbing on the yellow paint. At this point she sees that the swing is free and looks as if she were about to go over to it when Charlie rushes over and takes it. Rose, with brush still in hand, looks very dejected. The teacher brings over some blue paint. She takes some and dabs it over the yellow, then goes over it with red. The teacher writes Rose's name on the paper. She continues dabbing red paint with downward strokes over the whole mass, then uses the yellow, then the blue, in the same way. Occasionally she stops and looks over to see what the other children are doing. Her mother comes over and she shows her where "my name" is. She then strokes the mass of paint with her hand. Then dips (with a sudden spurt of energy and intensity) the three brushes into the yellow paint, then into the blue, and smears the mass on the paper with the three brushes. She looks at her smeary hands, wipes them on the wet paint on the paper as if she were doing finger-painting; next she dips her hands into the pot of paint and pretends to "wash" her hands with the paint. She then smears the hands again on the paper. She is giggling and smiling broadly as she washes and smears, and has a wonderful time until the teacher suggests that she wash her hands and start with some clean paints. The children get ready to go up on the roof so there is no further painting.

The painting of objects such as boxes, cans, clay, and dough products often supplies a satisfying outlet for the desire to mess. One little boy, who usually got paint all over himself and everything else, spent a happy half hour smearing an old box with yellow, ending up with the telling remark, "I love to get my hands dirty." The next two records revolve about a girl of four and one half years whose outstanding characteristics are fear of dirt, orderliness, and social inhibition. In the first excerpt, where she uses a brush on paper, she cannot break away from her need for order, possibly because of a feeling that while painting at the easel she is being observed. A child of this kind might be permitted to put the paper on the table or on the floor so that it will not be so obviously in the public eye.

Excerpt 1. Terry goes to the easel, puts a streak of yellow paint on the far right side, going from top to bottom. Then she puts purple over the yellow, red over both of these, and blue on top. She holds the brush easily and seems to have control of her movements which are slow and deliberate. She takes the yellow paint brush again and makes a downward stroke in the middle, not so long as the first line on the right. There is too much paint on the brush and some runs down the paper. She tries to stop it with the brush, making an upward movement. She seems to enjoy the movement for she continues the stroke up and around the paper (counterclockwise), dips the brush in yellow again, and, starting where she left off, finishes enclosing the area (with clockwise strokes). These strokes are easy, soft ones, not hurried. She puts on red, scrubs up and down, then around, in the middle of the enclosed space.

Now see how Terry gradually drops all restraint as she paints piece after piece of dried clay.

Excerpt 2. With the brush held in her hand, Terry goes around to the shelf where the clay is, picks out a flat round piece, and returns to the table. She surveys the various paint jars. The teacher says, "Here's some paint," handing her a jar of green. She sits down and begins to paint the clay. She seems to be concentrating intensely; first one side is completely covered with careful strokes, then the other. When this is finished, she puts it down on the table and goes to get more clay. She returns with four thin, long pieces and proceeds to paint them in the same methodical way. She holds the piece over the jar and just saturates it with yellow, filling the brush with lots of paint and letting it drip over the clay. Some brown paint has been spilled on the table. Terry pushes her brush forward through this paint, sopping up as much as possible, and wipes this on the clay. She then picks up the jar of yellow and proceeds to pour out a little on top of the already spilled brown on the table. She sloshes her brush back and forth mixing the two colors. She then proceeds to pour the contents of the purple jar, the black jar, the green jar, and another yellow into her own jar. She gets up and goes over to the easel, circling it to find some more paint jars, and adds red and green to her mixture. She plops one of the unpainted pieces into her big jar of "mixture" paint. She tries to fish the clay out but her hand won't go past the mouth. So she picks up the jar and slowly pours its contents into the yellow jar very carefully, watching to see when the clay will appear. She picks out the clay just before it slips into the other jar.

Then seeming to like the pouring process, she proceeds to pour the paint back and forth from one jar to the other, watching with interest as it flows out. She puts all of the pieces of clay in one jar and continues pouring, picking out the clay each time. Laurie joins her at the table and they both take jars of paint and pour them into one central jar. No words were exchanged. Charlie comes up to Terry and she threatens him with her paint-covered hands. He stamps his foot and says, "You do that to me and I'll - - -." Terry shuffles toward him with her hands outstretched, threatening but smiling all the time. Charlie runs to the teacher and says, "Terry is putting paint on me." Terry doesn't pursue him any further but smiles rather triumphantly and takes her place at the juice table. The teacher sees her paint-covered hands and tells her to go and wash them.

The importance of this thoroughly messy experience for Terry is suggested by the fact that she is able to threaten a little playmate with her dirty hands, for ordinarily she neither asserts herself nor defends herself against the attacks of others. In this instance it might have been helpful if the teacher had not merely asked Terry to wash her hands, but made some comment such as, "My, hasn't Terry done a good job of getting her hands full of paint."

2. Painting as a "De-inhibitor"

Easel paints are often used as a transitional release material. Children who are afraid to get into direct contact with messy materials such as finger-paints and wet clay show less hesitation in using easel paints, and after a reassuring experience with them they find it easier to forget their fears about the other materials.

Children who are usually overcontrolled, sober, and socially withdrawn seem to benefit greatly from the painting experience. Sometimes their response is hard to discern because they are characteristically rather muted in reaction, but some indications of special pleasure and increased freedom are usually present. The teacher's sensitivity to these cues can best be developed by exposure to many children responding to different kinds of situations. In the following records we shall try to point out a variety of these indications of release as they appear in the paintings of children whose inhibitions have had widely different sources.

The first child we shall observe is Shelley, a five-year-old girl who was described by her teachers as uninterested in any activity. Ordinarily she was outstandingly neat, rather "wooden" in expression, made no approaches to the other children, and persisted in following the teachers about. In the record that follows, notice first her progress from the use of rather similar colors to brilliant contrasts; second, the fact that she dabs paint on her apron; and third her rather excited giggling—all of which indicate growing freedom. The fact that she used all the colors in her "rain" pictures might also be an indication of increased daring, although there may have been a compulsive element in the repetition.

Shelley (age five) began to paint with orange and made an irregular bounded form (a rounded square) in the upper left-hand corner of the page. She proceeded to make two more of these patterns, progressing in a diagonal fashion across and down the paper. The second was yellow, the third blue. Next she added an orange tail to the first picture. She announced she was going to the bathroom and skipped off. When she returned she filled in the spaces enclosed by the boundaries—one with yellow, one with purple, and one with red. She then filled in more solids of the same shape as the first figures, and added tails indiscriminately. She used all the previous colors, adding green. She puts down her brush and calls, "Teacher, I want another piece of paper." "What is this?" asks the teacher, and Shelley says, "It's a lotta windows. . . ."

Her next picture was a series of straight vertical lines, going from left to right, including all colors (one each) beginning with orange and ending with purple. She continued the lines to the edge of the page, and about half of them were purple and the other half various colors. When asked what this was, she said it was the rain. The next picture was exactly the same except that she used all yellow. "This is yellow rain." She next began a painting of green rain. Liza paraded by all dressed up. Shelley looked down at her apron and dabbed a little paint on it. She then returned to her painting. The teacher said jokingly, "That's not green rain, is it?" Shelley threw her head back and smiled, "Yeah, green rain. I'm gonna make all the colors." There followed purple rain. Shelley giggled wildly. She then made blue rain, giggled hysterically, and then repeated purple rain. (Although Shelley was relaxed while painting, the observer had never before seen her have such an alert facial expression. She was absorbed.)

Barry, a little boy of four, was extremely accelerated intellectually, but very inhibited, expressionless, and withdrawn. His interests, in general, seemed to lie within the areas of mechanics and block building. Note his aggressive approach and the way he spatters, splashes, and drips the paints. The use of his fingers to paint with indicates his kinship with the medium. His full vigorous strokes and his smiles—rare for him—are good measures of his spontaneity.

When the easel was free for him, Barry slipped into his smock rapidly and went right to it with directness of purpose. He dabbles in the paint cups, swishing the brushes around in them. Then he selects a red-orange color and makes zigzag steps down the paper. He goes over this line, not to widen it, but to make it stronger in color. He attacks the paper with so much zest that he is painting with the heel of the brush. He stands back, looks at it a moment, then paints a line across and down the paper to the left. After this he dabs, filling the boxy shape with strokes and splashes, some of which land outside it. (At this moment he is enjoying the vigorous motion almost more than the painting composition. He smiles widely.) Next, he selects pale green and splashes a dripping brush on top of the right-hand top section of his design, smiling as he smears the still wet orange underneath. Putting down the green, he picks up blue, and lays this over the design, in swishing strokes, so strong that he is pushing the paper in. Before finishing, he adds a scalloped stroke down the right side, stands off to look at it, adds brief cross strokes going down. . . .

He starts a new painting. This time he selects the pale green, makes a swooping loop to the left, cuts off the end with a downstroke of blue. He next takes a brilliant scarlet, swishes this along the top of his design, covering the green line in several places. Then with his left hand he picks up blue and dabs on some dripping paint in one spot, over the red. The blue runs down the page, and he tries to wipe this off with his right hand, still holding the brush in his left. This seems to give him an idea and he paints a little with his finger. He seems little disturbed by the mess and much interested in the wetness of the paint. . . .

It is instructive to observe the general freeing of a child over a period of time. Sometimes the youngster who is pre-occupied with private difficulties shows little interest in paint-ing until something happens to bring him closer to the world outside himself. When this occurs there is often a cumu-lative growth of interest, vigor, and enjoyment in his painting sessions. This "snowballing" effect is clearly shown in the records of Ella, presented below. She was almost four at the time and had been in the center since she was two. Her teachers regarded her as definitely retarded in her use of materials, and reported that she had little contact with the children and would withdraw to a cubbyhole and sit in a little rocker for long periods of time. However, she was finally able to establish a relationship with one or two girls in her group, and began to reach out for more experiences. Then her painting came into its own. In the records, taken about a month apart, notice her increasingly animated and emphatic movements and her growing feeling of accomplish-ment. Possibly, too, her new ability to make social contacts was related to her success in externalizing feelings and preoccu-pations through smearing and messing with the paint.

Excerpt 1. At the beginning of this activity, Ella did not seem too interested. She stood in front of the easel holding a brush limply in her hand. Then she began to paint broad strokes in orange and green, after which she just smeared paint over the whole paper. She left her work and became interested in what the teacher had to say to some other children. Finally she returned to her work and smeared yellow paint around. She kept glancing at the observer and seemed more absorbed in playing with her gum than in painting. She turned back to her painting, but was content to hold two brushes idly. She then yelled to the teacher that she was finished.

Excerpt 2. Ella began to mix the red paint very vigorously with the brush. So vigorous was her movement that a good portion of the paint slopped on the leaf of the easel board. She had also been successful in spilling it on herself, but this didn't seem to bother her, and she casually wiped her paint-smeared hands on her slacks. She smeared the red paint all over the paper and the board. She took the paper off by herself and said, "Teach, teach." Then she began to use the blue paint, with which she made short strokes along the margin, thus providing herself with a border. In fact all her strokes are small, both in breadth and in length. Then with the yellow she filled in a solid mass. Then she ran the gamut from yellow to red to blue and then back again. She called out, "Teach, look what I made."

Excerpt 3. When the observation started, Ella was painting at a table. "Teacher," she called, and proudly displayed her painting. She said, "That's for my home." She made broad, thick strokes with the green paint and then dabbed a little black paint on top of the green. Next she banged on the paper with her brush and then looked up at me and smiled for several minutes. She proceeded to make a few strokes, using all of the available colors. She then brought the paper over to the teacher for inspection. Once again she used all the colors available. She took one cup at a time and emptied the cups of paint into the jars that were on the board of the easel. As she went back for another trip she knocked over the cup containing the black paint. While the teacher went to get a rag to wipe up the mess, Ella took a brush and smeared the paint all over the table.

3. *Painting for Release of Aggression*

Painting is sometimes an outlet for hostile impulses. This holds true for both inhibited and obviously aggressive children. For very restricted youngsters the release of hostility through painting sometimes serves as a preliminary exercise, as it were. Once they have given vent to their feelings without coming to harm, they can often go on to much more direct expression and healthier control. For those who find it difficult to control their aggressive impulses, paints offer a substitute outlet which often helps to relieve inner pressures.

It is not always easy to perceive how children release aggressive feelings while painting because their movements must necessarily be more controlled than those used in direct attacks against children or adults. However, the teacher who watches a good many children painting will become aware of distinct differences in the nature of their strokes. Some paint lightly with the tip of the brush, others attack the paper more assertively, pushing the brush down on it so that the bristles bend, still others seem to be scrubbing rather than stroking and a few even slap the brush against the paper. It requires, however, closer observation and deeper knowledge of the individual child to fathom the meaning of these strokes. Sometimes the child's remarks give a clue to his hostile intentions, and occasionally the activity is followed by a direct attack on someone who has frustrated him.

The most striking instances of release of aggression usually occur with normally mild and inhibited children. It may be that we take special notice of their behavior since it is so unexpected—although, on the other hand, it is widely accepted that the quietest and mildest individuals are often the ones who feel most strongly and deeply. We do know that constrained children are frequently covering up a seething mass of angry feelings which they dare not release directly, and

it is more than a mere guess that painting gives them a means
of expressing and relieving these feelings without forcing them
to recognize what they are and without risking punishment
for them.

In the record below, we see Josephine, an extremely withdrawn five-year-old, "letting off steam" in a very direct
fashion. In her case, the pleasure and stimulation which
she derives from the painting precipitate a good deal of verbal
aggression. It may be significant that after this painting
session she continued to giggle excitedly and spontaneously
joined the others in group activities lasting two full hours.

Josephine is asked if she will play with clay and she replies,
"I don't wanta play with clay." She continues the "wrestling"
game with Vi and they both say, "Come on, stop it," and
laugh. At this point Josephine is just beaming with delight at
her "fun" and Vi is asked to paint. She assents, whereupon
Josephine says she wants to paint, too. . . .

Josephine has her arm around Vi and says to the teacher, "I
want blue." The paper is not on an easel but on the table
and the two girls are standing side-by-side. Josephine takes her
brush and makes some straight lines down and across, then she
fills in the lines and smears. She now has a big blue blotch.
She giggles and says to Vi, "That's you. No feet you've got.
No hands, look at you. You've got a chimney on your head."
As she says this she takes the brush and makes lines going up
from the blue mass. "I'll do a horn on you—W-hee, whee—another great big horn," and she makes more lines up. Her expression gets more intense. She says to the teacher, "I want some
yellow." She says, "No," when asked to wash off the brush.
Now she continues letting off steam and directs this at Vi.
"Look at your big hand. Slap in the face. O.K. you wo wo.
Some water on your head, some ink on it, clay in your mouth,
punch in the nose, give you a black eye then." She says all of
this while giggling. Suddenly she begins to menace Vi with her
paint brush and bares her teeth, although she is still giggling.
Vi runs to the teacher for help. Josephine makes a few more
lines going up and smears a little green paint over the blue and

makes a few lines up and down. To the teacher she says, "I'm finished. Here's mine," and again giggles. To hear Josephine use all this invective was a surprise and I felt that for once she really had an opportunity to "let go."

Josephine's behavior presents a more obvious picture than that of most inhibited children who are fearful of their hostile impulses. Such behavior as using up all the paper available or mixing all the paints together are more usual expressions of the less transparent kind of release experience. Mark, four years and nine months old at the time, was rather a "sissified" little boy who talked very well but was completely unable to attack others or cope with their attacks on him. He tended to play with little girls almost exclusively and gave other evidences of being uncomfortable about his masculine role. Note how restrained he is at first when he pats the paper gently with his brush and carefully wipes the surplus paint off before beginning to make a stroke. Later he relaxes and becomes more assertive, using all the paper, mixing all the colors, and finally reaching a climax of pounding and splashing.

Mark: "Want to see me paint?" (I nod.) "See!" He takes the brush with blue paint, makes a stroke, then sort of pats the paper with the brush. Next he uses orange and gets paint on his hand as he does so. He seems disturbed at this and tries to rub it off. Maida comes to paint on the easel backed against Mark's easel. She comes over to Mark's side and takes a jar of green and another of yellow. He goes to Maida's side, talks to her, and tries to get her to give him back his paints. Finally he takes them. Maida to Rita: "He's taking all my paints." Rita, the assistant, takes the paints from Mark. Mark to Rita (in a wailing voice, quite distressed): "But these were mine." He goes over to Maida's side and watches her paint. Although he makes a great pretense of interest, it is obvious that he is really just biding his time to get his paints back. Mark to Maida: "You had a whole hour, Maida. You had a whole hour." He takes the paints, and puts them on his easel. He paints with red. Mark to me: "Look how much colors I have. One, two, three, four, five, six. I have six colors." He is all smiles now. He paints with black. "See all those colors I have?" He dips into the red, makes strokes, and then makes several strokes with black. He pats the paper with the black brush, then makes a jagged line at the upper left corner. To the teacher: "I'm finished." The teacher puts Mark's name on the painting, while he tells her about it. I couldn't hear what he said, but she wrote on his paper something about lions and bars. She took the painting off, leaving a new white piece ready for him to paint again. . . . He uses in order, red, green, and blue, which he merges with the green. He swings his feet and kicks my shoe. Mark to me: "What did I kick?" "My toe." "I'm going to step on your toes." He does. I pretend to feel pain. He laughs and steps on them again. I scream softly, as if in pain, and suddenly pull my foot out from under his. He laughs and repeats this game a number of times before tiring of it. He takes the red paint, holds the brush in his fist like a spear, and pounds the paper with it using a strong stabbing motion. He makes big splashes on the paper. Mark to the assistant, "I'm finished, teacher, I'm finished."

Boys and girls who are ordinarily rather spontaneous in their behavior often use the paint brush in a consistently aggressive fashion, slapping and banging it against the paper. Among children who have no particular difficulty in expressing hostility, and who are successful in the give and take of childhood, this may indicate only a vigorous and self-confident approach to the world. Among others it may signify a special need for releasing aggression. To discover its meaning we must observe how the child behaves immediately before and immediately after the painting, as well as the customary quality of his behavior with other materials and activities. Below we present an example of an all-out attack on the easel by a lad who often seemed rather sullen and withdrawn. Compare his behavior in painting with his actions somewhat later in the day when his teacher invites him to join the others at games.

The teacher leads Duncan to the easel, saying, "Do you want to paint?" He nods his head unenthusiastically. She ties an oilcloth apron around him. Grasping the brush between thumb and index finger he quickly puts it in the first jar on the right side, brushes firmly on the paper, makes downward dominant strokes of blue paint, then short downstrokes, small circular ones around these, and tiny dotted ones over this whole figure. He takes a brushful of red, and makes scrubbing movements in the center of the page, sweeping freely from top to bottom, and diagonal, jerky, banging strokes at the bottom center of the paper. A light mass of yellow is painted near the bottom. With a dripping brush of green paint, he paints assertive strokes boldly over the entire blue area again. Surplus paint runs down the border. He does not notice it. . . . He continues overpainting the same spot with centripetal strokes. The teacher asks what he was painting. He answered, "A stinker." He bangs a green brushful downward and seems to attack the paper aggressively making a heavy circular line at the extreme left. .

(Later in the morning.) The teacher says, "Let's play games." Duncan shakes his head negatively. She places her hands above her head, stamps her feet, then slaps her hands. The children imitate in puppetlike fashion. Teacher: "Let's see if you can do this, Duncan." He turns around with a disgusted air and slumps in his seat. Seeing food brought in for dinner, he jumps up and makes a step toward it. She puts a restraining hand on him. Calling each child by name, she directs them toward the table. Duncan remains in his chair. The children shout his name several times. He slumps again sullenly and whines as the teacher tidies the book shelves and chair. She takes his hand and walks to the table with him.

4. Painting as a Release for Anxiety

Through painting some children are able to give expression to anxieties and become more relaxed. Almost all observers who have worked closely with young children and have used painting as a therapeutic medium assert that it lowers the level of anxiety. This effect is not easily demonstrated through records. The relief from anxiety is something that can only be inferred from aspects of external behavior rather than directly perceived. When a child is outwardly tense and uneasy, fearful of making contacts with others, or compulsively hostile toward them, we assume that he is carrying a considerable burden of anxiety, even though we may not know its focus or its cause. When such a child becomes perceptibly more relaxed, outgoing, or friendly, we assume that in some way the burden has been lifted.

In the nursery school it is an accepted fact that children show their tensions most clearly during the eating and sleeping routines. At nap time particularly, youngsters who are able to forget their troubles during the active part of the day often find themselves face to face with their problems, and one observes the sudden emergence of restless behavior, wriggling, and masturbation, and the need for the reassuring presence of an adult. It has been our exprience that these restless and unhappy children, if permitted access to the easel, will often dash off a large number of paintings in rapid succession, and then return to their cots and lie there composed and relaxed.

This, however, does not work for all children. In particular, for those who express their difficulties through overactive and overaggressive behavior, painting seems to heighten tension and to act only as an added stimulant. It might very well be that in these cases the experience increases the pressure of anxiety by permitting it to come to the surface. The following brief excerpt is a good example of this kind of effect. Bud, the child in question, has been referred to in other chapters of this study. Here it will suffice to say that he was an extremely disturbed four-year-old, although he had made a great deal of progress in social behavior, having moved from a phase of alternating between withdrawal and unpredictable aggressiveness, to a desire for acceptance and a recognition that his behavior was sometimes unacceptable to others. In this instance, the painting seems to have seduced him into doing something which brought a heavy burden of guilt.

Bud and Shelley had both gone to the easels to paint. Bud had become quite vigorous in his movements while using red. He suddenly turned to the use of green, dabbed at Shelley's dress and dirtied it. He was immediately contrite and took her to the bathroom and with great patience and industry attempted to wash off the paint with soap and water, using his hands. She watched grimly as Bud, almost wracked with distress and concern, was intent and eager in his efforts to make amends.

We found others for whom painting seemed to be a rather threatening experience. In the following record of Wendell, we see a decided reluctance to begin, and later a definite lack of freedom and enthusiasm. The final product of his rather forced participation is rigidly symmetrical and gives no evidence of spontaneous enjoyment. Since the boy's great difficulty lay in learning to restrain his impulsive behavior, it may be that anything that tended to lower his controls loomed up as a threat.

Wendell looks up and around. He doesn't seem to be too interested in painting. He takes his brush and haphazardly mixes some blue, red, and white paint in another tray. Then he draws a horizontal line in a reckless fashion on the top right-hand side of his page. He shows Peter how he mixes colors. This he does carelessly and vigorously. He seems to enjoy the mixing. . . . He quickly dashes some paint together, "Look, I made lavender." The teacher says, "Good." He takes up a brushful and awkwardly continues the horizontal line right off the paper onto the board. He runs away, plays with the blocks for a minute, then dashes out and upstairs to the director's office. He comes back four minutes later, hurries to one side of the room, then to his painting. Quickly he takes up a brushful of red paint and carelessly smears a vertical line on the right-hand side of the page. He strolls over to Peter, quietly sits down next to him, and looks into his book for a few moments. Then he rises and approaches his painting again, eyes it hastily, and draws a messy, thick, vertical line on the left-hand side of the page. He seems very restless at this point. Suddenly he rushes upstairs again.

On the whole it has been our experience that painting seems to offer more to constricted children than to those who are overaggressive. The latter frequently avoid the easel in favor of less limiting activities. However, this may be a function of the conditions under which the medium was offered, and it may very well be that with a change in the procedure the hostile and poorly integrated child will benefit more fully.

Clues to Understanding from the Child's Approach

We shall now turn our attention from the direct benefits of painting for children, to what it offers adults in the way of clues to their development and needs. Recently there has been a sudden growth of interest in the diagnostic possibilities of children's paintings and many a careful search for specific criteria has been made. One intensive study in particular has focused on the preschool years, Alschuler and Hattwick's monumental work on the relationship between painting and personality in children from three to six years of age. It is instructive to learn that after several years of careful work which involved a fairly large staff and several hundreds of children, the investigators could point to only a few tentative findings that might have general application. They were able to describe many individual cases in which certain aspects of the choice of color, the quality of strokes or the use of space furnished clues to certain events in the child's life and the child's feeling about them, but unfortunately for those who would like a prescription for "interpreting" children's paintings, different clues were found to apply in different cases. In other words, at this point in history it looks as if a child expresses himself as idiomatically through color and line and mass as he does through the use of blocks. The situation that really obtains seems to be the reverse of what teachers and clinicians are seeking. It would appear that one needs to know the child in order to understand his paintings. And conversely the paintings do not, in and of themselves, illuminate the child.

These observations, however, hold only for the use of very specific clues such as certain colors or types of line. Most workers who have studied the relationship between the child's paintings and his entire functioning agree that the sensitive teacher can perceive certain general trends of behavior and feeling through the way he approaches the whole painting situation. Since this experience is simply a small sample of his total life situation, whatever is basic and characteristic of the child is likely to appear in it.

By and large, therefore, one can expect to find a similarity between the child's behavior in painting and his behavior in other areas. For example, compare the description of Buck, age four and one half, with his teachers' report on his general behavior. They described him as hyperactive, never still for a moment. He never walked if he could run. His play was extremely aggressive and frightening to other children. He liked especially to bang on the piano and to engage in water-play so vigorously that he emerged from the sessions drenched to the skin. As to his painting, note in the description the violent motion of his body, the "scrubbing" use of the brush, the stamping of his feet, and the vigor of his scrubbing and brushing movements.

Buck picked up the yellow brush in his right hand, makes a big circle at the top center of the paper. He then put the yellow brush back. picked up the green, put it down again, picked up several others paint jars, moving them back and forth a few times, then picked up green again and started to cover up the yellow with green, scrubbing hard. He put the brush back into the jar, pumped it violently up and down, bending his knees and moving his whole body up and down as if violently churning butter, saying, "Up and down, up and down. . . ." Again he picked up the yellow brush and began to cover over the green. Suddenly he started to stamp his feet (right and left alternately) saying, three times rhythmically in a loud voice, something that could not be understood. As he continued painting with yellow he began to scrub with the brush more energetically. He had a determined look around his mouth and jaw. Then he put down the brush, stood looking at the painting, then turned to look at the teacher. He picked up the yellow brush again and started to cover up the red in the upper left corner as she walked away.

Quite different is the orderly and meticulous use of paints described in the next record. It will come as no surprise that the boy, Perry, is rather anxious, timid, and afraid of a tyrannical father. He tends to play with girls more than with boys, talks well, and is very imaginative in dramatic play.

Perry (four and one half years old) chooses very decidedly the farthest brush in the glass containing purple color and starts to make a very clear line, rounding it out. Then he makes red circles with heavy brushes. Then on the right side he uses light blue and fills in the open space with yellow, "Look, teacher, what I am making." (It is a truck.) Now he fills in with blue, using very sure quiet movements being careful not to go over it. He adds a new form and says, "Toot, toot, the horn." He seems to have clearly in mind what he wants to do. He always makes his basic forms first, and then starts to fill in. He makes the red wheels last. He speaks as he paints: "This is red, the motor is red. And you know what the door is going to be? Yellow!"

When a child's behavior at the easel is quite different from usual, it is a fairly good clue to his future development. In this connection we have already mentioned Sally who appeared to be quiet, timid, and uninteresting, until she began to work with paints. Her freedom in using the brush and her appreciation of the colors foreshadowed the time several months later when she blossomed out into a very attractive, vivacious little girl and became a great favorite with the other children.

Because it is a liberating activity and the source of so many satisfactions, the painting process encourages many children to talk more freely than at other times, and the sensitive teacher can learn a good deal about their private preoccupations by lending an ear.

Mary, age five, an extremely reticent and withdrawn little girl, found it easy to talk to a companion while she painted. Her remarks went like this, "I am going to Scarsdale and there is a giant there and he saves everyone from life." "This is Scarsdale," she says as she points to her painting; then, "Want to hear a funny name?—Hoskapotts." Apparently Mary was painting something that was confusing to her, although the connection between the giant, Scarsdale, and the "funny name" was not clear. However, a skillful teacher, observing that .she was in a communicative mood, might have broken her consistent silence and uncovered a clue to her withdrawn and inhibited behavior. Similarly, Carla, who showed an ambivalent attitude toward the paint, started to touch it, but being uncomfortable about its drip, announced that she was painting "a little girl sitting on a rug." Later, still busy with the same painting, she announced, "I am making a little girl sitting up on a big couch. *She'll hurt herself.*" Still later she said, "A big pink couch. She's gonna fall. She's on a big pink couch. Look what I did (dripped some paint on the floor). I'm stepping on it." Here again there seems to be some connection between a number of things and feelings. Perhaps if at that moment someone had been alert enough to ask why the little girl would hurt herself, their exact relationship would have come out.

Some youngsters spin out elaborate fantasies that give us an inkling of their personal problems. This occurred many times in the case of a very disturbed four-year-old who had lost his mother when he was two, and whose father frequently beat him and clearly expressed a preference for his older sister. In the following record, which is fairly representative, notice the inclusion of destructive animals. We do not know, of course, what they are supposed to represent—whether his father, himself, or the world in general—but it is clear that in the course of his painting he was externalizing some rather compelling feelings.

At the teacher's suggestion, Bernie decided to paint. He talked to the teacher all through his painting, telling her what he was making. His first picture was done all in blue paint, with the paint brush held in the right hand. He seemed to gain great pleasure from it, since he spoke with enthusiasm and showed a great desire for the teacher to understand what he was saying and doing. As usual, he worked very carefully with tight controlled movements. Here are his comments. "That's a crocodile. His hands—going to bite her toe off. She's going to cry. He makes a face, like that he is going to scare her. That's her face down here. That's her skirt way down there. The little girl is scared here. Should I make a doggie?" At this point he stops to see who is crying and gets a tissue for his nose. Then he takes the brush in his left hand, transfers it to his right hand, and takes a clean sheet. He works very hurriedly at this, his interest having waned. His only comment is, "This is a big bad wolf." He finishes the picture and leaves it.

Sometimes while children are doing what their teachers least expect or desire, they are furnishing the richest clues to their basic needs. A large number of our records show poster paints being used for "messing" purposes that could better be served by finger-paints or water-play. In most cases the teachers try in vain to persuade the youngsters to use the paints as they are "supposed" to be used, but everyone concerned would fare better if instead they would offer a material more appropriate to the interest of the moment. The following excerpt from a record of an anxious and aggressive four-year-old clearly suggests the need for a different kind of activity.

Jackie was very enthusiastic in his application of the paint brush to the paper, but he did not use the brush for long. He rubbed his hands in the paint and yelled out, "Look what I am making." He spread the paint over the paper with his hands, but soon became more interested in rubbing his hands together. He wasn't satisfied until he had completely covered both sides of both hands with the blue paint. Finally he had enough of this and went over to the washroom to clean up.

Occasionally the stirring and mixing process is more intriguing than the actual painting. One lad of four was attracted to painting only when the teacher challenged him to make light blue out of dark. After that he kept interrupting his work to experiment with various mixtures and to show other children how to produce brown, purple, and mustard-green. No doubt he derived from this activity a sense of achievement as well as a chance to mess. The following record suggests that a combination of water-play with use of color might have captured Jackie's attention and offered him a truly creative experience.

The teacher gets out the big jars of paint and pours some of the colors into small jars, asking the children to help mix. Jackie asks excitedly if he can help, and he mixes the paint and water so vigorously that the teacher asks him to be a little careful or the jar might break. He seems fascinated with the colors and exclaims when the yellow is added to the blue, "It's getting green!" Next he mixes the red, and the teacher pours in a little blue. He yells, "It gets black!" He is told he can take the paints he mixed to the easel. He quickly takes the purple, orange, and red and starts to make circles with them. Then suddenly he throws the brushes into the jars, shakes his head and gestures with his hands in seeming disgust, "I done wanna do dat."

The teacher can learn something about the child from his attitude toward putting his name on the finished product. Many youngsters are not concerned about this, since their satisfaction lies mainly in the process of painting. However, boys and girls who have received too little recognition and have been criticized too much at home are likely to insist on having their names put on their products. Often they "paint" them as part of the picture—usually in illegible heiroglyphics—and announce over and over again, "I painted my name." It is fairly safe to say that any child who gets anxious or excited about signing his work has some doubt about his abilities or his place in the world.

Bits of behavior such as an excessive desire to please or tearing up the paintings before they are seen, can often act as clues to the child's relationship with adults. Sometimes, however, the behavior reveals more about the specific teaching situation than it does about his basic nature. In the following record, for example, we find four-year-old Lucy constantly apprehensive about the teacher's attitude toward her actions. When a child works in a tense manner, asks an adult's permission too frequently, and calls attention to what he is doing in an insistent fashion, the teacher might do well to evaluate the kind of painting situation she has set up, since behavior of this kind can be the result of immediate pressures as well as of deep-lying emotional problems.

The teacher calls out across the room, "Only one jar of paint at a time." Lucy gives no sign of hearing, gets two jars out, tips one over, makes a generalized nervous movement as paint splashes onto the floor, and looks with apparent apprehension toward the teacher. The teacher says (not in a scolding tone),

"I said one at a time." Lucy starts to paint. The teacher says, "This will have to be cleaned up." Lucy goes to the bathroom for a rag, a tense look on her face, pushes Rob out of her way, grimacing as she does so, and rushes over to scrub up the paint. She rushes back to the bathroom with the paint-filled rag, then back to the easel. She looks in the direction of the teacher, then runs over to her locker, picks up the pants which have fallen out, and hangs them up. Lucy, in a coaxing tone: "Can we have the brushes?" The teacher nods and Lucy takes a jar of brushes from the shelf and returns to the easel. . . . She paints a broad vertical blue line a little to the right of center of the paper, then a vertical green line about four inches to the right of that, both running from the top edge to the bottom paints swiftly. Taking her painting down, she looks around in edge. She connects the two lines with green and fills in the connecting space with black; paint drips onto the floor. She the direction of the teacher. She dabs paint on Julie's picture, hopping up and down as she does. This movement is quick and jerky and she looks over her shoulder in the direction of the teacher. She makes three vague letters (LOP) on Julie's paper. Then she dabs some paint on the palm of her hand. She grabs Julie by the hand, saying hoarsely with an urgent note in her voice, "Come on—let's wash our hands." She takes Julie by the hand and runs with her to the bathroom, almost dragging her. The teacher asks twice, "What were you doing in the bathroom?" Lucy does not reply. The teacher says, "You are smiling. I think you are teasing me. I want you to stay out in the room where I can see you." Lucy goes over to the toy shelf.

Clues from the Paintings Themselves

Earlier in this chapter we pointed out that specialists trained in both personality theory and art are not in accord about specific meanings of specific characteristics of children's paintings, such as color, line, and form. This cannot be stressed too much, since many teachers persist in looking for a magical formula that will reveal the secrets of the child's inner world. However, just as we found some illumination in the various approaches to painting, so there are valuable clues in the general qualities of the products themselves.

Most specialists agree that the way in which the paper is used, the regard paid to the limits of the sheet, the relationship between the placing of the paint and the shape of the paper are all indicative of the child's approach to the external world in general. Likewise, they agree that color choice is indicative of a state of feeling although they do not at all agree about the specific state a given color signifies. These formal characteristics are within the purview of the teacher but interpretation of the symbolic content of the paintings is quite another matter. Most workers insist that the child himself must furnish a clue as to what a given line, form, or mass means, using his own mode of expression. This means that the skill needed to interpret the meaning of a child's painting closely approaches that of the experienced psychoanalyst.

As an example of the complexity involved in interpretation, consider the following list of criteria, all of which must be properly weighted. They were developed by one of the more careful investigators in this field: number of pictures in a sequence, contents of each picture in sequence, size of paper, format of paper, size of form elements, distribution of form elements, movement elements, details of form, continuity of the whole, organization and content, color, variety of form elements, quality of line, and perspective.

One of these elements, color, will suffice to illustrate the amount of disagreement that exists. One worker insists that yellow and red usually indicate spontaneity in the early years, before four years of age, and that blue and green indicate control over feelings and should be expected after the age of four. Others have found a definite relationship between the use of red and feelings of aggression and hate and ideas of blood and castration. While there seems to be a general agreement that muddy dark colors indicate a tendency toward depression, some assert that the use of black signifies an unwillingness to acknowledge any emotions, while others think that it shows a tremendous anxiety burden. A fondness for brown or brown and yellow mixtures is variously interpreted as indicating interest in anal processes or the presence of depressive feelings. There are some workers, moreover, who believe that one can not give a valid interpretation of or assign an emotional connotation to any color that will hold good for all children. In line with this, the writers would like to offer an anecdote from personal experience. Two little girls were discussing their preference for colors. One said, "Oh black—I hate black. Do you remember that kitten I had to give up two summers ago, and I cried and cried when it was taken away? Remember? That was black." The other said, "I like black. You know why? Because when I lie down at night, I don't feel comfortable until all the lights are out and then when it is dark as it can be, it feels so good."

While some believe that over-painting indicates a need to hide one's feelings, others think that it may simply be the result of a succession of experiences which the child goes through in the course of his painting. Jane Cooper Bland, who has combined an interest in personality with expertness in teaching art, relates that she has often seen young children over-paint as they tell a story. As the story moves from episode to episode, a new picture is painted on top of the old and although the result looks like a mess, this messiness obviously does not reflect the state of the child's feelings.

The meaning of a particular element in painting varies with the age of the child who uses it. If a child of four paints in the manner one would expect of a child of two it would be fair to assume that he is showing some regression. A child of three who paints only in carefully controlled lines and balanced form while all his mates are happily splashing masses of paint might well be under excessive pressure for achievement. When a child confines his painting to a small area of the paper, he may be showing a lack of self-confidence, or fear and timidity about his ability to handle his world. But again we cannot emphasize too forcefully that the meaning of children's behavior is a comparative and idiomatic thing.

Many teachers are intrigued with the possibilities of having an expert analyze children's personalities through their graphic art products. We must warn these teachers not to place uncritical faith in any system of interpretation at the present time. Even the criteria for testing a system are elusive. If painting serves to bring out certain aspects of the personality not exhibited in overt behavior, how are we to find out whether the statements of the interpreter are true of the child?

Nevertheless, there is no doubt that some few people are exceptionally sensitive to the clues that can be found in a child's painting. A few happy instances of this special ability were encountered in the course of this project. In one case, the paintings of three different children were presented to an art teacher[3] who was well versed in the psychology of personality. All three had been recommended for special study by their teachers because in one way or other they had caused some concern. The interpreter in question was able to show that two of the three seemed to be happy normal children, while the third was definitely coping with anxieties. Later events proved her to be correct. The first two were Vera and Sally (already referred to in this chapter); the third was such an anxious little boy that his teachers were not able to help him very much.

In making her evaluations, the worker seemed to be paying attention to the manner in which the space was filled, the quality of brush strokes, and the choice of colors and their relationship to each other. In examining Vera's work, she noted that the child seemed to be responding to the limits of the paper by developing designs which in some way conformed to its rectangular shape but without rigidly and literally following it. The quality of her strokes indicated a certain spontaneity of approach. She tended to work from large sweeping movements to filling in the details. Although she rarely attempted a symmetrical design, very few of her paintings were off center. The forms she produced indicated better than average perception and control of the brush. The interpreter also felt that her paintings gave evidence of some pushing by the teacher in the direction of more sophisticated and conventional forms, for which she was not ready. (This was true. Most of the difficulty in Vera's case came from the fact that her teachers could not accept her rather impulsive behavior.)

Sally, who was showing extreme withdrawal and lack of response to the preschool group, revealed surprising awareness and sensitivity through her paintings. The interpreter felt that they represented a "taking in" kind of child rather than one who "gave out." While her brush strokes were not so dashing and spontaneous as those of Vera they were not meager or overcontrolled. She showed extraordinary sensitivity to colors through their juxtaposition and while her designs were not so sophisticated as those of older children they were adequate for the space they occupied. There were no evidences either of inhibition in the use of the paints or of compulsion with respect to the limits of the paper.

Admittedly, this type of analysis makes generalization difficult since it seems to depend almost entirely on the experience and sensitivity of the person who is making the interpretation. Possibly, too, the results cannot be fully appreciated except by those who possess these same qualities or have access to the entire set of relationships involved in the child's life.

The comparison between work with crayons, easel painting, and finger-painting frequently tells more about the child than the examination of any one kind of activity by itself. Vera's crayon drawing, for example, showed more tension in the manipulation of the medium and the production of a large number of small tight details. This may have been a reflection of the experience she was undergoing at the time, when the adults about her were attempting to force her into controlled types of behavior for which she was not yet ready. Her attempt to conform to this standard may also explain why her finger-painting showed extraordinary restraint. This was probably a way of protecting herself against the threat of letting herself go, since this medium tends to seduce children into free and uncontrolled behavior.

Sally, on the other hand, produced finger-paintings which were even more attractive and indicative of relaxation than her easel paintings. She executed these with a smoothly flowing movement which showed a good deal of variation. Her crayon drawings formed an extreme contrast to both her easel painting and her finger-painting. These were made up almost entirely of tight scribbly lines or very small enclosed forms apparently drawn with great tension. We may therefore surmise that they reflected her actual behavior in the group when she was referred for study, while her easel paintings were more indicative of her potentialities.

The interpreter's analysis of the third child, Hadley, might suggest additional clues to teachers. She noted that his lines "walked" around the paper instead of swooping or flowing—indicating extreme care but no enjoyment or spontaneity. His designs were meager in detail and he did not use all the space available to him. He was influenced to a much greater degree than either of the other two children by the limits of the paper, and his designs repeatedly showed a need for complete balance and static symmetry. He might as well have used crayons instead of paint because he did not exploit the possibilities of the medium for effect. The general impression was one of rigid control, fear of exploration, inability to improvise, and lack of enjoyment.

Hadley's finger-paintings were gloomy affairs. Almost all were in somber browns and blacks, and where red and yellow were used, they were generally over-painted with black. There was no evidence of flowing or rhythmic movement; instead, they were covered with small marks indicative of inhibition and tension. The similarity of the impressions given by his easel paintings and his finger-paintings suggested that he had no means of adequately handling his difficulty and was in need of special help.

To balance the rather gloomy view of the present status of painting interpretation given somewhat earlier in this discussion, it might be well to offer one more "success" story. This tale suggests that no interpretation by a trained person, no matter how apparently far fetched, should be disregarded without further investigation. It concerns Cathy, who was mentioned in the chapter on the use of blocks. She was chosen as a good example when the project personnel were seeking outstandingly well-adjusted children as a control group to be used in the study of those who were having adjustment difficulties. Her teachers reported:

Cathy is so mature. She uses everything and likes everything. She can use things independently but will accept suggestions from her teachers. She works harmoniously in every area. She plays with anyone and is well accepted by the others. She eats well and sleeps well and is good about routines. She seems happy in every respect, loves to sing and dance. She has no specific problems although she wets occasionally during her naps, sucks her thumb, and cannot assert herself very well. She likes to tease her mother, but in a pleasant way.

The specialist[4] who was working with the project as an interpreter of graphic products gave the following analysis of Cathy's work:

> The over-all picture is one of marked contrast between regression and control. The first of the paintings available shows marked tension and introversion but is relieved by a feeling of movement, even though the attempt is somewhat tense. There is evident anxiety. The paintings then proceed to a markedly regressive pattern overlaid with marked depression and introversion. Later paintings proceed to show fluctuation; first marked regression, then a marked attempt at control. . . . The persistence of a feeling of movement in spite of the regressive pattern seems to indicate a capacity for development and for creative outlets for the underlying tensions.

The painting analyst knew nothing about Cathy nor did the project personnel have many facts about her background. Because of the striking discrepancies between the teacher's picture of her overt behavior and the interpreter's analysis of her graphic products, it was decided to investigate the matter rather carefully, and arrangements were made for the interpreter to observe Cathy at painting and for the staff to meet with the project personnel and the interpreter for a full discussion. The following record was made by the painting analyst.

> Cathy and Glenna started to paint, side by side at two easels. Cathy stood with her body fairly close to the easel; the brush was grasped firmly in her right hand and her left hand was held rather tensely at her side, elbow bent, fingers tensed. Her weight was on her right foot. With a brushful of red, she inscribed a large movement, producing an introversive pattern, and then added a few tense lines to the right side of the paper. Taking the blue paint, she executed wild, tense, anxious movements on the left side, completely smearing over the first pattern. She used more blue paint and dripped and smeared it. Marked intensity of emotion was shown by the way the paint was

applied. More tense angular movements were made with blue paint. The brush was bent against the paper. Cathy held an animated conversation with Glenna, then returned to her "scrubbing" with the brush full of blue. She rubbed her nose and rested. Then in the left-hand corner of the paper she inscribed a few marks with her finger. She adjusted her apron. She leaned over Glenna's painting, danced a step or two, pointed to the "face" Glenna was painting and said, "Ho, ho!" Much more social conversation followed as she rested for almost five minutes. Then Cathy picked up the green brush and smashed a pattern in the very center, over-painting all the other colors. She danced up and down and conversed some more. The teacher gave her a clean sheet of paper.

Cathy again picked up the brushful of green paint, started to paint, in the extreme upper right corner, a markedly angular pattern, very different from the preceding one. Four girls gathered around, conversing. Glenna made a yellow pattern in the lower left corner. Cathy took no notice. Using both hands Cathy made a jagged, heavy-stroked line. Then she picked up the purple, made a strong, assertive downward dual stroke, with space between. The scrubbing downward movement became tense as she worked. She then filled in this rigid pattern and added assertive red strokes, heavily and tensely applied. With orange paint way over on the left side of paper, another isolated form was made with introversive movement, and tense stroking. This was then overlaid with more red, and the entire form filled in with aggressive stroking of the red paint.

Note: This entire painting is markedly different from the preceding one. If one had not seen Cathy paint it, one could easily doubt that it was hers. This may well have been Cathy's attempt to imitate Glenna, but instead of her forms being circular like Glenna's, because of her marked tension they became angular.

Cathy added a yellow form to the left of Glenna's paper—much as Glenna had done on hers. This was more or less reciprocation of a friendly nature, with no evidence of aggression. Glenna proceeded to fill this in and obliterate it in her own circular fashion.

Cathy then turned her attention to her own painting. Slowly she filled an open space in the center with yellow, smearing the edge over the red. Now with the green, holding the brush down on the paper rigidly with her left index finger atop the bristles, she scrubbed tensely and slowly down the center next to the yellow.

By that time Glenna was joyfully smearing her careful painting. Cathy emulated this action. She picked up the red and slashed some jagged, tense strokes, growing more intense. The paper was then removed by the teacher.

Impression: The marked contrast between these two paintings would seem to indicate a deep conflict—tension, extremely marked anxiety, followed by deep effort at control, resulting in reaction of more tension and some aggression. The first open expression of aggression seemed to be overlaid with anxiety and depression. The "budding" assertion in the strokes was retarded by the evident tension and insecurity.

The conference with the staff of the Child Care Center which Cathy was attending brought out the following facts about her background. She lived with her mother, grandmother, and two brothers aged six and seven. One of the four rooms of their apartment was rented out. Her mother worked as a domestic and called for her when it was time to go home. Several months after the start of the study, the father, who had been separated from the mother rejoined the family. The father was known to be intoxicated frequently and abusive to the mother. It also came to light that Cathy often complained of pains in her stomach and would cry bitterly and sometimes vomit. The same thing happened when her mother was late. When her mother was called on the phone to come for her, however, she immediately became better. At four and one half years she was still taking a bottle at night when she went to sleep. It seemed clear from the discussion with the teachers that Cathy showed a good deal of aggression toward adults in a disguised manner, that is by teasing. She would tease her mother by running away from her at school and at home she would tease her brothers and run to her mother for protection. She seemed ambivalent about her self-reliance; although she could help herself, she insisted on being dressed by her mother. It was also discovered that another child in the group, somewhat older than Cathy, acted as a kind of mother substitute for her, babying her and helping her when she got into trouble. One particularly significant finding was that about the time the father entered the picture, her drawing and painting showed a definite effort at control, in addition to more evidence of aggression.

All in all, it was felt that the facts that emerged during the conference tended to support the painting interpretation in spite of its complete contrast to the original picture the teachers had given. The tendency toward aggression shown in the paintings was paralleled by Cathy's teasing; her anxiety was indicated by her psychosomatic symptoms; her regression and ambivalence about accepting control were amply demonstrated by attachment to the bottle, by demands for help when she could help herself, and by playing baby to the older child's mothering. But it is significant that it took the observation of several teachers to piece out the picture. One effect of the whole investigation was to make her teachers aware of the fact that Cathy, too, had her problems and could benefit from a little more consideration.

Unfortunately it was not possible to investigate every case as thoroughly as Cathy's, and we do have to recognize that there seem to be as many misses as hits in our attempts at interpreting graphic products. Attempts to predict the child's future adjustment are especially hazardous. One expert judged a three-year-old boy "capable of working out his own problems," on the basis of his paintings. Two years later he was diagnosed as definitely psychotic. However, in this case, events of great traumatic intensity intervened between the production of the paintings and the final breakdown.

One of the important points to be recognized concerning the meaning of children's paintings is that they change rather rapidly from time to time. If they do mirror states of feeling, these are usually temporary, changing with circumstances and events in the life of the child. The best we can do is to observe both the child and his graphic products over as long a period of time as possible.

Any teacher who wishes to work in cooperation with a painting analyst should know that between twenty and thirty pictures are usually required, the more the better. Moreover, the products alone are frequently not considered adequate for analysis. The child's thoughts about them, the remarks he makes while painting, the things he mentions when asked to talk about his completed painting are often necessary to give meaning to the painting itself. It is also desirable to learn how the child behaved during the day a given painting was made, what series of events led up to it, what followed it, and what was taking place in his home at the time.

Suggestions for Teachers

Perhaps the most important thing to remember is that children, at least those below the age of four, are not generally attempting to paint pictures. Rather they are interested in the experience of applying paint to the paper, and it is therefore inappropriate to ask what they are making. A better way of establishing communication would be to make some noncommittal remark about what fun it is to paint or how interesting the results are.

Secondly, it is important to bear in mind that painting may be the only means a child has for expressing certain emotional experiences he is going through. Therefore it is wise to arrange conditions so that children can paint whenever they want to. This means having an ample quantity of materials, including plenty of paper and a wide range of good richly colored paints. Older children, roughly between four and one half and six, might be shown how to mix the colors they want, using the three basic primary colors and black and white. However, this is not a very reliable method of helping them obtain what they want because their mixtures often result in rather muddy colors.

If budgets are small, it might be wiser to invest in an adequate supply of paints, brushes, and paper than to buy easels, for youngsters can paint with great enjoyment on tables or on the floor. Sometimes paper can be obtained free of charge from the local newspaper printing department. Paints can be made cheaply by mixing powdered pigments with water and adding Bentonite, which is available at art supply stores; it is an "extender" used in making ceramics.

Some people believe that the number of colors available to very young children should be limited to one or two. If this practice is followed, they should be contrasting, i.e., a warm and a cold color. Our records, however, reveal that this limitation is frustrating for some children, as indicated by their repeated requests for additional colors and their impatience while waiting for the teacher to take away the jar they are using and get another one. When the painting experience means the release of emotional pressures, irritations of this kind may actually discourage interest.

Mixing the paints should be as much a part of the experience as spreading it on the paper. Muffin tins or custard cups as well as tongue depressors, popsicle sticks, or old paint brushes might be provided for this purpose. It might be advisable to make this an accessory activity and provide paints specifically for those who like to mix and mess. This is the only satisfaction some youngsters can derive from the activity. Sometimes a genuine interest in painting itself can be aroused by permitting children to help prepare the paint. The setup should include low shelves for the very young and large jars for the vigorous.

When cleaning up is considered fun rather than a chore, children often enjoy it as much as they do the painting. Sponges and rags, and jars for clean brushes should all be set aside in easily accessible places. It is very important, however, not to force the children who have painted to clean up the easel corner, for it may be precisely those who are not yet ready to enjoy painting who get the most benefit from this cleanup activity.

Our records indicate that the general setup often needs correction. We should therefore like to suggest that a "help-yourself" program will avoid lengthy, discouraging waits and give the children greater freedom. Ready-mixed paint can be kept on a low shelf or table in pitchers with large spouts. Several sheets of paper should be fastened to the easel with clasps, clothes pins, or loose-leaf rings rather than thumb tacks. Smocks, aprons, or plastic ponchos that do not require buttons or ties should be kept on low hooks near the painting corner. The equipment should be located in an area that cannot be harmed by paint, with the floor protected by linoleum and a few boxes or old pieces of furniture at hand for those who are not yet ready for the easel.

To increase the availability of this activity, the equipment might occasionally be taken to the play ground during seasonable weather, and it might be made available to those who cannot sleep during rest time. Needless to say, we do not recommend painting as the standard means of occupying children who have been temporarily removed for unacceptable behavior.

Frequently the approach to the activity also needs overhauling. In general, the teacher should bear in mind that it is more important for the child to enjoy painting than to learn the best techniques or observe the rules about order and cleanliness. After the child has had a chance to experiment in his own way and has discovered the pleasure of the activity, suggestions might be made about handling the materials. Unfortunately many of our older children are extremely restricted and overanxious in painting because of an overemphasis on rules during the preschool or kindergarten years. Even the insistence on having the child wash his hands immediately after painting might spoil the enjoyment since it carries with it the suggestion that the activity is dirty or messy. The paint will not stain other things and unless the child is going to eat immediately after painting, there seems little reason to make an issue of washing up. A tentatively worded suggestion such as, "Would you like to wash your hands now?" should be sufficient.

Getting a hesitant child started on the painting experience is an art, and success most often depends on the general attitude of the teacher. Certainly "rules" for using the equipment should not be mentioned in the beginning. Having made the paint available to the child, the teacher might take the brush and say, "I'll make a picture first, and then perhaps you would like to make one," making a few strokes on the paper as she speaks. Sometimes inhibited children become intrigued if the teacher makes only one mark on the paper and then withdraws. Once a constricted child has gained enough freedom to use poster paint with enjoyment, the teacher might encourage him to use the messier materials such as finger-paints, various types of water and paint mixtures, clay and dough, with or without color added.

Occasionally we find teachers telling children what to paint or how to paint, even suggesting that they fill in the blank spaces on the paper (often done in an effort to conserve paper). This kind of direction takes painting away from the child and makes it a teacher activity. Sometimes children interpret such "advice" as lack of confidence in themselves; at best it shows a lack of respect for their way of doing things, and does violence to the meaning of the product. Also, it is not advisable to frame a suggestion in such a way that the child will feel he should paint in order to have a picture to give to the teacher or to take home. It is far better for any youngster to paint for the fun of it than to paint to please adults.

CHAPTER VIII

The Finger-Paint Experience

THE ADVANTAGES of finger-paint as a play material for very young children are being more and more widely recognized. Aesthetically speaking, it encourages creative expression through direct contact between creator and product and through novelty and lack of arbitrary standards to limit its use. Psychologically, it has been found effective for both children and adults in overcoming certain inhibitions, in evoking a free flow of fantasy life among disturbed people and in exploring such aspects of personality as expansiveness and sensitivity to sensory impressions.

Many investigators have attempted to use finger-painting for diagnostic purposes. Of the studies available, Arlow and Kadis[1] have reported material of the most direct relevance for the preschool age range. In using finger-painting in the psychotherapy of children they found that the ability to create recognizable objects paralleled improvement in adjustment, and that the choice of colors was "an almost unfailing index of the mood of the patient and the theme of the painting." Black and brown were used for themes indicating depression and hostility, blue and green for more cheerful themes. Inhibited, frightened, and insecure children were partial to the darker colors and, in the younger groups, used only one color as a rule. A few very disturbed children used red as the sole color, and seemed to associate it with destruction by fire. They found the handling of the paints equally indicative: "Inhibited, frightened, and insecure children . . . may be unable to adapt themselves to finger-painting as such; instead, they may dip an individual finger into the paint jar and use the finger as a pencil or crayon, thereby indicating reluctance to avail themselves of the less formalized means of expression which finger-painting permits. Those children who fail to cover the sheet completely with paint may be suspected of being inhibited or frightened. Conversely, the inability of a child to limit himself to the paper is important diagnostically. Such a child may be suspected of being too aggressive or insufficiently inhibited. He can no more limit himself in painting than he can in other life situations."

With promising reports about the usefulness of finger-painting emerging from the clinic and the therapist's office it seemed worthwhile to investigate its utility in preschool groups. We had the following questions in mind: If it can help deeply disturbed people overcome their inhibitions and express their fantasies and emotions, would it not be even more helpful to growing youngsters whose problems are still in an emergent state? In the usual preschool group, where it is not integrated into the child—teacher relationship and where interpretation of the child's feelings is not attempted, does finger-painting still retain some of the same values it has in the more intimate therapeutic situation? And are teachers aware of its unique values and the possibilities it holds for the child's development?

As to the actual use of finger-painting, we found that it was included at some time in all the centers cooperating with this investigation, but it was available at all times only in one group. For the most part it was used, like water-play, as a rainy day activity and was rather heavily controlled by the teacher. In no center was there any provision for other than group work, and the number expected to work together varied from two to twelve. The teachers generally took the finger-paint from the containers but asked the children where they wanted it placed on the paper. In some groups only one color at a time was offered, but even when more were offered the children were permitted to choose only one color for each painting. The amount, too, was generally restricted. The orientation of the teacher seemed to be similar to her orientation toward clay and easel painting. She seemed to feel that the major "job" of the child was to learn how to deal with the material so that it would remain within the boundaries of the paper and retain the consistency necessary for achieving graphic effects. In all centers the so-called pictures were meticulously dried, preserved, and displayed on bulletin boards in the same manner as crayon drawings and easel painting. Remarks made to the children frequently included phrases such as, "What a pretty picture you are making!" Thus there was an emphasis on the product, similar to that found in our observations on the use of clay. There was rarely any conversation between teacher and child about the painting, and few names for the creations were reported.

On the whole, teachers' reports of the effects of finger-painting on children were favorable. The most universally noted effect was that of relaxation and the most frequent comparison was with water-play. They all noted, however, that it could not be offered as frequently as water-play since it requires more of the teachers' time for supervision. While most reports indicated that it was one of the generally preferred activities, one teacher said that her group of very young children with personality difficulties did not enjoy it and seemed disturbed by its messiness.

Interestingly enough, any comments made by the teachers about its usefulness in helping them understand their youngsters were negative. Teachers insisted either that they could not learn much by watching children with finger-paint or that they could not see any change in them while they were using it. There were no spontaneous references at all to the meaning of the experience from the child's point of view. For an understanding of this aspect of finger-painting it is necessary to go directly to the children, as we shall do through our illustrative records.

Appeals

Theoretically, finger-paint offers several different kinds of appeal and satisfaction. According to its originator, Ruth Faison Shaw, it should be a means of expressing ideas, emotions, and deeply personal experiences in a graphic way. On a less complex level its use involves a variety of sensations—visual, tactile, and kinesthetic. It can appeal to interest in color or interest in abstract form and design. In addition, it might be a useful substitute for playing with mud or exploring body products, the handling of which is forbidden and prevented. The remarks already made in relation to the importance of exploratory and substitute materials in the discussion of water-play would also apply here.

We offer the record of Bill below as an example of the variety and intensity of pleasurable experience implicit in the activity. He is an extremely inhibited four-year-old, always absorbed with himself or with daydreams, interested in manipulating materials, but apparently completely unable to make contact with children.

Bill has just finished his first painting of the day and is sitting back in his chair, watching the assistant teacher put down another sheet of paper. He smiles in a pleased manner, stretches backward a bit against the chair, holds his red hands up, and widens and closes the fingers slowly. With an anticipatory look he asks for the red and yellow, and points to the jars with a dripping hand. He notices the hand and laughs to himself as though pleased. The assistant teacher puts a dab of red at the center top of his paper, then a dab of yellow (about a teaspoonful). Bill looks as if he were "itching" to begin, and immediately after she has finished he puts three fingers of his right hand into the red dab. He pulls down a long, triple, vertical line, luxuriating in the feeling. He then puts the other hand into the yellow, swooshes as though in a puddle, running it into the red, and sucking his lips in a smile, eyes alight. Then with his right hand he starts to make a horizontal arch of the red and yellow paints together, using the fingers, then the palm of his hand, fingers wide so the paint can ooze through. Then he rubs it zigzag, up and down, now standing up next to the table to get more force into the stroke. He notes Miss H passing; as she smiles at him he smiles back, a wide happy grin. He points to a jar she is holding; his face expresses exuberance and expectation. He smears with both hands together, right and left across the painting, and says, "I make a nice one," half in question and half in a statement-of-fact manner. Miss H ladles out some black paint, putting it at the center top of his painting. Bill watches with excited eyes, barely able to wait. He almost seizes upon it, pushing it across back and forth with both hands, running over the edge of the paper. A boy stops by the table, and Bill grins. "This is black paint," he says, pushing hard, covering all the paper now with cross swoops and arches. He sits down a moment only, then gets to his feet again in order to push better. He sees an assistant teacher, "I want more red and yellow and black," he says to her. He sweeps the paint around the paper in up and down strokes, crisscross strokes, figure eights, and up and down again. He is more relaxed now, experimenting in direction and feel. The colors are all run together in a dark brown effect.

Bill stands back a little, holds up his covered hands, and smiles at them; he seems pleased. He sees Miss H and asks, "Miss H, a little more?" She smiles and ladles out some red. Bill watches with his mouth open, head a little on one side. As she puts the paint on the paper, he watches her, rubbing his hands slowly back and forth and up and down, as though using a washboard.

He sits down, swishes the new red and yellow and black allotment of paint. He is quiet now; the exuberance is gone but in its place there is real relaxed joy. He looks up from the painting to note the seven jars of paint at the other edge of his table and smiles at them. He has a look of King Midas regarding his gold.

Another boy comes up, dips out paint for himself as Bill watches and laughs to see it drip from the end, a real spontaneous gurgle of enjoyment. He asks for more paints, continues smearing until he announces in a relaxed way, "I think I'm through." He asks for more paper and goes through much the same procedure again.

The observer later made these comments: "Of all the mediums used, Bill seems to get the most complete pleasure from finger-painting. During this session he let go with the first spontaneous laughter yet noticed. While he enjoys miniature toys and seems absorbed in them, there is not the outgoing *joy* he seems to feel about finger-painting."

Clare, a well-adjusted five-year-old, exhibits a somewhat similar variety of sensory experiences in the record below. Neither of these children seems to be "projecting" any definite ideas, but since the teachers do not converse with them, it is impossible to know what they may be trying to communicate. From records like these we can appreciate somewhat more vividly what they are taking in from the experience, but we are left almost completely in the dark concerning what they are giving out.

As Clare watched the others prepare their paper, she said, "Rub it more. Rub it all over. Rub, rub rub." She spoke these words very fast and moved her hand in rhythm as she spoke. The teacher put a large dab of paste on her paper, "What color do you want?" "I want red," Clare called out very quickly and very loudly. She took the red paint jar and spilled some of it on top of the paste mound. She stood up straight and put both hands in it, then rubbed them together. "Look at my hands. Blood," she said, turning to the girl standing next to her. She continued rubbing her hands together until they were both thoroughly covered with red. She picked up some of the paste—paint mixture that was still in mound form and squeezed it. She made wide full rubbing motions in the air and looked about to see if anyone else was rubbing his paper yet. She picked up the red paint jar and spilled some more of it on the paper. Then she put both hands on the paper, palms flat, and began rubbing it well into the paper. She used very fast movements. Now and then she would make a small design with one finger; often she would use all her fingers as they swept over the paper to make designs. She lifted her hands and squeezed them. . . . Now she used the cushion edge of her palms and slid them about the paper. With her left hand resting on one side, she made quick large marks covering the entire paper, using the finger of her right hand. She rubbed the marks out with the palms of both hands, covering them completely. "Oh, Ma," she said in mock despair, "My hands are bleeding." She rubbed her hands together and smiled happily. Clare made a few more marks with the finger of one hand and then lifted the paper to hand it to the teacher.

From close observation it becomes clear that the appeal of finger-paint is not primarily an aesthetic one. At any age within the preschool range, the children's primary concern seems to be with "messing" and tactile pleasure, similar to that shown by the subjects of Stone and Murphy in their experiments with cold cream. This appears so frequently in the records that it suggests a common need for experiences with touch beyond those usually available to these children, i.e., urban apartment dwellers.

Some observers have suggested that the way finger-paints are handled is related to anal interests and toilet training. This may be true, yet there often seems to be a delight in sheer sensation and pleasurable feel apart from the more intense aggressive manipulation which has been accepted as indicative of unresolved anal curiosities. Contrasting records will illustrate this difference more dramatically than any abstract description. The first is that of a boy almost five years of age who was very belligerent toward other children and frequently wet himself. He had four older sisters but was reported to be his father's favorite child, the only boy and the "baby" of the family. There is evidence of some rejecting attitudes on the part of his mother and it is known that he was subject to a good many controls, impulsively and aggressively imposed.

The teacher comes over and puts an apron on Jack and sits him down at the finger-paint table. After the paper is wet, he asks for red paint. He sticks his hand right into the center of it and sweeps it around and around. Then he makes a straight line with one finger and slaps on the paper with both palms. Then he goes around and around again with both hands and stops to cover his arms with paint. The teacher stops him. He draws a circle with one finger. Then he asks for blue paint and spreads it around with his palm. The teacher tells him to use his finger-tips. He does so and runs them up and down on the paper and across the page. He then scratches the paper with his fingernail and picks up a piece of the torn paper and smells it. He makes all sorts of lines on the paper and then makes curly figures and looks at them closely. Then he looks all around him and sings and keeps working his hands on the paper, but does not watch what he is doing. He looks back at his work and again makes circular motions with his palms. He then rubs blue paint into his arms up to his sleeve above his elbow. He scratches a design with his fingernail and claps his hands together. Then he says he is finished.

The record of a four-year-old named Ron, who was considered both aggressive and withdrawn, described the same kind of vigorous smearing and scratching with a good deal of banging thrown in. In contrast to these two, we offer a report on a little girl of four who had long been constricted in her movements and withdrawn when with other children. She had recently shown more sociability, but until the day before this record was taken, had evinced little or no interest in finger-painting.

Fanny is eager to begin; she is restless, rolling on her heels and moving up and down the table. Miss H brings paper and immediately Fanny dives for the red paint jar. She dabs it around with the wooden ladle, making a design, and tipping her head to one side to watch how it comes out. Except for the alertness of her bright brown eyes, her face is expressionless. She then helps herself to dabs of blue, and places these in balance with the red just arranged. She leans to her right to whisper to Ellen who is now smearing her paint with vigorous arm movements. Fanny watches this for a moment, turns to her own paper, and pushes both hands down into the paint, smearing in wide circles and ovals. Her movements push from the outside, up, down the center, and around the bottom in rotation. She leans across Ellen to pick up the jar of yellow, dabs a large drop into the center, and immediately smears this into the same round form. Miss H stops by and Fanny looks up at her. "Can I get some on myself?" she asks, wringing her hands to cover them entirely with red paint. (While she used blue and yellow also, the red predominates.) She regards her spread fingers with her characteristic poker face, turns them over, stretches and wrings them, then rubs her arms with a dainty finger up to her elbows. Now she gets a dab of blue and rubs this in with side and up-and-down movements. She now tries to draw with her right index finger the outline of a large cross, but swooshes it together almost immediately. She adds yellow, smears this in, so the paint is now a fairly uniform terracotta red. She is experimenting with feeling the paints, rolling her hands sideways, on their backs, and on the palms. She tries all sorts of swirls and zigzag strokes. Her pressure is firm, but not heavy. For a moment she stares off into space; her face is without expression. Then she looks at her hands, still in a semi-daydream. Then, as if the sight brought her back, she runs around the tables and shows Miss H her painted hands and arms.

There seems to be a third type of tactile experience, between the sheer immersion in sensation just illustrated and the energetic smearing and squeezing and slapping found in Jack and Ron. Connie, whose behavior is described below, obviously enjoys both elements in the experience. She is about three and one half years old and considered well adjusted.

Connie leaves the easel and wanders over to where Jill and Penrod are finger-painting. "I wanna do that, too—right here." She sits down to wait for the paint, with her tongue sticking out of the corner of her mouth. When she gets it she chants: "Just use this hand, this hand, this hand—gotta have some white." She rubs the paint around in circles. Miss U tells her to put it all over the paper. "Yeah." She rubs slowly and hard in circles with both hands. "Look—I got it all over my hands! Red gloves." She begins to move her hands independently, in vigorous circles. Then using her right index finger and left palm she rubs slowly and in no apparent pattern or design. Then she brings her hands together again, pressing hard, and rubs them around and around. She says to Miss U, "Red, red, gloves—but it gets on the table." Miss U gives her more paint. She grunts, and says, "Mix it up, you see. Mix it all up." Miss U says, "Oh look, you got it on your sleeve." "That's all right. That's why you wear a smock. It's all right. Hee! Hee! Will you please get a little more paint? Over here—look, I covered the whole picture up. She rubs her hands luxuriously in the paint, apparently with great satisfaction. "I'm making a picture. Look. I'm making a big, big bathroom. Water in a can. I'm trying to make a train track. I'm making—mmmmm. You see, look! . . . ."

She rubs the left-hand corner of the paper, and bouncing up and down in the chair, rubs the middle furiously. Then she quiets down and returns to the slow hand movements. She says to Ann, "Gil is his mamie." She laughs and vigorously bends her knees and rubs the paper hard and fast. She picks up the paper from the table with two fingers, and screams out a laugh. She rubs the paint onto the table with a slow sensual movement of her hand and her whole body moves, too.

Release

Some children exhibit a crescendo of release progressing from a first delight in the feel of the paint, to somewhat more vigorous experimentation such as rubbing or slapping, to a final frenzied smearing which does not seem to retain any sensuous component. The following report of Ted, an anxious and aggressive boy, illustrates this sequence, although the final movements are not very completely or vividly described.

Ted leaves his playmates in the house and says he wants to put on his smock. The teacher puts it on. . . . Ted sits down with his paper before him. He has no paints, but he rubs his hands across the paper and hums a tune. The teacher asks what color he wants. "Yellow." He squeezes it between his fingers, then works at a varying pace. Sometimes he spreads the paint with what appears to be intense interest and speed, while at other times he does not have his mind at all on what he is doing. He asks for some red and pink, but Chester, who has some light blue, comes to Ted's table and drops some of it on his paper. Ted spreads it all over the paper, some on the table. He seems to enjoy making lines through the paint and screams like a siren as he does this. His face bears an expression of delight and he frequently talks to himself. Occasionally he says a word or two to Chester and Ann. He rubs paint up both his arms and says, "I'm painting my arms up. Now I'm dark people. Now I'm all blacked up." Ann says, "What are you— tokey?" "Yes, I'm tokey." He covers the entire paper with his pink paint and makes lines with his forefinger through it. He lifts his hands up: "Look at my black hands." He picks up some paint from the other table. Chester says, "Wait, I need some." Ted puts it down. "I don't have any," he says. Mrs. H hands some to Ted, who says, "Good, good, good." He takes some and spreads it on the paper with intensity. After spreading a new color over a large area of paper Ted runs his fingers through the paint, making lines. He then rubs them out.

A crescendo of freedom and intensity of expression can frequently be observed when children are allowed to work on one finger-painting uninterruptedly without any artificial limits of time or material. This release expresses itself in every possible way—in color choice, types of stroke, use of hands and body, and even in social attitudes. Roland, the anxious five-year-old whose behavior is briefly described below, gives us an excellent example of this progressive achievement of freedom and spontaneity. Notice the sequence in his color choices from green to yellow, and in his strokes which range from limited inward turning movements to more assertive lines to large outgoing movements, finally culminating in smearing. Notice also the comparative constriction of his first approach, with only the finger being used, then the whole hands; the intense appreciation of the paint-covered hands, and finally the defiant bit of bravado in which he openly expresses the impulses which are merely suggested by his use of the paints.

There were three different colors available, red, green, and blue. The teacher asked Roland which one he wanted, and he chose the green. He dipped his fingers in the paint and began to trace circular figures from the outside moving inward, then reversed to the inside moving outward. He kept looking at his paint-covered hands and laughed about it, appearing more interested in the observation of his hands than in the painting itself. He held them a few inches from his face and shouted as if frightened. He seemed intent on putting on a show for a little girl who was standing by his side, watching him attentively. He'd stand up from his chair every once in a while and shout and laugh, making growling noises in addition. Then he asked the teacher for some blue paint and began to make some short up-and-down strokes and returned to making circular figures in a clockwise movement. Then he requested yellow paint with which he stroked in short narrow diagonal lines. Then he began to smear paint over the whole paper and on the table as well. He lifted up the paper and pressed the painted side against the wall. He called, "Teacher," and laughed when she came. He knew he had done something wrong, and seemed rather pleased about it.

Definite evidences of kinesthetic pleasure abound in the records. Children make anticipatory movements in the air before they start or continue to move rhythmically after the painting has been removed. In the course of the activity itself, the pleasurable experience spreads and extends from the local stimulation of the skin to include sensation and movement of the whole body. Undoubtedly the paintings record present, immediate sensation far more than past experience. The following record of a withdrawn three-year-old girl illustrates this keen kinesthetic enjoyment.

The teacher placed some yellow paint on the page in front of Elsa. She moved her hand around in the air without doing anything. Finally John said, "Go ahead, paint." In the meantime Elsa kept muttering to herself, "Mommy." Suddenly she plunged both hands into the paint and spread it around a little. John and Elsa showed their paint-smeared hands to each other. Then Elsa turned her attention back to the page and spread the paint in all directions over it. Then she called out, "Look at mine, mommy, look at mine, mommy, look mommy, I'm finished." She lifted the page off the table and showed it to the teacher. Then she replaced it and said, "Give me more." The teacher placed some more yellow paint on the page. Elsa was rubbing her hands together as if she were washing. Then she requested some light blue paint, and was very intent on covering the entire bottom half of the page. She called out to the teacher, "Teacher, I'm finished." Then she began to clap her hands together in front of Pam's face. Pam complained, but Elsa didn't stop until the teacher told her to go to the bathroom and wash up.

Self-Application

The tendency to smear paint on themselves was very common among all kinds of children. In fact, it was often more intriguing at the start than the painting process itself. Extremely aggressive and uninhibited youngsters did not hesitate to spread the paint all over themselves, but the extremely inhibited ones were somewhat more restricted. Colored "gloves" were a simple delight to all types. This "disguise," moreover, seemed to stimulate the more timid and fearful children to throw off their inhibitions and become almost promiscuously aggressive and threatening. Extreme messing and smearing of the face as well as of the hands and arms was encountered only once, when three very disturbed and aggressive children in a special guidance nursery were allowed to play with finger-paints.

It is interesting to observe that one child, Fanny, whose deeply sensuous enjoyment has been described, put the paint on herself the first few times she used it, and then put herself on the paint by writing her name in the middle of her creations. This would suggest a more intimate relationship between product and child than we have encountered with any other material.

The following protocol describes the behavior of an "anxious" three-year-old girl who was ordinarily extremely hesitant about entering activities and about using materials and making contacts with other children. Note the social value of the hand smearing.

Nell asked for green paint and made gestures of delight and pleasure as she smeared it all over her hands and arms. She looked at the other children at the table and said, "Look, look." She asked for more green paint, immediately put a very little on the paper, but seemed to take more pleasure in smearing it on herself than on the paper. "Look, look," she exclaimed to the student teacher. The teacher replied, "What a nice picture," evidently ignoring the fact that Nell was showing her her hands.

Nell did, however, make an attempt to try her skill at creating a design. She rubbed the paper with one finger making a white mark on the paper, but she no sooner made it than she smoothed it over again, covering up the white spot. She got very vigorous just once, when she moved her whole hand rapidly in an up-and-down motion. After doing this she decided to wash her hands.

Approach

The initial approach and early handling of finger-paint seemed to be characteristic of the child's general attitude toward life. As Arlow and Kadis have suggested, timid children tended to hesitate before beginning to paint, then used a single finger or tentatively the finger tips. It took them longer to "warm up" to the situation, and they showed more anxiety about paint sticking to their hands than did either the well-adjusted or the overactive and aggressive children. Spontaneous and uninhibited youngsters, on the other hand, usually plunged in with both hands, swung their arms in wider arcs, worked at a faster tempo, and more frequently smeared the paint past the boundaries of the paper. The differences in approach are so striking that they might well be used as a preliminary screening device early in the semester to help the teachers differentiate those children who will need encouragement and stimulation from those who will need firmness and restraint. Below we present an example of the characteristic approach of an inhibited child.

Very gingerly, Tillie (two years and five months old) put out her right index finger and touched the paint. Then she noted the paint on her finger and smeared the finger on the paper. When it left a streak her face lit up in a pleased smile. She looked at her hand, then stroked the paper some more and during this time kept looking around. . . . Then she looked again at her finger and said, "Take this off me." Mrs. H said, "When you're finished." However, in a few minutes she brought a rag saying, "You can wipe it on this." Tillie wiped her hands at intervals throughout her activity with the finger-paint. Then she got both hands into the paint and put her entire right hand into it, palm down. "Look at this," she said to no one in particular as she made semicircles with her right hand. Again she looked at her palms and kept wiping them automatically on the rag.

Now compare Tillie's approach with that of a well-adjusted lad of three and one half years.

Charles looks at the paper and proceeds to finger-paint with complete abandonment and unself-consciousness. He dives into it with both hands enjoying the slippery sensation; he tries both hands simultaneously making circular motions in perfect rhythm. Then he takes a stick and makes straight lines on the pages. Other children are lining up chairs nearby making a great deal of noise, but Charles is oblivious of them. He bangs on the paper with his fist and with a chuckle states, "I am done."

Freedom and Restraint

This sharp contrast is found only in the initial approach. It is perhaps the chief virtue of finger-paint that it very quickly frees inhibited children for greater spontaneity. It is not at all unusual to see morose and lethargic youngsters gradually brightening to open laughter and moving in ever increasing tempo with their whole beings expressing pleasure. Fanny and Bill, whose behavior was described earlier in this chapter, were characteristically extremely restrained. Yet when the description of their behavior with the finger-paint was read to a group of experienced nursery school educators, all were impressed with their "freedom and spontaneity." Unless one has witnessed the transformation which can take place in a fifteen-minute session, it is difficult to be convinced that it can happen. Not only are the children palpably happier, but they are also more approachable socially. This is easy to understand, for when we feel good we want to share our satisfying experiences. The record reproduced below depicts a five-year-old who is ordinarily timid, shy, and rather passive. Although she is not so completely free in the use of the material as many others already cited, nevertheless she gives unmistakable evidence of enjoyment and openness to contact.

Sitting down at the table, Sally looks at the other children with a frown on her face. The teacher places an apron around her. She then stares at her hands for a moment with a worried look. The teacher puts a blob of red paint on the sheet before her. A smile breaks out on her face and she slowly but firmly moves both of her hands in two circles in the paint. After watching her own work with intense interest for a few minutes, she looks at what the other children are doing, never removing her hands from her work. Finally she removes her hands and looks at them with interest; they are all covered with red paint. She holds them up for the others to see, but not at all in a menacing gesture, saying, "Look, I got red gloves!" The teacher shows them black paint to put on the sheets, but Sally refuses it, saying in a serious tone that she wants blue instead. The teacher gives her a blob of blue paint. Sally rubs it into her red-colored sheet, with the same expansive yet firm movement as before. The blue mixing with the red brings forth a joyful exclamation, "Oh, look at the purple! What a nice color!" She laughs as if at a personal joke, and continues rubbing the paint. Turning towards her younger brother, Bruce, seated next to her, Sally says that his is dark. She stops her finger-painting and looks at her paint-covered hands. "Oh, do we have to go home like this?" This is said not too seriously. She no longer paints, but watches the work of the other children. She tells the teacher that she is finished.

When children like Sally are enjoying themselves and are open to contact, teachers have a golden opportunity to promote their social relationships in the group. It is important, however, to choose the group members carefully, to include some of the blessedly spontaneous and friendly children and avoid those who are overwhelmingly aggressive.

The finger-painting session often brings out energetic and apparently aggressive behavior in unaggressive children. Elly, for example, was described as "not an aggressive child. . . . Doesn't attack others, cries out when hit, and very seldom hits back." Yet with finger-paints (see p. 287), she was extremely vigorous and apparently released aggression without guilt. This little girl is four years old and considered well adjusted by her teachers.

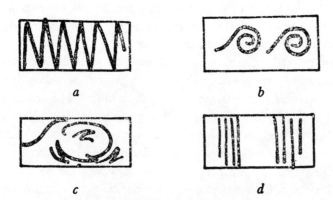

a

b

c

d

SKETCHES OF ELLY'S FINGER-PAINTING

Elly is absorbed in smearing the original pattern with strong jagged down movements which continued right off the page. Now with two hands, she makes two concentric circles and scratches over these vigorously. Now with strong arm movement she starts to swing a circle, inscribes half of it, and then cuts off this movement with horizontal swings centralized on the paper.

With the fingers of her right hand, she again scratches the right side of the paper. Her nose is almost on it, so closely is she working now. There is more smearing with two hands. Now with downward, vertical, scratching movements toward the body, she makes double verticals on both sides of the paper using both hands.

She picks up the paper, holds it ready to give to the teacher, then lays it down again. Vigorously, with up-and-down jagged movements, she overlays the design, turns the paper over, and repeats this on the back where enough paint is smeared to give the pattern form. She picks up a rag and works over the design. She bangs the paper aggressively, and with extreme vigor makes a huge concentric circle with a finger of her right hand.

The effects of this type of release can be remarkably beneficial. Ron, the little boy whose smearing and banging have already been mentioned, used to start the day in an irritable and hostile frame of mind, but after free use of finger-paint, his black moods would subside and he would engage in vivid dramatic play and all other activities.

In direct contrast, we sometimes see children who are ordinarily very spontaneous and impulsive working with finger-paint in an extremely cramped manner. The reason is somewhat obscure, but since this medium tends to lure its users on to greater freedom, it may sometimes be experienced as a threat, particularly by those who are having difficulty in curbing their impulses in order to be acceptable to adults. It may also have too close an association with certain anal interests to permit free expression, and its messiness is so prominent and unrelieved that it may produce particularly acute conflict among those who are rebelling against demands for orderliness. At any rate, when children are noticeably restrained in their use of finger-paints, one can be fairly sure that they are subject to greater requirements for cleanliness and conformity than they can easily assimilate.

Such children may be withdrawn or aggressive, depending on other aspects of their history. The aggressive ones, who ordinarily wade in slapdash, will join the group but handle the material in a constricted manner, while the timid and fearful will usually refuse to participate at all. The following report of Milly, an extremely hostile four-year-old, illustrates the former case. The mother was profoundly annoyed by her messiness: "I can't stand to look at her, she's so messy when she eats." Though nothing is known about her toilet training, she did refuse to play with water and even hurried while washing. She once identified clay with feces and with a wickedly gleeful expression threatened to throw it at another child. It may be that she is thinking of finger-paint in these terms, as some children have been known to do.

Milly sits alone at the table. She asks Miss C to roll back her smock sleeves. She looks at the finger-paint a moment, very seriously, seeming to study it. Then she puts both hands into it rather gently and begins (using her full palms) to smooth it out carefully, working from the center out, and then from the edge inward. She begins to experiment with first the right and then the left hand, using the index finger of each hand in turn. She makes marks, first circular then straight, then obliterates them with both hands. She next uses her right palm in a circular motion. Now she uses both hands and carefully brushes the excess paint from the paper onto the table, and then onto the floor. She now returns to dual hand motion, but uses only the tips of her fingers. She looks up and with an ingratiating smile says, "Teacher, I need some more." Miss C complies. Milly notices a clump of paint on her smock and is absorbed for a few minutes in fingering it (using only her index finger). She now returns to gentle motions with the middle finger of her right hand, making straight, fairly short lines from the top to the bottom—but not over the whole width of the paper. She calls to Miss C, "Come look at my design. See I've made some bananas for you." Milly's posture throughout was erect. She merely bent her head to look and moved her arms and hands.

In the case of a child like Milly, the alert teacher might encourage conversation about the finger-paint and even participate in the activity, saying, "Isn't it fun to mess this around?" or "My, my paint feels good," or "Doesn't it remind you of something? It reminds me of butter"—(or some other innocuous substance). This could easily lead the child to state her resentment in words, and perhaps reduce overt attacks by reinforcing verbal expression of hostility. It would be essential, of course, for the teacher to be able to accept understandingly any free expression of resentment or interest in body products.

Meaning

On the whole, very few overt indications of fantasy occur in our records. All authors who have referred to the fantasy-releasing qualities of finger-paint had developed a warm, accepting, personal relationship with the child and had stimulated him to talk about his products. These two conditions, which seem to be necessary for the communication of fantasy through finger-paint, are seldom present in a single classroom session. In our own records, the few faint traces of thought processes that did emerge were not followed up and no effort was made to discover their meaning. In one instance we found Jules, a three-and-one-half year-old boy, incising three human forms in red, saying "That's my mother, my father, and Mike." (The identity of Mike is obscure.) Then he asked for some more red paint, and as the teacher poured it over one of his figures, he protested, "No, not on my mommy." He followed this by wiping out the figures himself, saying, "My mommy all gone, my daddy all gone." Then he began to trace similar patterns, explaining that he was making his mommy, and naming parts of her anatomy as they appeared. After that he said, "There is my daddy in big feet." This child was very spontaneous but seemed particularly infantile and had difficulty in accepting school routines. He needed an unusual amount of reassurance about the separation from his parents when he first came to nursery school, and whenever he was disturbed he would ask for his mother. It may very well be that drawing his mother was a form of reassurance. This is especially likely since the drawing came after a period of very messy handling of the finger-paints during which he over-painted green with red, and red with black. The act of wiping out the first figures may be variously interpreted, but in this instance it did not seem to indicate a hostility.

One gains the impression that Jules relied on the support of his mother to overcome his infantile impulsive behavior— which was perhaps represented by his smearing at the beginning of the session.

In a record cited earlier in this chapter, three-year-old Connie, using red finger-paint, announced that she was making "a big, big, bathroom" and quickly followed this by making a "track." Later she referred to the red paint on her hands as "blood" and seemed preoccupied with that idea, but rather gaily so. This combination of events suggests some connection in her mind, but exactly what it could be can not be determined without further investigation. However, sequences of this sort sometimes suggest symbolic meanings rather clearly. Just before one session, a lad named Phil indulged in a boasting jag, insisting that he was bigger and older than anybody else, and that the toy cars he was playing with were bigger. When he began to finger-paint, he first outlined his hands in the paint, then made an ocean liner with five decks. As he was working on it he said, "Wow! It's up to the sky. It's almost to the top of the sky." This was followed by a "fish" and finally by a "doubledecker bus." The connection between the boy's talk about being big and his insistence on making "big" objects out of the same substance in which he first made an impression of himself— that is, his hand—seems fairly obvious.

We must emphasize, however, that the meaning of a finger-paint product is essentially private and personal, not to be derived except through the verbally expressed association of each child. One little boy took particular delight in mixing different colors to make brown. Said he, "Look at my hands. My hands are brown—I don't like the smell much." A special interest in anal processes suggests itself immediately. However, he followed these remarks by, "This is frosting color," and later, "I don't care if I have paint on my face, I'll wash it off when I get home." These later remarks cast considerable doubt on the first interpretation.

Color and Form

Almost all the children observed (approximately 40) mixed the colors in a smeary fashion. Most of them wanted some of each available color, and they swooshed them together with great delight, later adding several colors separately. Occasionally a child would begin to work in one color, then add a second and a third, in each case spreading the mixture completely over the paper before adding to it. We could not find any special pattern of needs or behavior to distinguish the children who used one color from those who mixed several together. Only three in the whole group used several colors separately on the same sheet. The manner of approach, the extent to which the hands, fingers, and body were used, the vigor and types of movement, seemed more revealing than the choice of color in most instances.

The combination of color choice and type of stroke seemed to offer a more valid clue to the child's inner state than any one factor alone. Thus, while all the children used dark colors and black at times, the anxious ones used them more frequently and had a greater tendency to use their fingers for making lines, hooklike markings, and cramped curves. It seems clear, too, that outstandingly well-adjusted children tend to experiment with a large range of colors and work in broad rhythmic sweeps—although the latter factor may also be related to the level of development since the true rhythmic sweep does not emerge until about the fifth year.

By and large, the children seemed more interested in having plenty of material and several colors to mix than they were in pattern, form, or final color effect. Interest in form was almost completely confined to lines traced in the paint with fingers, nails, or sticks—only one child indicated appreciation of the undulations and shading of his strokes. These patterns were, in general, of the same abstract variety that one finds in the easel painting of preschool children. To relate them to personality organization or emotional status, it would be necessary to make continuous sketches or photographs as the finger-painting goes on, since the final production cannot represent the whole rich sequence. To show how much material is concealed by the final product—and how much is revealed by observing an entire sequence—we should like to present sketches based on a record of Tanya, a four-year-old girl, made during one finger-paint session. The report accompanying the figures notes that the little girl sat quietly at a table of noisy children, waiting for the material. When a red blob was dropped on her paper she began to stir it slowly with her hand to form the patterns in *a* and *b* on page 294. The rest of the designs were made sometimes with one hand, sometimes with both, often with the index finger only. Movements were careful and usually tense but she seemed to enjoy smearing her hands with paint and rubbing out the designs. Her concentration span was unusually long and she remained on after the entire group had left the table. The observer comments, "Tanya derived an extraordinary amount of satisfaction from this medium, and noticeable release of tension."

A glance at these drawings reveals a remarkably even succession of inward moving, curved forms, and assertive straight lines or jagged angles, as well as a repeated splitting of the page into two halves or four quarters. One might suspect that this child is rather constricted in her approach to life, due to a conflict between aggressive outward movement and protective withdrawal. This is reinforced by an examination of her easel paintings, which show the same duality. Her behavior in the group bears out this hypothesis; she is described as "quiet, but there's a lot pent up," and as a "lone wolf" who is extremely neat and conforming but at times assertive and

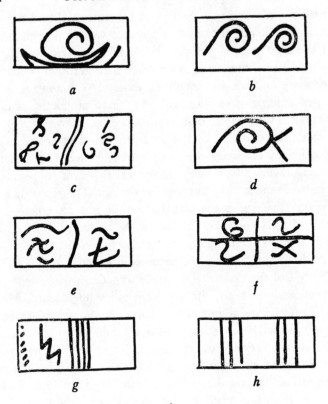

SKETCHES OF TANYA'S FINGER-PAINTING

aggressive toward other children. Her home situation, however, suggested a more specific and illuminating interpretation.
We find that Tanya has a six-year-old sister but is the favorite
child of her father, an overanxious and ambitious man, who
is home all the time because of illness. It may very well be
that she is representing her family situation by splitting the
paper repeatedly into four segments, with three containing
rounded symbols and one a straight line pattern. Similarly
she may be indicating her emotional isolation from the other
children and her aggressive tensions by the succession of spiral

and jagged angles. These ideas are, we realize, still in the realm of conjecture. However, it does seem likely from the care and absorption with which Tanya works that she is attempting to express matters that are of deep significance to her. An interested teacher might well use this opportunity to encourage such a child to talk and thereby gain more insight into her difficulties in the group.

Implications and Suggestions

This brings us to some implications of our finger-paint observations. Since the principal gratification lies in sensory experiences, including the chance to smear and be messy, we raise the question whether the usual method of presenting finger-paints and the usual procedure of preserving the end products are appropriate for these youngsters. Why insist on designating the last phase of the experience as a "picture" when it is not an attempt at art and is actually the least important part of the process to the child? When the teacher shows so much interest in these dried paint masses, she may be indicating that she is not sensitive to his own values in the experience, and at the same time, may be rather subtly indoctrinating him with a philosophy which endows only externals with positive values.

There seems little doubt that finger-paints are close relatives of mud pies and that the kind of sensory immersion we have observed could also be served by cold cream, mud, or the white base which is used in the preparation of the paints. In fact, mud was actually substituted for finger-paint among the younger children in one school. However, the children's usual desire to have some of each color available seems to indicate that the visual experience is an additional stimulation. We strongly recommend not only that many colors be available, but also that the children frequently be permitted to take them from the containers and use as many as they wish at one time. We also recommend greater leeway in the net amount of paint they can use, since each addition seems to give new impetus. Furthermore, when a child appears to be absorbed in the feel of the material, it might be well to offer him a small pan in which to mess. Preferably, such a pan should be on hand at all times for the overflow of paint. Also, for children whose primary interest is smearing, we suggest white oilcloth in place of the usual coated paper, since it can be washed off and used again. This would reduce the cost and encourage the teacher to think of finger-painting as simple enjoyable activity rather than art work.

It is not to be assumed from these remarks that none of the children appreciated the aesthetic aspects of finger-painting. Some of our younger but more advanced children showed considerable response to color mixtures and some of the older children produced forms of great artistic appeal. As a matter of fact, there were indications in several of the records that response to finger-paints could be expected to follow a general sequence, starting with delight in feeling the substance and some joy in indiscriminate color mixing and smearing, going on to experimentation with patterns, and finally developing into an appreciative exploration of both the form and color potentials of the material. For the children who have reached this stage of development, it would be wise to continue the present system of using sheets of coated paper which can be preserved. They should, however, be free to ask for new sheets and to indicate when they are ready to leave the activity.

The optimal method of using finger-paints would then provide for those who need an opportunity just to mess, for those whose pleasurable experience lies in kinesthetic and tactual sensation, and for those who are ready to express themselves aesthetically. This would mean offering a free choice of paper, oilcloth, and a shallow pan. But it would also require great tolerance on the part of the teacher and sharpened awareness of both the need the child brings to the experience and the kind of gratification he is extracting from it. When finger-paints are presented without the usual limitations, they offer the child a new world to explore and a unique opportunity not only for self-expression but also for self-discovery. As a consequence we believe he will become a freer and richer person.

CHAPTER IX

Music and Movement: Fruitful Combination

CO-AUTHOR OF THIS CHAPTER: MRS. ELLEN SCHINDEL

IN THIS CHAPTER we shall be discussing music together with movement executed to its accompaniment. Many specialists in the field of both the dance and musical education believe that the two are inseparable when working with young children, and our own investigations have lent support to this point of view. In this part of our project we have asked, as always, what peculiar advantages, what benefits and values the medium has to contribute to the process of healthy growth, and· we have discovered that the list is a long and impressive one.

The immense potential of this combined medium has been recognized by a number of specialists in child development and in psychotherapy, particularly Bender and Boas, Lowenfeld, Altshuler, and Coriat. As a background to our own discussion it will be useful to mention the specific contributions that have impressed them most. First, it affords release from crippling impulses by stimulating primitive and infantile movements and attitudes, by relieving instinctual tensions and expressing "shapeless emotion," and by evoking deeply buried fantasies. When one recalls the manifold limitations of the crib, play pen, and carriage, as well as the constant insistence on order and cleanliness in most households, the need for so many avenues of release becomes more than clear.

The specialists find that music and movement make a second contribution in helping the child sublimate aggressive and destructive urges and channelize disorganized energy in socially accepted ways. Third, the effect of releasing emotion and achieving order and self-control through rhythm is to give the child "harmonious contact with himself," and through this, increased integration of body and mind and enhanced self-acceptance. These benefits may, in turn, account for the value of musical experiences in promoting participation, adaptation to others, and social growth. Finally, the teacher can often find in the child's movements and comments, and the roles he chooses in the dramatization of music, a wealth of clues to his innermost thoughts and feelings.

When we turn to recent literature that deals with the educator's concepts of what music and movement can offer children, we find a more limited approach to the subject. For the most part the major emphasis is on the achievement of skills; the psychological implications and the wealth of experiences are hardly mentioned. Two exceptions to the general emphasis may be noted. Sheehy stresses the importance of permitting a child to express himself musically in his own way to give him a feeling of respect for his own expression. Buttolph[1] claims that music should have its place in everyday living, and points out that all children are capable of a joyous response to it, and that out of their constant "calls and shouts, stamps and jumps, walks and runs, bendings and swayings, our great symphonies and modern dance forms have developed." With more widespread recognition of this point of view, the traditional gap between the educator's orientation and that of the psychologist may well be bridged.

With our awareness sharpened by the ideas just outlined, we have analyzed the records of 144 children taken while they were participating in some kind of musical experience. The observations were made in 21 different groups, at 13 different preschool centers. In addition, we also surveyed common procedures in the use of music and conferred with the teachers of the groups involved to discover their views on the significance of the musical experience.

In analyzing the records we were interested in the following questions: How, in general, do the children use experience with music in their growth and self-adjustment efforts? What special values does it have for children of given behavior patterns—aggressive, inhibited, anxious, etc.? How much do musical experiences further group integration? What *unique* values does music have that other materials or activities do not have? Above all, we were interested in the extent to which teachers are aware of the possibilities offered by music for helping children individually and in groups to work out some of their adjustment problems.

Common Types of Musical Periods

We found that the musical experiences in preschool situations fall into four general categories: (1) The most common is called "rhythms." During these periods music is played by the teacher on an instrument such as a piano or a drum, or by means of a phonograph, and the children are encouraged to respond in some overt fashion. Some teachers permit them freedom in interpreting the music by means of movements, but far more often they are told what to do as the music plays either by a hint or a direct suggestion from the teacher. Even when phonograph records are used, a narrator often suggests appropriate movements. There is remarkably little variation in the musical selections, especially when phonograph records are used. (2) A frequent, often daily, practice is to have children listen to phonograph records. The records used are about equally divided among instrumental selections, children's songs, and stories told to a musical accompaniment. In most instances the children are requested to remain seated and quiet as they listen. Occasionally they are permitted to sing with the record, but they are not expected to move around at this time. Sometimes they operate the machine and choose the records; this provides the most spontaneous of all the "listening" experiences. (3) Group singing is also very popular, either as an integral part of the music program or occurring more spontaneously—introduced by the teachers, for example, when they want to keep a group together during a waiting period. Occasionally the children are encouraged to accompany these songs with rhythmical, interpretive actions. Usually these are the prescribed, customary movements accompanying folk songs such as "The Farmer in the Dell." Very often no bodily movement of significant proportions is permitted during group singing. (4) The most frequently encountered procedure is to have children play music on simple instruments. They take turns in using drums, triangles, tambourines, and cymbals, etc., which they are asked to beat in time to a piano accompaniment or a teacher's or a child's signal.

The most outstanding characteristic of these musical experiences is the amount of control and direction involved. Teachers who would not dream of telling a child how to paint do not hesitate to describe the exact type of movement to be used to accompany musical phrases. Perhaps the greatest lack of opportunity for creative effort in the whole preschool program was observed during the so-called "music periods." For the most part, then, music seemed to be imposed rather than evoked, and little or no teacher participation in the movement aspect of the experience was noted. "Quiet periods" almost always brought forth disciplinary measures. "Active periods," during which children were permitted to move around, were much more successful, even when they were executed under the complete control of the teacher. The following records of "passive" and "active" periods suggest the differences the children find in these experiences.

Passive Period. The children were very noisy. The teacher told them that when they were ready she would play the record for them; it was a record that they would have to listen to. When they were quiet she put the record on. . . . The children were noisy again and were not listening to the record. "Shall we turn it off?" the teacher asked. . . . The children were very restless. They got up and down, talked to each other, and giggled.

Active Period—Controlled. The teacher, seated at the piano with the group standing around her, says, "Mark time." Terry and Moira mark time. The music stops and one child says, "Do it with one foot." The teacher plays music as the group marks time with one foot. As the teacher stops playing, Terry says, "Do it on your toes," and the teacher plays skipping music. The group starts to skip around the room, except for Moira and Terry, who stand on tiptoes holding hands. The teacher says, "When we finish, Terry." She stops the skipping music, and tells the group to walk on their toes. They do. Terry and Moira walk around on tiptoes, holding hands. The teacher then says, "Doris wants to dance," and starts to play music. Terry turns around in small circles on her tiptoes, as does Moira. Terry, however, has her hands at her sides until she sees Moira turning around with arms outstretched, whereupon Terry stretches her arms. The music increases in tempo and both girls continue to keep time, spinning faster and faster. They both end on the floor, dizzy, as the music stops. Throughout the rhythm activity both girls kept time to the music perfectly.

Active Period—Spontaneous. "What would you like to hear?" asked the teacher. "The Magic Record," said a few children. During the record there was general conversation. At Roy's request they had to hear the Geni drink his milk again. During the circus part Roy and Johnnie ran around fast. Roy was smiling. Frank and Sarah joined them. They all showed with their hands the shortest and the tallest man, in time with the record. Roy and Johnnie got on their hands and knees and pretended that they were lions; they roared like lions also. Then they were cats. Toby and Alice clapped hands and ran around. Alice, Frank, Toby, and Sarah ran around the room lightly. Frank started to crawl around and then Alice followed him.

Teachers' Evaluation of Musical Experiences

When discussing the values music has for children, individually and in groups, the teachers gave the following reasons for offering it:

I never use music to calm children down; on the contrary, I use it after rest, to follow the quiet time with the more active rhythms.

On rainy days we use music to help children calm down.

Music helps the children by bringing them into the group as they recognize melodies.

Children are more relaxed after music.

Rhythms are popular; children like to march.

All our children enjoy rhythms.

Music has helped some children physically and helped their coordination; it has also been an opportunity to make up songs about things.

When children realized there was no pressure involved at music, they liked it better.

There are some children who can't enjoy music and never do, but those who do participate like it.

By and large, the thing that stands out about these statements, is the teachers' appreciation of the children's enjoyment of the activity. However, it is striking that the reasons given by any one teacher for the use of music were rather fragmentary. Although some had noticed the effect of the musical experiences, none seemed aware of the variety of effects possible. Unfortunately, also, many seemed to assume that a child's nonparticipation or inability to enjoy music was simply a characteristic to be expected, something in the nature of a constitutional defect. When we remember, however, that most of the musical periods involved a consistent and sustained conformity which was not demanded in any other aspect of preschool living, we can understand the reluctance of some children to participate. For example, one teacher repeatedly called her group together to make sure that all those doing rhythms do the same thing; another removed a three-year-old boy from her group bodily when he deviated from her instructions, remarking, "You can play again if you do what I say."

There is no question about the primary appeal of music to children when it is not complicated and vitiated by adult impositions and demands. The following records were chosen almost at random as exemplifying the happy, exuberant participation so often to be seen in active music periods.

Record of Amelia. Amelia runs into the music room, gallops four steps, hops around. Then the music starts; she, Elsie, and Kitty form a trio. Amelia gallops with one knee stiff. She runs over to Linda, "You like to dance, Linda?" She gallops back to Kitty and Elsie and grins gaily. She uses the entire floor space to run around. She bounces up and down to the new music and shakes her hand like a rag doll. She smiles at the assistant as she lies on the floor ready for the scissors exercise. Her body is relaxed but she is alert and looks around to see whether she has left enough room. She moves over, and starts to do the scissors with well-coordinated arm and leg movements. In bicycle riding she bends her elbows as if grasping handle bars. She kicks the floor when pretending to be a drum. When the game of horses begins, Amelia runs to Elsie and the two play together, leading the others. When the group forms for singing, she runs over to sit between Elsie and Kitty. She remembers the words and music of the songs very well. Elsie places her hand affectionately on Amelia's thigh, as she sits comfortably cross-legged. Amelia says suddenly to Elsie, "Let me kiss you." She kisses her. Teacher asks for suggestions for new words for an action song, and Amelia offers "Spank your sides," which is accepted enthusiastically. The teacher picks up Amelia and hugs her. Amelia runs across the room and out.

Record of Jory. Someone starts to play a record, "Sunshine." Jory smiles, walks exactly in step with the rhythm, and is the first one in line. He stops, and now the children are all rolling over. Jory rolls much better than the others; he laughs, swings, sings the words, and is completely masterful in all his movements. I never saw a child change so completely the moment the music started to play and he could move and express himself as he listened to the words—"Now the grass is deep and soft"—and "while you are resting." He is absolutely absorbed and lies and moves in a dreamy lazy way, stretching his arms, closing his eyes, and getting up very slowly. Then during "bicycle riding" he is very active, performing with quick exact movements; he seems completely happy.

Record of Zita in Free Rhythms. Zita jumps up with the other children when the teacher begins to play a lively tune. She follows Margaret, running around and around the teacher, who is sitting in a chair. They follow the music well for three-and four-year-olds. They run and run. The music stops and the teacher says, "Rest now." The children either sit or lie down on the cement. There is much hard breathing and quiet laughter. The teacher plays soft, low music while the children rest.

The music changes to lively dance music. Several children jump up, sway, and twirl in time to the music. Margaret and Zita are facing one another; they dance forward and backward, swaying and keeping very good rhythm. They have happy smiling faces. Margaret turns and prances around and around the teacher. Zita follows along behind her, imitating her movements.

Special Values for Specific Kinds of Children

OVERACTIVE AND AGGRESSIVE CHILDREN

Sensitive teachers have noticed that well-guided musical experiences have several salutary effects on hyperactive and hostile, aggressive children. They tend to be soothed, relaxed, and less tense; their interest is challenged and they want to explore their own abilities in relation to the music; they have an opportunity for channeling explosive behavior; and finally, through the use of dramatic roles, the emotions underlying their behavior can be given a socially acceptable form.

In our records, it was noticeable that the most disturbed children were frequently those who reacted most sensitively. It was also striking that the effects were quite different for different children, although in almost all the cases they operated in a desirable direction.

As one illustration of the rather subtle effects of music on a disturbed child, we should like to present a few excerpts from the record of Bud, a three-and-one-half-year-old boy. His mother had placed him in his preschool group because, as she confessed, she could no longer handle him. At the Center he was overactive and aggressive, in constant conflict with the other children, at odds with routine, and often destructive with materials. The first record gives a fairly typical picture of Bud's usual day at school.

Bud is drawing when the boys make clanging noises with the train they have made. Hears, "All aboard! Let's go!" and rushes over with his drawing and his can of crayons. The boys tell him he cannot get on because the train is full of coal, and he stands there saying, "No, it isn't. The coal is at home." He says, "Clang, clang," with the rest of the boys as they go off on the train. The motorman says, "You can't go," and pushes Bud away. Bud pushes him, and the whole train collapses. The motorman lies so still on the floor that Bud is frightened. Then he says defiantly, "Well, you did something to me." Liza comes to look for crayons. By this time although Bud is still holding the can, the crayons are all over the floor, some of them broken. The teacher says, "Who brought these here?" "Bud did! Bud did!" everyone choruses, and Bud looks very guilty and doesn't say anything. He is now straddling the train all by himself. . . .

The following record of Bud at music was taken on the same day. Notice how relaxed he seems as he watches the rather violent reactions of the other children, and how quickly and cooperatively he responds to the teacher's challenge about being a "good horsie."

The teacher has brought her accordion. Bud has not left the phonograph or made a sound during the entire half hour of listening. He is sitting on the table, swinging one leg as he watches the group almost going wild as they listen to various rhythms. . . . The teacher says, "I'll bet Bud would make a good horsie." Although he has apparently been dreaming, with a far-off gaze, he almost falls off the table in his eagerness, throwing himself on the floor on all fours and progressing noisily and bumpily in a sort of strenuous hop. He moves to the far end of the room, instead of heading for the other children. Following his example and the music, all the others become horses. Then some of them take riders. Bud is the willing horse of Liza, moving energetically and quickly on hands and knees until he collapses from weariness. By this time everyone else is tired, too, and someone suggests "Rockabye, Baby." The teacher takes Jack's hands and swings his arms back and forth to the song. Watching them, Bud looks about eagerly for a partner. He goes to one boy and says, "You want to rock?" and without waiting for an answer, he grabs him and says force-fully, "Rock, play rockabye." He seems clumsy and has a rhythm all his own, not related to the music, but enjoys himself in this quieting manner.

The relaxation that music induces in tense children some-times frees them from preoccupation with themselves and opens the way to participation in the group. Neil, the boy in the next two records, was also brought to the preschool center because his parents could not deal with him. He was five years old when he entered, extremely aggressive and over-active and often distraught and destructive. In addition, he spoke only Spanish in a group where no one else could speak it. The first indication of kinship with other youngsters came when he wanted to join groups of elementary school children who sometimes had musical games near the quarters of the Center. The following excerpt shows him joining one such group.

Record 1. Neil went to the door, looked out, evidently saw something which interested him and disappeared. The observer went after him and saw him run to some children who were skipping around in a circle to the sound of music from a piano which was being played by one of the teachers. He still had the lady's shoes on and had four or five fingers in his mouth as he tried to imitate the others ("shake, shake—I turn myself around"). He squatted, jumped, and ran to the music; finding the shoes an impediment, he ran to the corner, took them off, and went back to the group.

Later on, when he was with his own group in a musically centered activity, he seemed to comprehend what was going on and could perform as others were performing. This was not the first time we found that foreign-speaking as well as nonspeaking children responded to the stimulation of the music.

Record 2. The teacher played the "Fire Engine" song. Neil and Paul were on the floor keeping time to the music very well. The teacher told them to sit down. They sat for a minute then Paul got up and ran around in a wide circle. Neil joined him and then they jumped in circles. Paul started all the motion and then Neil would try to copy him. . . .

The sense of well-being derived from musical stimuli often has a beneficial effect on unhappy children. Benny, described as a very aggressive three-and-one-half-year old, seemed unable to participate peacefully in any other activity. Though ordinarily "never still for a moment" he is able to show sustained interest for an entire half hour, and though at other times he teased and annoyed his groupmates, he now kisses another boy and ignores two teasing attacks made on him. Note that his keenest enjoyment is shown when he is permitted to behave spontaneously, as in skipping to the waltz music.

The teacher now returns, and Benny immediately asks her for "Genie, the Magic Record." He squats on his small chair, toes hanging out behind, and leans far over the table to see the mechanism. As the song begins, Benny and all the others sing loud and clear. . . . He sways his head to the rhythm of the song and a far-away daydream look comes over him. He turns his head and sees Donnie next to him, leans over impulsively and in a generally buoyant mood, and kisses him. He throws an arm over the child's shoulder, as if to move closer for a better advantage. . . . As the record ends, other children get up and go off to play, and only Benny and Donnie are left, sitting side by side. Benny's body is completely relaxed; he sits on his haunches and lets his mouth drop half open. . . . He turns back slowly to the table and sees one little girl waving a paper jacket for a Victrola record toward him. She leans over and quite deliberately pokes him in the face with it, giggling. He pays little attention until she slaps his face with the paper. At this he grabs the paper jacket, manages to get it away from her without tearing it, and announces that it is his turn to choose. He repeats firmly that he wants "Genie, the Magic Record."

Now he sits back on one foot, watching the teacher put it on. He is very quiet now, completely at rest. The song comes to a part suggesting that the listener dance. The other children do so, as if they are used to this part and like it. Benny leaps from his chair so swiftly one can scarcely imagine he was ever in it, and dances with considerable fluent abandon. He skips and sways to the waltz rhythm, covering more floor space around the room than most of the children. He waves his arms over his head, and his whole body takes part in the action.

The dance stops and another part of the record begins, and as quickly as he had left his chair, Benny returns, sits down, and assumes the former quiet immobility as if he had never been active at all. As the record continues he participates by clapping in rhythm or singing "London Bridge"; sometimes he just stares into space—yet he has an intent look on his face throughout.

Free musical periods give energetic youngsters a much needed chance to "throw their weight about," to use their bodies vigorously, to experience the delight of muscles moving smoothly. Even ordinary ground games executed to music can offer this release. Tuffie, a four-year-old youngster who was usually in trouble with someone, found in some of the school music periods an opportunity to be "wild" in a constructive fashion without infringing on the rights of others. The next two records show him in action—with and without musical accompaniment.

Record 1. Tuffie was running and scuffling and sliding up and down on the floor. He was waving his hands and grinning happily, making a lot of noise with his shoes. . . . The teacher says crossly, "Tuffie, I don't want you to do that anymore." He took two more flying leaps, at the same time yelling, "Yippee," in a loud shrill voice. He glanced teasingly at the teacher. Noting her stern expression, before she could reprimand him he ran to the other side of the room where Millie and Bob were.

Record 2. A new record was going to be played. "Shall we listen to the engine or the horses?" asked the teacher. "I want to ask for the horses," Tuffie exclaimed breathlessly, jumping up. "O.K., sit down and we'll listen to the horses." He ran to his seat with short hopping runs and sat forward in his chair, flipping his lower lip with his right three middle fingers and making the sound "Blub, blub," until the record started to play. Then he immediately jumped up from his chair, stood erect with his left foot forward, shaking his hands in time to the music. Anticipating the words of the record, he lay down on his tummy and began to crawl. "We are going to listen first, Tuffie," said the teacher pleasantly. He jumped up quickly and obediently sat down. He began to stamp his feet impatiently, his right hand beating time to the music. When the record was finished, Tuffie immediately jumped from his seat, throwing the chair over in his excitement. He stooped and picked it up and thrust it under the table carelessly. When the record was played again he became a horse and was the first one to start the action. He alertly lifted his feet high and jumped around, his hands flying in the air, yelling, "I am the horses." Before this action was completed on the record, he lay down to sleep. He lay on his tummy, his arms bent, and his face resting on his folded arms. He slept very quietly, not moving a muscle. Once again before the activity on the record changed, he jumped up abruptly and became a horse in the forest. "Bzzz, Bzzz, Bzzz," he yelled, running with quick lively steps into the forest. Suddenly he became a fish, hurling himself to the floor on his tummy and crawling vigorously, waving his arms and bending his legs. As soon as the record was finished he ran to a wheelbarrow.

Music-making as well as movement to music may offer an outlet for the children who need to "let off steam." For Benny, a boy whom we have already met, the beating of a drum seems allied to the satisfaction of whirling in a dance. Since he shared a one-room apartment with his parents and often found it hard to stay within the boundaries of his group room, his desire to "let go" is more than understandable. His attempt to reduce his vigorous drumming to a rhythmic form which followed the piano melody is a clear example of the way music can help children impose order on the expression of their chaotic feelings.

Benny started to beat on his drum vigorously as soon as he got it. He half clenched his teeth and had an aggressive glee-ful look on his face. He stamped his feet alternately as he beat. The teacher began to play a simple rhythm on the piano with a slow regular beat. Benny picked up the rhythm almost immediately, keeping in time but seeming to have a hard time holding himself down to the slow rhythm; a determined smile was on his face.

The next rhythm was faster and he got away from the time completely, beating madly on the drum as rapidly as he could. The teacher suggested that they have a parade. Benny joined in enthusiastically, walking around beating wildly as the line was becoming organized. When the teacher asked for quiet, Benny said very vigorously, "Shhhhh!" As the parade started, he was at the end of the single line. He ran ahead for a moment and got in front, but almost immediately he circled around and got back at the end, following along beating time and marching with vigorous stamping steps in time with his beating. In a moment the parade speeded up. Benny speeded up even faster than the others, stamping, then running; he had a grim aggressive smile on his face, and his teeth were clenched. The parade broke up in general chaos, Benny joining the others in beating madly on his drum. The teacher then started a very slow rhythm. Benny kept in rhythm with the piano most of the time, but occasionally broke loose and put in three or four extra very vigorous beats. He looked up and watched the teacher intently as she played, swaying his body in time; then he joined another mad drumming as all the children made as much noise as they could and the rhythm broke up. During this noise the teacher started again to play slowly and Benny tried to get into rhythm with her, even though many of the other children were still beating madly and paying no attention to the piano.

Music can help children perform difficult feats of self-control at times. While responding to the musical stimuli, immature, impulsive youngsters often behave in a comparatively mature fashion, accepting frustrations and maintaining themselves under circumstances which are hard for them to sustain at other times. To illustrate this point, we offer the following record of Hal, an anxious and often aggressive three-year-old who was considered by his teachers to be "infantile." Notice his spontaneous recovery from his first angry reaction, and his later acceptance of necessary control.

Hal went immediately to the phonograph and started to turn the handle. The teacher said, "Don't do that, Hal. . . ." He remained by the record-player. The teacher said, "Sit down, Hal, and listen with the other children." He sat down whining, "I can't see." He poked his mouth out and pushed himself far away from the group and pouted, then said angrily, "I'm going to tell my daddy." (The other children were enjoying themselves immensely.) He stuck his tongue out at any who looked at him. No one said anything to him. He inched slowly back to the group. . . . He jumped up off the floor, got a chair, placed it beside the phonograph, and began to clap his hands to the music like the others. He sang "Ding, dong, ding, dong," opening his mouth wide. The teacher put another record on. It began with "Ouch." He jumped up laughing and said, "Do that again." The teacher stopped the record and started it again. All the children laughed and repeated joyfully, "Ouch." The children asked for it again and the teacher said, "Now this is the last time, children. . . ." Hal worked his mouth to the music and clapped his hands. The music stopped, he stood up, pointed to "Three Blind Mice," and said, "I want to hear that." The teacher played it. He sang the song, nodding his head to each word. He stopped abruptly, scratched his leg, and talked to Karen again. The teacher stopped. the music and looked at them. Hal said, softly, "Teacher, we'll be quiet." She played "Humpty, Dumpty." He sang, lifting his feet up and down to the music.

STIMULATING THE INHIBITED CHILD

A certain number of children who lack previous social experience with their peers cause their teachers considerable concern because of their apparent lack of interest, timidity, and general inhibition. Sometimes they manifest no perceptible interest in any materials or activities for months on end, but spend their time sitting and staring vacantly before them, wandering about or following the teachers. A few show more serious symptoms such as mutism, echolalia, grimacing, and unprovoked silly laughter. Teachers who have used music and movement in a spontaneous fashion, participating with the inhibited children, report that their interest is generally aroused and their behavior more focused. The less seriously disturbed children respond to an even greater degree; the intrinsic fascination of the activity seems to help them forget themselves long enough to become absorbed in what is going on about them.

It is not always easy for a teacher to recognize an individual child's response to the music hour when she is occupied with ten or fifteen others. This is especially true in the case of these underactive children because their responses tend to be on a subdued and muted level in the beginning. The excerpt below is fairly representative of the early behavior of an anxious and inhibited child in the music situation. Freddie, the little boy in question, was three and one half years old when the record was taken. Ordinarily, he seemed bewildered by the group and spent most of his time sitting close to one of the teachers and doing nothing. Here we see him participating, although at a minimum level.

Freddie is sitting with five children in a group near the piano. The rest have musical instruments and are marching. Freddie has a drum which he beats occasionally. Instruments are put aside and Freddie sits in his chair as most of the others do rhythms. He watches, swings his feet, and smiles when Frankie and Paul tumble over. He pats his knees as music is played, gets up from the chair and goes to a table nearby, and then comes back to his chair. The teacher calls the group together and suggests that they all do the same thing. Freddie kneels in his chair and smiles as he watches them skate, skip, and march. He puts one foot on the floor and the other knee on his chair, moves back to a kneeling position, and then stands as the other children do lively rhythms.

Some children who drift about the periphery of the group most of the time can do things *with* the group when stimulated by the musical experience. Donnie was one such child. At three years of age he spent his days pretending he was a lion, crawling about, and growling at the world. At the time of this record he seemed to be completely isolated, apparently absorbed in solitary play. The music period described below is obviously a rather uncreative and controlled period, but even so, Donnie performs with more zest and spontaneity than he ordinarily shows.

. . . . The group all sit together in a line of chairs against the wall. Donnie doesn't join the others and says, "I'm the teacher, I'm going to sit *here*." "Here" is next to the victrola. The teacher tells him to sit somewhere else, then he protests with, "I wanta put the record on dere." His voice has a whining quality as he asks this, and he looks dejected as the teacher refuses. Then he sits down and listens to Terry who is singing, "I Love My Rooster." He is much absorbed. Taking the lead from the others, he shrieks with glee at the parts the group laugh at and listens quietly to the rest of the record.

Donnie is chosen by the teacher to go into the middle of the room and follow what the record says. First he "walks" in a circle and as he walks in good time to the music, he holds his head up a little self-consciously, and rather erectly and proudly. Then the record and music tell him to "run," which he does, but not with much speed or exertion. Then he is told to "roll on the grass" which he does in a very relaxed and limp fashion. He gets up and yawns. Then he is told to "jump," then to "swing," which he does with a little more vigor than he showed in running. His part is over so he returns to his chair, is told how good he was, looks pleased, and sits with his hands folded; however, he seems much more awake and interested than before and watches the others.

Even a routine music period works magic for some children. Molly, a five-year-old, was described as timid, solitary, overly "good," adult-oriented, and unspontaneous. Her responses to listening to music were in line with this characterization, but observe her reaction when she was able to do something in relation to it.

Record 1. The teacher instructs the children to sing softly when they sing about the sled coming and to sing louder and louder as it gets near. Molly kneels on the floor and holds her ankles. The children are singing and when they begin to sing loudly, she continues singing in the same tone. The teacher gets the toy instruments. Molly, "I'll play the bells." She puts the bells on her wrists and shakes them, smiling at Patsy. The teacher plays "Jingle Bells" on the piano as the children begin to sing. The teacher says, "Now bells. . . . Good, Molly!" Molly swings her hands in and out, "Like this?" She shakes her wrists up and down vigorously. The teacher plays the piano once more and tells the children only to sing this time. Molly sings along. Teacher: "Now jingle bells, play with me." Molly swings her arms out and in with lips slightly parted.

She now slaps her hands on her knees to make the bells ring, then claps her hands, and shakes her wrists once more. The music ends.

Record 2. The teacher plays the piano and tells all the children that they are to be rag dolls now. They all stretch themselves out on the floor. Teacher: "Molly, you're a wonderful rag doll. [To all children] Stand on your toes now. Try and touch the ceiling every time I play a loud chord." All the children comply. . . . Teacher: "This is marching and clapping. Who would like to march and clap?" Children: "Me, me." Molly leads Angus, Rita, and Wilfred around the chairs then in a circle in the middle of the floor. They march and clap as they go. The music stops. Teacher: "Now who would like to skip and clap?" Molly skips quite vigorously with open mouth and tongue in cheek. The music stops and they gather around the piano once more.

Music and Social Integration

It is common observation that children who are disorganized and aggressive or timid and withdrawn have as great difficulty in gaining acceptance as group members as they have in coming to terms with themselves. The tense, subdued child behaves as if an approach to the group is quite beyond his capacities, as if he has not the energy to initiate nor the power to sustain group contacts. The anxiously aggressive and hostile child, on the other hand, although he breaks into the group and makes contacts with other children very frequently, rarely finds himself accepted because of his threatening and unpredictable behavior. It is interesting and instructive to observe that music serves these two kinds of children quite differently. The shy, withdrawn child seems to have more vigor, more power, more ability to maintain contacts during music; the aggressive child finds in it a challenge to the exploration of his abilities and the mastery of his own movements, as well as an integrating agent that calms his anxieties and opens the way to constructive relationships.

As the children come into the room they grab for drums, cymbals, and a tambourine. Jennifer does also but fails to get anything, then says, "I don't want any." She stands and watches a boy march and beat a drum to a rhythmic record. The other children are sitting on a bench clapping hands to the rhythm, but she stands on the other side of the room. They march to the tune of "Yankee Doodle," which the teacher is humming. But Jennifer just stands around, occasionally putting her finger in her mouth and half watching. The different moods of the music do not seem to affect her at all, but her fingers are always moving. She handles the instruments but does not attempt to play them. Then she invents some game of her own which consists of climbing on a table and jumping down from it, apparently oblivious to what the others are doing and to the music. The group then plays a game called the "Squirrel Game" with the musical accompaniment of a record. In this game there is tag play and Jennifer, who has been asked to join in but refused, watches with such keen interest that one wonders why she doesn't play it too. As the others are playing she swings her arms around with excitement and for the moment is in the game in spirit if not in body.

Absorption in something that contributes to the group experience is another road to integration. Donnie, to whom we have referred several times before, apparently cannot sustain much close contact, but because of his pleasure in manipulating the simple musical instruments of a rhythm "band," can be a part of the group without having to tolerate or contribute to personal relationships.

As Donnie helps the teacher bring musical instruments to the corner he sings in a mischievous tone, "And I'll be the boy with an arrow and I'll knock you out and I'll knock you out cold." He lays out the instruments on the floor for the children and says to Eric: "Sit down or you won't have anything." Eric obeys. As the boys and girls get ready, Donnie looks around; he takes cymbals as does Rex and says to him smilingly, "We both have these." Rex changes to a triangle and Donnie to the wood knock. Donnie to Rex, "Do you want to change?"

No answer. The group sings "John Brown." Donnie's face is intent. He purses his lips and gets into the song, beating the primary rhythm mainly. Rex leaves and Donnie gets the cymbals. He strikes them with the right emphasis and with visible pleasure at the end of "Yankee Doodle."

The familiar circle games and exercises executed to music are valuable aids to many severely withdrawn children. The stimulation of the music, the security of oft-repeated movements, and the relaxed atmosphere of the group combine to give them the reinforcement they need. The effect is a cumulative one and they frequently need a long period of watching before actually joining in. Moreover, since they sometimes begin to participate only after the more spontaneous members have had their fill, it may be desirable to continue the activity a little longer than planned to give them an extra chance. All these points are clearly illustrated in the following record of Perry.

Mrs. W plays "Here We Go a Tip-Toe," while Mrs. H sings. Mrs. H stands up saying: "Let's see how we can tiptoe." All the children except Perry stand up and tiptoe gingerly to the music. When the music stops someone suggests "the pony one." Mrs. H: "Do all the ponies want to come in the barn?" Perry remains on the floor watching, but the others come and stand in a row. . . . All are asked to come back to the piano, and Mrs. W tells them about a new song about "all kinds of clocks—big clocks, small clocks, and the little tiny clocks." The song is played and sung for them. Mrs. H suggests that they could make the clocks tick on the floor with their hands. . . . Mary then requests the engine song, and as soon as the music begins she leads the group in crawling away "Puff, puff . . . puff, puff." Then comes "Run a little, run a little." Mrs. H, "Now the piano is going to tell you to do something else. Let's listen." When the music begins Mrs. H asks, "What is it?" Mary: "Jump!" While the children are jumping to the music, Perry slides on his stomach and then rolls over, nevertheless watching the children. Rocking music is played and the children move their legs up and down on the floor. Perry who has already been lying on the floor begins to raise his legs. Mrs. H calls attention to him by saying, "Look how high Perry's legs are—'way over his head."

Under the spell of music some children blossom forth dramatically. If a complete outsider were to observe Melinda's behavior, as depicted in the next record, it would be hard for him to believe that this four-year-old girl as a rule seemed totally overwhelmed and constantly sought to cling to the teacher. Although she is not definitely interacting with the other children, she is among them and participating without apparent inhibition.

A teacher is playing the piano and there are three other children running around the room. Melinda joins them and for the first time this morning seems to be really enjoying herself. She is free and relaxed and smiling. She is not running as fast or as energetically as the other children but she is waving her arms about and making some attempt at keeping time to the music. This is also the first time she has been without her doll which she has left in the playroom. Now she is even laughing out loud. The teacher stops playing for a moment and Melinda runs over to the piano and tries to play it herself. She has both hands on the keyboard and is making quite a lot of noise. When the teacher starts to play again she begins to skip and run around the room, almost dancing.

After the first few months a withdrawn child sometimes pairs off with a more spontaneous "pal," who supplies the support he needs for group participation. In the next record, notice how Jerry acts as a guide and catalyst for Betty, helping her relate to both the music and the group.

Betty is squatting near the piano. She looks very comfortable until the group uses her name in the song; then she becomes very fidgety and shy and does not sing with them. She seems very much relieved when they sing other children's names. When children play the "fooling game" (with fast and slow, loud and soft clapping of hands) the first time, Betty does not clap—she just moves her hands and feet restlessly. Now she moves next to Jerry and watches him pretend to be a conductor. When he puts his arms up for "get ready," she puts her arms up; next he claps and she does too. She seems to be guided by Jerry rather than by the music. She seems to like the "Jack Frost" song; she sings it without caring what Jerry does and doesn't even notice that he isn't singing. For fun, Jerry begins to move about the floor. Betty laughingly joins him, leaning hard on her left arm and pulling her right foot with her right arm. Now she is back on both arms with her knees up and her feet on the floor, really singing loud enough to be heard. The teacher comments on how nice her voice sounds. "Jingle Bells," say Betty and Jerry in almost the same breath when the teacher asks for another favorite song—Betty knows how much Jerry loves that song. They grin at each other while singing loudly, catch each other's hand and stand very close to each other.

Sometimes children who are neither withdrawn nor timid do not find it easy to become part of the group. During most of the day they may be constantly embroiled in conflicts because they have not yet developed any appreciation for the needs or feelings of others and find it difficult to wait or to accept substitutes for the things they want. During the music periods, however, these children will often hover on the periphery of the group, as if aching to join. The record of Barry, age four, cited below, gives a very clear picture of an intermediate stage in group integration, in which a youngster begins to show definite sensitivity to the other children and a real desire to join them. A little teacher assistance at this point might have sent him far along the road to group membership.

The teacher has just sat down at the piano and is playing softly as the group gathers around. Barry saunters over from the rocker, hands in his pocket, watching closely as the Birthday Queen crown is set on Martha's head. He smiles slightly, looks from one to the other as they sing "Happy Birthday," but does not sing himself. He stares at Martha with a rapt expression. His eyes seem glazed. Suddenly he whips his hands out of his pockets and, using his thumb and index finger as a gun, shoots "bangbangbang" to the left of the group and skips lickety-split around the edge of the room. He skips back to the group who are singing "Itsy-bitsy Spider," stops but a fleeting moment, and skips around the room again, at a slower, more measured pace this time. He returns to the group around the piano—his hands are thrust into his pockets and on his face is a shy half-smile; he stands so that he can see the faces of the children singing "Down at the Station." (Barry doesn't sing.) He moves over to the side of the piano, climbs on the foot, and hangs over the keyboard. He walks over to Eddie and puts his face very close to his as he mouths the words of the song. Barry laughs in delight. The group are forming a train, the end of which passes close to Barry. He makes a quick tentative move to join. The music begins, the train starts off, but Barry decides not to go; he retreats, walking backwards three steps to the piano, and with hands in pocket watches it chug along the room. He smiles broadly, his eyes alight. He starts off at a run after the racing train, but stops short. With a hop and a skip he is over at the party table; he twists his body so he can look into Miss H's face, "My mamma made a party cake and I ate it all up." He seems insistent and eager, the words tumbling one over the other, but nevertheless his voice is clear and carries. Miss H smiles indulgently and in soft, lilting tones says, "Yes, your mamma made it for you. She told me." Smiling brightly, his eyes luminous, he skips back to the piano, just as the train arrives. . . . He stands while the others are sitting down at the party table. He chimes in the end of the song "Up like a Bird," making the motions of a bird flying. . . . The others assemble and start off on a grand march. Barry smiles a wide open smile, ducks around a stationary post, and hop skips, taking a route parallel to the group's and arriving at the table at the same time the marchers do.

Sometimes teachers overlook the subtle cues that "periphery" children offer to indicate their readiness to participate in group experiences with music. They trail after the others or stand in a corner making slight imitative movements that are perceptible only to the seeing eye. Although often extremely eager to join in, they cannot take the first plunge without the support of the teacher.

In the following record of Carla we see an example of thoughtful handling on the part of the teacher, who not only seems to know what to say at the proper time, but also senses that the little girl wants help in learning how to do the things the rest are doing.

In the music room Carla sits down to let the teacher help her change to her sneakers. The music teacher suggests that bare feet might be fun, and wouldn't Carla like to try it that way. She doesn't respond to this. She sits on the edge of her chair as if ready to rise, but she does nothing except watch the other children. She smiles as the teacher begins to play a gallop. The teacher urges her to join the game but she refuses. Near the end of the first gallop, however, she says, "I want to dance slowly." The music teacher plays a slower dance, but Carla does not participate. She sticks her tongue out and runs it around her mouth. She leans back comfortably and smiles. . . . She stands up and announces, "I'm just gonna stand here." She nods her head in time with the music. . . . She moves over to sit closer to the teacher and taps her toes quietly as part of the game calling for foot stamping. She bites her lower lip, then begins to laugh as the teacher says something to her. . . . "Their socks are getting dirty," says Carla, nodding her head knowingly. The teacher says, "Why don't you see how your sneakers work, Carla?" She gets up and smiles delightedly as she runs around the room holding the teacher's hand and sighs in disappointment as the dance ends. She puts her finger in her mouth and stands watching the children play elephant. The teacher shows her how to make a trunk with her hands. She joins in the game, and when squirrel music begins, she slowly develops her own idea of imitating a squirrel. She smiles and chuckles during this, and when she finds her efforts are successful, she giggles. When everyone starts to imitate camels, Carla uses the technique she learned for the elephant.

The social effects of the music period can be as telling with aggressive children as they are with the timid and with-drawn. The direction given by structured movements as well as structured sounds seems to have a reassuring influence on them, and the pleasure and comfort they derive helps them not only to withstand attacks upon themselves but to reach out to others as well. It seems clear that when any child is comfortable and happy and active he is in a good position to make positive group contacts.

Since the records cited in our previous discussion of the benefits of music for aggressive children involved some degree of group participation, we shall mention only two additional examples. Melita, in the record below, was reported as an extremely hostile little girl who spent many hours at school in open conflict with teachers and with children—boys particu-larly. (This behavior was understandable in the light of the home situation, since the mother openly preferred a brother to Melita.) Although some aggressive acts occur in the first record, they are provoked by another child and she displays a fairly advanced degree of socialization by including her tormentor in her dance. In the second record, we see Melita calm and peaceful, sharing her happiness in a tender way with another child—a boy.

Record 1. Melita runs to sit under the piano with Jimmy and Cal. Leila joins them. The piano starts and Melita, look-ing up with an impish grin, presses down the pedal with vigor. The teacher explains that that will hurt the piano and Melita stops. The music continues and Melita follows the words with her lips. The teacher selects Melita, Leila, and Eddie to sing. Rob is annoying all the children. He pulls Melita's skirt and darts away. Melita runs over to him and hits him three times. She then calmly returns to the piano. Rob comes over and lifts Melita's skirt. Still singing, Melita hits him. The teacher suggests they become snowflakes. Melita makes light dancing movements. Leila imitates. Melita then takes Rob's hand and says, "There must be one girl and one boy." She does the leading. The next song is a lullaby. Melita still holds on to Rob's hand and pulls him gently back and forth.

Record 2. The teacher plays a song about an engine. Karl is on the floor next to Melita, who is seated on a chair. Melita puts his head on her lap and strokes his hair gently, lovingly, saying, "Go to sleep." She fondles his ear. Karl wants to sit up after a few moments, but Melita persuades him by words and caresses not to do so. Each child is having a turn at the piano. Karl moves closer to Melita and puts his head up and pats her arm. She pats him back. Melita now gets her turn at the piano and then returns to her chair. She, Karl, and Leila play the game of switching chairs.

Sometimes the music periods can be used to confer a much needed bit of importance on a child who has some special musical ability or who feels comfortable enough to lead the group in familiar songs or movements. Ellen, an anxious hostile three-year-old who was constantly in conflict with other children and frequently also with her teachers, responded with an unexpected degree of maturity when given a chance to lead. The value of this experience for her is indicated by the fact that she continued it even after the others had gone on to something else.

The teacher starts with "The Muffin Man." Ellen sings with the group, occasionally glancing at the music book in her lap. When it ends she comes up to the teacher with the page turned to "Jingle Bells" and suggests that the group sing that song. The teacher says, "All right," and they sing with Ellen, as the leader, holding the page of "Jingle Bells" for the group. She stands right next to the teacher and looks very important as she sings. She now sits down and turns to the page with "London Bridge." She comes up again to the teacher to suggest it. The teacher agrees and again Ellen leads the group. As they sing, she swings in rhythm. At the end of the song Ellen smiles and then sits down. Then she chooses "Loopty

Loo," "Lazy May Will You Get Up?" "Twinkle, Twinkle, Little Star," and "The Farmer in the Dell." Ellen smiles once during each song and sways in rhythm. She thoroughly enjoys leading the group. The teacher announces that it is time to eat. The group proceeds to the tables, but Ellen sits down in a rocking chair in the bedroom, singing "Three Blind Mice" while she rocks. She sings half a minute to herself and the teacher approaches Ellen and asks, "Don't you want to eat?" Ellen answers, "No." Ellen goes to the library unit, takes a mitten from the shelf, puts it on, then goes back to the bedroom rocking chair, and still holding the book open, sings "The Farmer in the Dell."

Specific Needs Satisfied During the Music Period

In addition to the more general effects which we have been discussing, observation reveals that some children use the music period in a way that is peculiarly their own. The tendency to return to primitive forms of movement, for example, can be noticed in any children's group which is permitted to do as it wishes in response to the music. Some children will crawl or walk on all fours whenever they can, and will even refuse to take part in the music situation unless they are permitted to assume this "primitive" posture. Such children do not fare very well in music periods that are completely directed by the teacher, since they usually participate only on the rare occasion when she suggests the imitation of an animal. Careful observation of when a child participates and what kind of movement he enjoys, will help the teacher tailor the music periods to individual needs.

Music helps some children to assume dramatic roles that are especially meaningful to them but which they do not ordinarily play out. In Chapter III, we related that Tessie, an impulsive and demanding child, chose to play a "mean Easter bunny" during rhythms. This seemed to give her an opportunity to play out her vindictiveness without actually injuring anybody. Miss Bird tells of a boy whose mother had recently had a baby. He appeared to be perfectly happy at all times, but during the dance periods suddenly began to choose the role of baby bunny. If others chose this role, he had to be the *littlest* baby bunny, a role which necessitated being carried about by the mother bunny (the teacher). Only after a long period of playing this baby role could he give it up. Then he decided to be Superman and never returned to the baby role again.

The fantasy play children carry out in response to music can be very revealing to an observant teacher. Tuffie was a child who revealed himself strikingly in this way. In school, as the youngest member of his group, he was alternately fearful and aggressive. At home he was the victim of an older brother, a severely disturbed child who continually attacked or threatened him. In his assumption of roles, Tuffie plainly showed his need to be strong and big and his anxiety not only about his brother's superior strength, but about the fact that everyone in the preschool group was larger than he. When the rest of the children were hunters, he announced that he was the wolf; when others were farm animals, he became the farmer. Unfortunately, his need to stand out was neither well understood nor accepted by his music teacher, and any attempt at original improvisation brought forth censure and punishment. The following excerpt exemplifies the kind of experience the music period often brought him.

. . . . Slow music. Tuffie rolled over on the floor, quickly and not awkwardly. Rising rapidly, he turned around several times. His right hand was held high, his left low. Stopping his turning, he kicked his right foot high and gracefully in the air. Then he stopped and put his hands in his pockets. The music teacher stopped playing the piano and announced loudly and with some feeling, "Those who don't want to play music can sit down!" With this she walked swiftly to Tuffie, picked him up in her arms and placed him in one of the chairs against the wall. He started to cry immediately. The classroom teacher who had been sitting quietly all this time slid over to Tuffie and picked him up and placed him in her lap. . . . The music teacher now said to Tuffie, "Come over and play if you do what I say." She was not angry and her voice was more or less pleasant. Rubbing the tears from his eyes, Tuffie walked slowly and rather hesistantly over to the piano. He stayed on the fringe of the group.

With more understanding of what Tuffie was trying to do, his teacher might have utilized his departure from her directives to permit him to take the leadership role and also to find out more about what he was trying to work through. In a record of a more spontaneous music period, conducted informally by his group teacher rather than by the music specialist, Tuffie reveals a different side and also shows that animals have special emotional appeals.

When the music begins, Tuffie leans farther out of the window and smiles. The vocalist is singing a lyric about a galloping horse and he says, "Listen to that horse gallop." Fran calls to Tuffie, "Come on down." He hurriedly climbs down the ladder and joins Sarah. They join hands and pretend to be horses galloping around the room. They are very happy—laughing, skipping, and giggling. Anna, pointing under the chairs says, "This is our stable." Just at that moment the vocalist mentions birds, and Tuffie cries out, "Let's play birds. Birds are awfully happy." They all jump around holding the edges of their pants or dresses with their hands and making squeaky noises in an effort to imitate birds. Now and then, they say "We're birds." The music stops and so do the children. Tuffie suggests, "Let's play birds again."

Children often reveal in rather subtle ways their feelings about themselves and their relationships with others. In the record below, Lester, an extremely anxious child of four and one half years who had difficulty in adjusting to the routines and activities shows a desperate attempt to compromise between being one of the group and opposing the group. He says he wants to fly like the others but announces that his airplane is "new and not going to go." When the other children return from their "flight," he insists that he wants to sleep. When everyone else wakes up, he continues to lie quietly.

The teacher played some marching music and Lester marched the way he pleased and not in the prescribed formation. When the music stopped Lester said, "I'm tired." The teacher told them to rest for a while, so they stretched out on the floor. Lester: "I'm sleeping." He gave his neighbor a nudge with his foot. "When you say 'Good Morning' I'll wake up." Teacher: "Good Morning." They all got up except Lester. He remained sleeping. They all sang a song to wake him, but he did not move. The teacher moved him to the side so that they could all be airplanes in their hangars. . . . Suddenly Lester became "an airplane" too. He ran with his hands outstretched and was the last to "land," and to get into his "hangar." Lester: "I'm a new airplane, teacher. Don't give me no fuel. I want to fly now. This airplane is not going to go, teach." They all take off but he remains again. When they return he lies prone on the floor and says, "I want to go to sleep."

Often the more active and aggressive youngsters need the stimulation of something novel in music or movement to arouse and hold their interest, while the timid and infantile tend to respond better to what is known and familiar. To do justice to all types, the teacher would do well to offer a varied fare and at the same time give the children the freedom to show what they need. In the record of five-year-old Sharon, we have an example of the initiative and verve that suddenly animates an apathetic child when she is allowed to take the lead in something that is both familiar and close to her heart. In the course of her triumph, her need to dominate and control others reveals itself, giving the teachers a hint of the reason behind her usual reticence.

Sharon has brought her records to school, and the teacher sets up the machine. Sharon sits down and calls the others, loudly and commandingly, "C'mon, ya kids, c'mon, you kids. Here they are, kids. Come over!" Sharon talks authoritatively to the teacher, giving many instructions. All the children sit as close to the machine as they can, especially Sharon, who practically crawls into it and seems utterly absorbed. They sit as quiet as little mice. No one talks except Sharon, who has command of the situation. She sings along with the songs, which she seems to know quite well, and beats out the rhythm. A record is passed to another child for inspection. "Don't break it!" admonishes Sharon severely, frowning. When the record comes to a part about pulling, Sharon follows each pull with grimacing and grunting.

At "Girls and Boys" she wrinkles her nose and makes a face. She sings "Cats and Beans and Barley." She really throws herself into singing "Oh, Dear, What Can the Matter Be," practically shouting and indulging in histrionics such as the observer has not seen her use before. She burlesques "To Market," making silly faces and singing in a high-pitched voice. Teacher suggests that since the children have been sitting so long they play some music they can get up and run around to, but Sharon objects to this. The teacher says, "Just for a little while." Sharon declares, "You can't play your records. Play the other side of this one. You can't play mine if you play the others."

Suggestions to Teachers

We must emphasize again that there seems to be a more complete lack of spontaneity in the music program of most preschool centers than in any other activity. Due perhaps to the tradition of music and the dance, no real middle ground is recognized between passive listening and skillful performance. The folk attitude which accepts music as a form of expression for all people is completely forgotten in many schools. Even where the period is not limited to listening or to purely imitative singing, the teacher or the phonograph record dictates the children's movements, and the children have little chance to find their own level of satisfaction.

Many teachers feel that they are not sufficiently well trained to conduct a music program because they do not have the skill for finished performances. Yet specialists in the field of music and dance think completely otherwise about the need for skill. Sheehy[2] points out: "Music is not an intellectual experience; it has to do with feeling . . . settle yourself into the mood of the child." Bird[3] says that the only prerequisites for a teacher who wants to work with children in a music-movement situation are "a good sense of humour; a healthy imagination; a willingness to crawl on all fours." It might help the teacher to remember that the quality of the experience for the child resides in what he feels as he is going through it, not in how graceful or how perfect a performance the teacher presents.

It might be helpful to review the variety of possibilities for music periods, breaking them down roughly into music-making and responding to music. For music-making, we might use rhythm instruments, singing, the piano, the phonograph, informal chants, and clapping or stamping for percussion effects. Drums, tom-toms, cymbals, bells, gongs, triangles, castanets, rattles, etc., can be used quite effectively by even very inexperienced persons, and such instruments are portable, so that the teacher can follow her group. In addition, they are so easy to use that the children are encouraged to try their hand at creating effects. Variations in tone quality are possible even with these simple musical devices, and the teacher can use her voice as an accompaniment to achieve tune. (There are many times, indeed, when the use of the voice alone is quite adequate for the children's purpose.) Another way to encourage experimentation is to supply noisemakers of various kinds—sticks, blocks, hollow containers filled with dried beans or pebbles, segments of pipe, and chains or glasses filled with water at different levels. The prime requirement of these homemade instruments is simplicity, since if they are complicated they may prove to be a source of frustration instead of encouragement and satisfaction.

In response to music, movement comes first to mind, but this might be accompanied by singing or by informal music-making. It may take the form of completely free expression, unnamed and unchanneled, or it may consist of imitation of animals, wind, birds, streams, different kinds of people, etc. It may involve the use of a dramatic theme revolving about the teacher in a directing role, or it may develop spontaneously as one child and then another makes suggestions.

As to the source of control, it is possible to have periods completely controlled by the teacher, completely by the children, completely by phonograph records, or any combination of these. The important thing for the teacher to realize is that each kind of music period offers unique benefits to some children. Therefore different periods may be planned for different objectives—to stimulate, to soothe, to integrate isolated children, to challenge the interest of the anxious and scattered, or to achieve spontaneity. Small rhythm instruments placed where children can reach them easily offer them an opportunity to try their hand privately, without too much supervision. Likewise, the phonograph also permits a good deal of freedom if it is so placed that children can manipulate it themselves. The doll corner is a very attractive location for those who need to get away from the overexuberant play of the group.

Many teachers have complained that try as they may they cannot persuade certain children to participate in "rhythms" activities. In these cases the first thing to do is to examine the kind of music period that is being offered. If it is too rigid and controlled, some children will hold off for fear they cannot perform satisfactorily, and at the very least the period will be robbed of a good deal of its spontaneity. Over and over again we see notes like the following in our records: "He always waits for other children to start, watches, then joins in." It is not unusual to find a child stimulated by a recorded song or story but inhibited by the teacher's attempt to channel the responses in a certain direction.

An extreme form of the controlled period is described in the record below. Unfortunately it is all too typical of what is happening every day, particularly in groups where the musical experiences of the children are directed by "specialist" teachers who come in only for brief periods during the week. In view of the remarkable advantages of music as a form of release, a means of self-integration, and an invitation to group membership, we wonder what it offered Wilkie, the little boy in the following account.

The music teacher plays a little tune, thus instructing the children to sit down on their chairs. They seem to understand this musical language. Wilkie sits at the edge of his chair. He picks his nose, scratches his head. Now the music says, "Stand up." His hands fly up in the air; he jumps up, and throws himself down on the floor with great ease. "Look, I am down." He squirms on the floor; he shifts to the right, now to the left, while the other youngsters first march and then run around. . . . The children perform one by one, stepping into each hoop made of rubber tubing, to the music. They must listen attentively for the music directs them forward or backwards or tells them to remain in place. Their feet must be within the hoop without disturbing its position. It is Wilkie's turn. He stands up, walks leisurely to the starting point, places his feet firmly on the floor, turns his head to look at the music teacher, listens to the music, and does very well up to the end of the hoops, turns around in place and is ready for his "climb down the stepladder." He turns to the youngsters who are his audience, makes a comical grimace, is encouraged by their laughter, takes two steps forward, flops down on the floor, and with his hands and feet scatters the hoops all over the floor. Two other boys join in the rampage. The music teacher stops playing and with an angry expression collects the hoops and reprimands the wild youths. She puts the hoops into a box on the piano, sounds the chords for sitting down and instructs them in the next procedure which she calls "statues." The children keep in step with the music, and when the music stops playing they stop too, and remain in that last position as still as a statue. Wilkie runs with the others except much faster, arms swinging at his sides. His facial expression is one of expectation and apparent pleasure. The music stops, he flops down on the floor, and rests his head on his elbow. When the music teacher reaches his place he tries to maintain a still position. The music teacher says, "Stretch and fall like a rag doll." Wilkie falls on top of another boy. The music teacher scolds him and sends him to his seat.

Equally compelling samples could be offered to show the effects of "listening" periods when children are not permitted to move about or to accompany the music with sounds. Moreover, it seems a highly questionable practice to demand that little children listen to music when they are clearly not interested in doing so. Some teachers claim "they should have that kind of listening experience," but we might ask what kind of experience it would be and what possible values could accrue from a situation that has no meaning for the child. If the object is to develop an appreciation for music, would these teachers not get farther by making the occasion one of definite pleasure and satisfaction, and by encouraging participation instead of sheer passivity?

The self-consciousness and timidity shown by many children who are reluctant to participate with a large group might be overcome by cutting down the size of the group. In some of these cases and others as well, it may be possible to build groups around the children who need help by choosing those with whom they already have some contact. We do not, however, recommend the practice of asking timid or withdrawn children to show the others how to do things such as imitating high-stepping horses, etc., hoping thereby to inspire them with more self-confidence. It often does the very opposite and destroys their budding enjoyment as well. In general, it seems better to keep participation on a group basis rather than to single out individuals to demonstrate movements.

Even under good conditions, some children are too inhibited to participate freely. To help them achieve release and the full use of their bodies, Bender and Boas[4] suggest primitive, rhythmic activities such as cartwheels, somersaults, leap-frog, and childhood stunts as well as "rolling on the floor, and crawling on all fours, or running in circles," leading into animal fantasies. They also recommend "a circular formation with some rhythmic or dynamic activity, such as skipping, leaping, running, and Indian steps." As to the musical atmosphere, "the constant beating rhythm of a drum, gong or cymbal . . . seems to provoke movement reactions. It also causes a group reaction which seems to force even the more difficult children into participation"; and when the sounds are built up to a climax, they lead to a salutary release of tension.

Sometimes teachers are afraid to permit children to respond to music as loudly and as boisterously as they would like to because of practical considerations, such as the possibility of disturbing others or hurting themselves. Instead of curbing them, one solution is to have the activity in the outdoor play space, using simple instruments or a portable phonograph. Another is to introduce dramatic games through which the children can expend some of their energy in a positive fashion. Bird, for example, pretends she is a strong wind blowing leaves—the children—and they run and tumble about with great glee. Reversing the roles, she sets up a structured, yet guilt-free, situation in which she is a leaf, at the mercy of the children, who play the wind. In so doing she gives them the opportunity to chase her, the grownup, who usually represents the symbol of strength to children. This type of game has a twofold objective: it frees children to be more childlike, both physically and emotionally, yet keeps them within the limitations they need in order not to feel that they are being destructive or "bad."

Occasionally children take refuge in music as a form of escape. They sit alone playing records for hours at a time, or listen with others without participation in group musical activities. When a child is actively trying to relate himself to his world, quiet, relaxed listening may offer a needed chance for rest and recuperation. But when he goes from solitary block building to solitary painting, to solitary, dreamy listening, the positive contribution of the music is extremely dubious. Here is a chance for the teacher to be of real assistance— by sharing the "listening" experience, unobtrusively building a sense of mutual pleasure, and by keeping her eyes open for signs of outgoing, active responses to encourage by her own responsiveness. She will find, too, that records with songs or stories usually animate these children more than unrelieved instrumental music, and when they are permitted to manage the machine themselves and to listen with only one or two companions, they are still more likely to come out of themselves.

One of the most fruitful ways of helping children understand themselves and their world is to follow their own fantasy leads. If they are encouraged to sing and act out classical nursery rhymes and delightful folk songs, the roles they choose and the way in which they interpret them may be extremely significant in the light of their own personal adjustment problems. It is important, however, that spontaneity of interpretation be permitted. Much can be learned by the teachers and a good deal of release can be achieved by the child from parts like the spiders in "Little Miss Muffet," or the mice in "Three Blind Mice." When Tessie (in Chapter III) chose to be the *mean* Easter bunny, the teacher might have encouraged her to act it out more fully in order to discover why the bunny felt mean.

An observant teacher can always help a child take a role that fits his need of the moment. In the following record of Lonnie, the teacher might have suggested a role for him (such as being the wind for scattering clouds, or a mother duck with her babies, etc.), thereby turning the rather colorless circle game into a dramatic situation, and making him feel a welcome group member. Moreover, this might have given the boy a chance to express the need that made him break away, and the teacher might have gained an opportunity to learn more about him and find a way to work with him.

The music teacher explains the next routine. The children are to hold each other's hands and form a circle, and walk and run around. "I'll hold your hand," Lonnie says to Janie as they stand up. He is smiling and seems happy and less tense and pensive. He runs around in a circle for a few minutes, and then quite suddenly lets go of Janie's and Billie's hands and walks towards his chair. The music teacher stops the music and asks, "Lonnie, why did you break the circle?" "Huh?" he asks. "All right," she adds, "You can sit down." He places his thumb in his mouth; his feet are firmly planted on the floor and he watches the children with a wide-eyed expression.

Bird suggests a dance-play form which she has used successfully with groups of young children. The teacher describes a situation—a train rushing home, boats sailing on the sea, the wind making leaves swirl in the fall, people climbing down a mountain, etc.—and the children's suggestions for improvised dramatization are asked for and followed out, much like the old game of "rigmarole." Each child who wishes to is given a chance to direct the action, and his directions are followed until another child makes a suggestion. A special virtue of this kind of activity is its fluidity, which permits the teacher to create situations in which the group flows around the timid child, luring him by a variety of fantasy invitations. Often this child's first movement is the decisive one, and once a fantasy appeals to him, he is no longer withdrawn.

The importance of the teacher's participation in this kind of activity, and indeed in all musical activity, cannot be overestimated. If she merely stands by and directs, the children tend to feel estranged, isolated, and at loose ends. But when she is also hopping, skipping, tumbling, or acting like a gust of wind or a rabbit, the situation is structured so that a feeling of "we-ness" predominates. She can be used by the children in any way that fits their needs. She can play a cherishing role for those who need "mothering" and are too shy to ask for it, or she can be a mild menace which is, in the end, overthrown and outwitted by the children. As long as she remains within the group, she also offers support to those who are not yet ready to sustain continuous contact on their own. We must not forget that many of these preschool and kindergarten youngsters have not yet reached the point at which they can initiate and maintain any sort of direct bond with other children; they need the good offices of the teacher to help bring to fruition their feelings of friendliness and their desire for companionship.

Summary

We have been discussing the ways in which music and movement can serve children by freeing them from painful self-consciousness, by making them better acquainted with their peers, and by offering channels for the release of energy and the integration of movements. We have presented many protocols as evidence that music has special values for those who suffer from a variety of difficulties. But we also recognize that we have only begun to explore the contributions a knowledgeable use of music can make to the mental health of children. Only as teachers gain more respect for the quality of their own contribution to the children's development and regain some measure of spontaneity for themselves, will we be able to develop further the promise that music holds.

APPENDIX

THE FOLLOWING Suggestions to Observers and Suggestions for Recording were used in training observers who participated in the project on which this book is based.

Suggestions to Observers

Please read the following suggestions carefully. They may be very important for the success of your performance as an observer.

RELATIONSHIP TO TEACHERS

Try to keep in the background as much as possible. The good observer is unobtrusive, so that both teachers and children forget she is there.

Please do not question teachers about anything while they are working. If possible, do not question them at any time.

Observe what is going on in the group sufficiently to keep out of the teacher's way when she is directing activities and routines.

If the teacher approaches you, accept what she has to tell you graciously, but do not take the initiative in extending the conversation.

Even if the teacher should ask you to participate, please try not to do so. Be gracious if you have to refuse, but remember that you are an observer and should assume no responsibility for the children.

RELATIONSHIP TO CHILDREN

Again, keep in the background as much as possible. You cannot record if you are participating.

Try not to approach children or engage them in conversation.

If children ask what you are doing, say something that is truthful, but noncommittal, like "Writing."

If children ask for your help, direct them to the teacher whenever possible.

If the children get into serious difficulties, help them *only* if the teacher cannot be summoned quickly.

Try to ignore children who seem to be bidding for your attention or who are following you.

If children talk to you, smile or nod, but do not encourage them.

Try to keep far enough away from the children so that you do not get in their way.

Try to follow the child you are observing closely enough to lose nothing of what he does or says, but try to keep him from being overly conscious of your attention.

If you are observing a group that plans to go to the playground or on a trip, go along with it and continue your observations.

If you are sufficiently unobtrusive, the children will soon learn to ignore you.

MATERIALS FOR OBSERVATIONS

1. You will need a watch with a plain face and a large minute hand.

2. Have a plentiful supply of paper that is easily handled. A writing board with a clip to hold the paper in place is useful.

3. Be sure you have your assignment sheet with you on observation days.

4. Keep the group enrollment list with you. If new children appear in the group, add their names.

SUGGESTIONS ABOUT RECORDING OBSERVATIONS

1. Learn the names of the children in the group to which you are assigned and be sure you can identify them correctly before beginning the recording of the observations.

2. Be sure to note the time you begin and the time you end each observation unit. If you can, indicate the end of each five minute interval. This can be done simply by writing the time in the margin of your recording paper every five minutes.

3. Be sure to indicate the order of each child observed; e.g., first, second, third or fourth child in the group assigned for the day. Also, indicate on each record whether it is the first, second, third of fourth record for that child on that day.

4. Adequate records will require continuous recording as you are observing. It will be necessary to develop some set of short-hand or abbreviated symbols as you go along.

5. Records should give a description of the situation in which the child was observed, and should report other children and teachers present in that situation. Everything the child says and does, and everything that is said and done to him (or her) should be recorded exactly. Tone of voice, expression of face, attitude of body, quality of movement should also be included whenever possible.

6. Because of the demanding character of recording, 5 minute rest periods between observations are recommended whenever possible. If the time allows, some observation of the situation before beginning recording is advisable.

Suggestions for Recording

ADAPTED AND ABSTRACTED FROM MIMEOGRAPHED COPY OF
"CHILD PSYCHOLOGY," BY L. J. STONE, SECTION ON
RECORDING AND OBSERVING CHILDREN'S BEHAVIOR

RUNNING RECORDS are at once the most difficult and the most valuable records that you will make. Here it is your task to record so fully, so thoroughly, and so vividly that you *reconstruct* the scene you have observed. You must actually freeze what you have seen in writing. The prime requirements are for you to *see* what happens in as clear and unbiased a manner as possible and then to *communicate* what you saw and felt as fully and vividly as you can.

A good running record should include the *gross activities* of the child in a clearly stated *context* and within a definite *time* framework. By gross activities are meant the actual locomotions

of the child; where he is, where he goes, what he does, what he
says and to whom he says it. The setting and background should
be stated and the passage of time clearly indicated.

2:27. Johnny has been riding a tricycle with two other children since
rest-time. Three other children whom he has largely ignored are having
a parade near the sandbox. The others, including his special friend Dick,
are absent today. One teacher is in the cloakroom; a student stands
near the sandbox.

John rides behind Carol, occasionally saying "beep-beep" and almost
bumping into her. He stops suddenly and watches the 'parade' (one
of the children is clanging pot-cover cymbals together). He gets off his
bike and runs over to the 'parade' group. Shouts, "Hey, I'm a soldier!"
He picks up a stick and falls in line between Edith and Billy.

This record of gross activities usually focuses on the child's
adaptive or *purposive behavior* and tells what he does and how
he occupies his time. Often, however, such a record is incomplete just because it is likely to omit *nonadaptive* behavior—the
inconsequential but highly expressive movements and activities
of the individual. We want to know what the child *does*, but
we want our records also to tell what *kind* of a child this is.
To be sure, the content of activities tells us something of this.
The child who is constantly riding a bicycle and climbing the
Jungle Gym is different from the child who is usually swinging,
rocking and pushing a doll carriage. But to understand the
child better we need a more complete record and the second
step is to give the *finer details* and the *nonadaptive* aspects of
his behavior. Thus (the times are omitted in these examples) :

Johnny has been riding a tricycle with two other children since rest-
time. *He constantly glances around him as he rides, and hunches his
shoulder as he approaches other bikes.* Three other children whom he
has largely ignored are having a 'parade' near the sandbox. The others,
including his special friend Dick, are absent today. One teacher is in the
cloakroom; a student stands near the sandbox.

John rides behind Carol, occasionally saying "beep-beep" and almost
bumping into her. He stops suddenly and watches the 'parade' (one of
the children is clanging pot-cover cymbals together), *frowning, rubbing
his cheek and shifting his feet on the pedals. He is flushed and perspiring.* He gets off his bike with *sudden and superfluous energy, knocking the bike over and leaving it in his wake. His arms and legs go out
from his body in wide sweeps as he runs, knocking over a doll carriage
as he goes.* Shouts, "Hey, I'm a soldier!" He picks up a stick and falls
in line between Edith and Billy.

The inclusion of these details and expressive movements helps one to visualize the child's activities far better than is possible from a mere record of gross activities and locomotions. But still more is needed to round out and complete the picture of the individual if this behavior is to be presented vividly to someone who has never seen him before. We need to know not only *what* he does but *how* he does it.

The addition of the "fine details" begins to round out the picture of the "how" but it is necessary to convey the *quality* of behavior; to characterize it in such a way that the personal stamp of the individual, always visible in all his actions, is also conveyed in the record. Sometimes using an apt and vivid verb rather than a general one will accomplish this; sometimes descriptive phrases and adjectives must be used:

Johnny has been riding a tricycle with two other children since rest-time, *tramping the pedals in his characteristic, superenergetic fashion, emphasizing energy rather than precision and often missing a pedal for a half-turn.* He constantly glances around him *challengingly* (*as though expecting interference?*) as he rides, and hunches his shoulder (*protectively?*) as he approaches other bikes. Three other children whom he has largely ignored are having a 'parade' near the sandbox. The others, including his special friend Dick, are absent today. One teacher is in the cloakroom; a student stands near the sandbox.

John rides behind Carol, occasionally saying "beep-beep" and almost bumping into her. He stops suddenly and watches the 'parade' (one of the children is clanging pot-cover cymbals together), frowning, rubbing his cheek, and shifting his feet on the pedals. He is flushed and perspiring. *He is utterly relaxed now, his body limply poured and draped over the tricycle—all his exuberant energy turned off as by a switch. Now he is completely oblivious of the other bikes, even when one jars his own. Just as abruptly the switch is turned on again*: he gets off his bike with sudden and superfluous energy, knocking the bike over and leaving it in his wake. His arms and legs go out from his body in *clumsy and violent* wide *lunging* sweeps as he runs, *his arms held awkwardly, elbows close and fingers spread wide, face very intent and tongue protruding from the side of his mouth;* he knocks over a doll carriage as he goes. Shouts *stridently, voice pitched high,* "Hey, I'm a soldier". He picks up a stick (*gun?*) and falls in line between Edith and Billy. . . .

Finally, it is important to add your *impression* and *interpretation* of the behavior you have recorded making it perfectly clear how you have seen it. In a few instances this has been done parenthetically above. For example—

Johnny's behavior in this episode is a good sample of what can be seen every day. He shows remarkable *focus* on what he is doing—usually completely shutting out everything else that is going on. He is remarkable for his energy and whole-hearted attack on whatever he is doing, putting his soul into it completely. For so vigorous a child his ability to relax is surprising: he is either completely in action, using every bit of himself, or utterly passive and quiet. These relaxed interludes seem to come at regular intervals (this needs to be checked) and usually occur when he has finished one thing and is about to start something else. He rarely "flits" from one thing to another: there is generally a clear beginning and end.

It seemed to me that he had a chip on his shoulder today. He seemed to expect interference from the other children on the bikes and once or twice ran his bike into theirs as though to see what they would do about it. Also, when he joined the parade, it looked to me as though he expected to be rejected by the other children: he announced his intention to join them belligerently and he almost shouldered his way into the group.

Note the importance, for example, of the last paragraph. The quality of belligerence might not be evident without specifically calling attention to it, yet it may be the most important point of all in understanding Johnny's behavior at this time. The interpretation may even be erroneous, but it can be checked against other evidence. A pseudo-objectivity which omitted this interpretation would simply deprive us of what might be our most significant information. At the same time, even if we assume that the interpretation is not correct, it may tell us a lot about the child. It might, for example, indicate how very intensive an energy-output Johnny shows—so that to someone who does not know him very well even his ordinary actions show so much drive that they seem hostile.

Recording of this type "takes on many of the aspects of court reporting, with the added difficulty that it requires not merely mechanical speed and skill but judgment and sensitivity on the part of the observer." It is essential to be free of encumbrances and to have a prepared notebook, so arranged that one does not need to look at it as one writes but can devote all one's attention to the child. Abbreviations and symbols for common words and objects on the playground are very helpful. "Frequently the recorder's greatest difficulty is not in setting down actual words or obvious locomotions and activities, but in noting the subtler characteristics of movement and expression which serve to convey the child's mood and the emotional import to him of the events taking place. It is usually safest to set down some cue word or phrase along with some marginal indication that will readily catch the eye and not risk the danger of falling behind the whole action in seeking the *mot juste*. Immediately after the event the recorder can look for these cue signs and while the events are still fresh, elaborate the description as necessary."*

Whenever possible the recorder should go over the record *immediately*, filling in in this fashion, making sure that everything is legible and adding the interpretation. Only then is it safe to set the record aside before transcription, if necessary.

Suggestions for Training Classroom Teachers to Observe Children at Play

THE INVESTIGATION on which this volume is based clearly indicated the desirability of giving nursery school and kindergarten teachers some training in the observation of children's play. The nonteaching observers who participated in the project frequently mentioned the wealth of understanding and stimulation they derived from their record-taking, and there is every reason why teachers should share that wealth. Although each teacher will inevitably develop her own ways of observing, several general suggestions might be in order.

It is highly desirable to keep some sort of running record on each child in the group. Brief notes might be jotted on filing cards every week—ideally, every day—showing not only the activities the child engages in but the way he reacts to them. To gain the necessary insight, the teacher should put herself in the place of the child as far as possible, and focus her attention on the child more than upon the activity. Brief notes

*L. J. Stone, Group Play Techniques. *Monogr. Soc. Res. Child Development*, 6 (1941), 105.

on the general setting and atmosphere, the number of children involved, and the tempo of the play, should be included. It will be found that these daily or weekly notes will not only provide an overall impression of the child but also will indicate the direction in which he is moving.

As a training procedure, it will be helpful to have the teachers-in-training make their observations in pairs. In some cases they might choose the children they wish to observe, in others they might observe the same child and compare notes afterwards. It is important to set a limit in time—say, five minutes—for these practice observations, so that they will learn to grasp all the major aspects of the child's play behavior in a brief period. Judgment of the child should be avoided, and personal impressions should be put at the end of the record. All practice periods should be followed by a thorough discussion with the supervisor.

The specific suggestions which follow were used in training the observers who participated in the project. Although they are too detailed for general use by teachers, we believe the broad pattern will be instructive, since it will serve as a reminder of the major aspects to be observed, such as absorption, indications of feeling, and relationship with other children. A second reason for their inclusion in this Appendix is to show how the project was conducted.

ASPECTS TO BE NOTED WHEN OBSERVING CREATIVE ACTIVITIES

In observing a child engaged with any creative medium, several objectives might be kept in mind:

To discover what the material means to the child; i.e., is it something to be explored in its own right? to make something else of? to be manipulated? to be exploited in helping the child?

To achieve a more penetrating understanding of the emotional needs of the child.

To discover the unique values of the specific medium for given children.

In order to achieve these objectives, reports should include some material on each of the following points:

1) *The situation in which the child is operating.* This includes other activities going on, number of children at the

activity being observed, proximity of teacher, general atmosphere in room (noisy, peaceful, boisterous, rigidly controlled, etc.), availability of material being used, method of presenting it, time available for its use, restrictions set by the teacher. Can the child get the material by himself when he wants it? Is it set before him or are suggestions made that he use it? Can he have it if he asks for it, without specific direction on teacher's part? Is the amount or kind available controlled by teacher? Is the child permitted to remain with it as long as he wishes?

2) *The child's approach to the material.* From what activity is he coming? Does he come at his own request, at teacher's suggestion, or because others are already engaged with the material? Is he eager, reluctant, or neutral about using it? Is he slow in getting started or does he plunge right in? Does he seem apprehensive about the messiness or dirtiness involved? Does he ask for any change in the material, i.e., more water for clay, or different colors in paints? Is he selective, haphazard, or impulsive in use of the material? Does he seem intent on making something, or is he absorbed in manipulation alone?

3) *Degree of child's absorption with the material.* Does he seem intent on what he is doing, or does he seem interested more in what the children near him are doing and work in a desultory fashion. Does he seem to be daydreaming without any real relationship either to the material or the other children? Is his concentration span long or short? Is he easily distracted from what he is doing? Does he seem to use the activity as a means to social contact rather than as an end in itself?

4) *Energy expended.* Does he work on a fairly even keel or does he use a great deal of energy in manipulating the material, in his body movements and his verbalization? Does he seem to persist in an activity to the point of tiring himself? Does he start to work slowly and then gain momentum until he is very energetic in his actions or vice versa? Does he seem listless, lethargic, lacking in vitality?

5) *Development or movement apparent in each session.* Is there any change apparent from the initial approach to the end of the session? Does he become progressively freer and more venturesome? Does he start rather "wildly" and later show more integration, or does he continue at one level throughout?

Does his mood change in any way as he works; i.e., does he seem to relax or become tense? If ordinarily quiet, does he become more articulate, or does he start vociferously and then quiet down?

6) *Manipulative action.* Is child free or tense in his handling of the material? Is he careless or careful? Are his movements large and sweeping or small and precise? Smooth or jerky? Does he use material in the conventional way and stay within the limits set for its use, or does he explore it for less conventional possibilities that it may offer; i.e., by splashing, splattering, or smearing paint or clay over self, floor, or furniture?

7) *Attitude toward material.* Is the child willing to share the material with others or does he seem more intent upon collecting and hoarding it? Does he ask for more than he uses? If there is a shortage of material, does child make the best of the situation and use his share constructively? Does he use a great deal or very little?

8) *Tempo of work.* Does child work rapidly or deliberately? Does he seem to hurry to finish what he is doing or is he leisurely in pace? Does his pace vary with different situations and activities or is it always about the same?

9) *Body movements.* Does the child's body seem tense and his movements constricted, or does he seem relaxed and able to use his body freely? Are his movements uncertain, jerky, or poorly coordinated? Is there a sureness about the way he does things and do his movements give evidence of good coordination? Does he move his hands and arms freely and incorporate his whole body rhythmically as he works, or does he stand or sit rather rigidly, using parts of body only? Does he use right, left, or both hands?

10) *Verbalization.* Does he talk, sing, hum, or use nonsense phrases as he works, either to himself or with others? Does he ever giggle or shout? Are his voice tones loud, shrill, excitable, soft, aggressive, tense, enthusiastic, or matter-of-fact? Exactly what does he say, in his own words? Judging from his intonation, what is the purpose of his verbalization?

NOTE: The form in which the suggestions above have been cast may tempt the observer to try to summarize, interpret, or analyze the behavior he witnesses. That is *not* what we are suggesting. The specific items mentioned are only limited samples of many possibilities and are included only to help sensitize the observer to aspects of behavior that might otherwise not be included in the report. The good record is made up of *detailed descriptive* material from which answers to questions like those put above could be derived.

Additional Suggestions for Observing Specific Activities

IN OBSERVING the use of clay, finger-paint, easel paint, and blocks, the following aspects should be noted in addition to those mentioned above, which apply to observation of all creative activities. To avoid excessive repetition, many of the suggestions apply to several of the activities but are included in one list only.

Clay. Does the child pound, scratch, squeeze, roll, slap, throw, tear, or pick at the clay? Does he grimace, suck his lips, blink his eyes, change his facial expression often? Does he make large or small objects, with or without definite form, and resembling actual objects or not? How does he achieve form—by pounding, rolling, etc.? Does he state what he is making, copy what others make, show an interest in their products? Does he use large "gobs" or small bits, spread it out or smear it outside the board? Does he use water and if so does he spatter and splash or wipe up the excess? Does he call attention to his product, compete with others or compare it with their creations? Does he state that he is making something for a particular person? Is he eager to save it or does he destroy it? Does he clean up of his own accord or by teacher suggestion? Does he linger over the cleaning process and play with the water? Does he comment on the dirtiness? What is his mood after finishing—more aggressive, relaxed, talkative, etc.? Does he act in his usual manner or differently in the activities that follow?

Finger-paint. Does the child start spontaneously or touch the material hesitantly? Does he want to wash his hands immediately or later? How long does he remain at the activity? Does he inspect his hands, wipe the paint off, say anything about the paint on them, keep from getting it on his wrists or arms? Or does he smear it on his face and arms, on furniture or other people? Does he want many colors, consistently choose the same ones, mix them together, or keep them separated? Where does he place the paint initially? Does he spread it over the whole paper, go outside its limits? What is the direction of his strokes—in, out, up, down, concentric, zigzag? Is there a repetition of pattern or stroke? Does he let off steam by banging, slapping, squeezing, etc.? Does he attempt to make a form or pattern, and does he name it or tell a story about it? Is he concerned with symmetry? How does he react when others comment on his products or when they get smeared or torn? What seems to be the principal source of satisfaction—the feel, color, design, chance to mess?

Easel paint. Is the color choice free, suggested by other children, restricted by the teacher or situation? How does the child grasp the brush? Is he careful about the amount of paint he uses or does he use a great deal? Does he drip it on the paper, himself, the floor? Does he wipe it up carefully? Does he scrub, pat, attack the paper with the brush, or use exact, meticulous strokes? Does he over-paint? Does he ignore boundaries or emphasize them by making borders? Is he merely experimenting with the paint or does he make patterns? Does he always make the same kind of patterns?

Blocks. Does he play by himself, always with others, or both at times? Does his behavior with blocks differ from his behavior at other times? Is there a relationship between his block structure and his own body form or the conditions under which he lives or his attitudes toward others? Does he often repeat the same design? Does he use his structures for protective or aggressive purposes? Is he more concerned with neatness or alignment or balance than with creating things he can use? Does he talk to the blocks as if they were human? Do they appear to represent people in his environment? Do the themes of his block-play echo his family life? What is the general tone of his play—casual, hostile, protective, etc.?

Music Research Project

Suggested Musical Selections

TEACHERS may wish to experiment with recorded music as a means of quieting the children down at nap time. Preliminary explorations indicate that simple melodies are most effective, particularly when played on wood winds. The following list includes some of the selections tried out.

1. Bizet. Introduction to Carmen. (Flute and clarinet melodic line; soft, soothing with lilting quality.)
2. Britton, Benjamin. Ceremony of Carols. Morristown Boys Choir (young voices and harp; very ethereal quality; simple and charming).
3. Chadwick, George. Symphonic Sketches: Noel.
4. Delius. On Hearing the First Cuckoo in Spring.
5. Ethnic Series. East Indian Music. (Exotic, weird, enchanting, unusual.)
6. Humperdinck. Hansel and Gretel: Evening Prayer; Sand Man Prayer.
7. Liadow. Cradle Song.
8. Moussorgsky. Pictures at an Exhibition.
9. Moussorgsky. Prelude to Khovantchina.
10. Ravel. Mother Goose Suite.
11. Tallis, Thomas. Spem en Allium Nun Kuam Habui. Cond. by Michael Tibbet.
12. Recorder and Guitar Music. (Simple, soothing—lullabies, etc.)
13. Weber. Bassoon Concerto. (Light, airy, gay, classical.)

NOTES

Chapter I: The Function of Play in the Child's Development

1. Macfarlane, Jean. The relation of environmental pressures to the development of the child's personality and habit patterning. *Journal of Pediatrics,* 15 (1939) : 146.
2. Kubie, Lawrence S. Problems parents can prevent. *Child Study,* 26 (1949) : 38.
3. *Ibid.,* 26:37.
4. Erikson, Erik H. Studies in the interpretation of play. *Genetic Psychology Monographs,* 22 (1940) : 561.
5. Slavson, S. R. Play group therapy for young children. *The Nervous Child,* 7 (1948) : 320.
6. Gillies, Emily. Therapy dramatics for the public schoolroom. *The Nervous Child,* 7 (1948) : 336.
7. Tipton, Gertrude. Mental hygiene in a war nursery school. *The Nervous Child,* 4 (1944) : 218-9.
8. Kubie, Lawrence S. Problems parents can prevent. *Child Study,* 26 (1949) : 56-57.

Chapter II: Dramatic Play: Mirror of the Child

1. Erikson, Erik H. Studies in the interpretation of play. Genetic Psychology Monographs, 22 (1940) : 561.
2. Isaacs, Susan. Social Development in Young Children, p. 425. Routledge, 1933.
3. Lowenfeld, Margaret. A new approach to the problem of psychoneurosis in childhood. *British Journal of Medical Psychology,* 11 (1931) : 226.
4. Isaacs, Susan. Childhood and After, p. 69. Routledge, 1948.
5. Isaacs, Susan. Social Development in Young Children, pp. 215-18, 428.
6. *Ibid.,* p. 315.

7. Markey, Frances V. Imaginative Behavior of Preschool Children. Child Development Monographs, 18 (1935): 63-68. Teachers College.
8. Figures in parentheses indicate the average number of 15-minute periods during which the child was observed to engage in the type of activity noted.
9. Markey. Imaginative Behavior of Preschool Children, 18:70.

Chapter III: Dramatic Play: Instrument for Growth

1. Isaacs, Susan. Social Development in Young Children, p. 453.

Chapter IV: In the Block Corner

1. Johnson, Harriet. The Art of Block Building. 1933. Cooperative Schools Pamphlet No. 1, John Day.
2. Alschuler, R. H., and L. W. H ttwick. Painting and Personality, A Study of Young Children. 1947. University of Chicago: Vol. I, 134-6.
3. Lowenfeld, Margaret. Play in Childhood, p. 321. London, 1935.
4. Homburger, Erik. Configurations in play: clinical notes. *Psychoanalytic Quarterly*, 6 (1937): 170.
5. Lowenfeld, Margaret. Play in Childhood, p. 62.
6. *Ibid.*, p. 222.
7. *Ibid.*, p. 208.
8. For fuller presentation of Bud's play behavior see Growing Through Play. Ruth E. Hartley, Col. Univ. Press, 1952.

Chapter VI: What Clay Can Do for the Child

1. Bender, L., and A. Woltmann. The use of plastic material as a psychiatric approach to emotional problems in children. *American Journal of Orthopsychiatry*, 7 (1937): 283-99.

Chapter VII: The Use of Graphic Materials

1. Alschuler, R. H., and L. W. Hattwick. Painting and Personality, A Study of Young Children. Vol. I, p. 6. University of Chicago, 1947.

2. Liss, Edward. The graphic arts. *American Journal of Orthopsychiatry,* 8 (1938): 95-96.
3. We are indebted to Mrs. Jane Cooper Bland for these interpretations and for many of the suggestions to teachers.
4. Mrs. Mary Greenwalt, a psychologically oriented artist, served as interpreter of most of the paintings collected by the project personnel.

Chapter VIII: The Finger-Paint Experience

1. Arlow, J. A., and Asja Kadis. Fingerpainting in the psychotherapy of children. *American Journal of Orthopsychiatry,* 16 (1946): 144-45.

Chapter IX: Music and Movement: Fruitful Combination

1. Buttolph, Edna. Music for young children. *Childhood Education,* May, 1946: 443-45.
2. Sheehy, E. D. Lecture given at the Caroline Zachry Institute of Human Development, 1950.
3. Bird, Bonnie. Lecture given at the Caroline Zachry Institute of Human Development, 1950. Miss Bird, a professional dancer and teacher of dancing, often uses dancing for its therapeutic value. She and Miss Sheehy were among the experts who participated in a program of lecture demonstrations offered as part of this project.
4. Bender, Lauretta, and Franziska Boas. Creative dance in therapy. *American Journal of Orthopsychiatry,* 11 (1941): 237-39.

BIBLIOGRAPHY

Chapter I: The Function of Play in the Child's Development

Adlerblum, Eleanor. Mental health begins school. *Mental Hygiene,* 31 (1947): 541-55.

——— Beginning school guidance early. *Mental Hygiene,* 34 (1950): 600-10.

Axline, Virginia. Some observations on play therapy. *Journal of Consulting Psychology,* 12 (1948): 209-16.

Barker, R. G., J. S. Kounin, and H. F. Wright. Child Behavior and Development. McGraw Hill, 1943.

Baruch, Dorothy W. Therapeutic procedures as part of the educative process. *Journal of Consulting Psychology,* 4 (1940): 165-72.

Bollinger, Dorothy M. Group therapy at the Children's Center. *The Nervous Child,* 4 (1944): 221-27.

Despert, J. Louise. The meaning of the young child's play. *Nursery Education Digest,* 3:1-12.

Erikson, Erik H. Studies in the interpretation of play. *Genetic Psychology Monographs,* 22 (1940): 557-671.

Frank, L. K. Projective Methods. C. Thomas, 1948.

——— Genetic psychology and its prospects. *American Journal of Orthopsychiatry,* 21 (1951): 506-21.

Frank, L. K., and Ruth E. Hartley. Play and personality formation in preschool groups. *Journal of Personality,* 1 (1951): 149-61.

Gillies, Emily. Therapy dramatics for the public school-room. *The Nervous Child,* 7 (1948): 328-36.

Hartley, Ruth, L. K. Frank, and R. M. Goldenson. New Play Experiences for Children. Columbia University Press, 1952.

Koenig, Frances G. A group therapy experiment in a city elementary school. *Understanding the Child,* 18 (1949): 40-44.

Kubie, Lawrence S. Problems parents can prevent. *Child Study,* Spring, 1949: 37 ff.

Lowenfeld, Margaret. Play in Childhood. Gollancz, 1935.

—— The theory and use of play in the psychotherapy of children. *Journal of Mental Science,* 84 (1938): 1057-58.

—— The world pictures of children: A method of recording and studying them. *British Journal of Medical Psychology,* 18 (1939): 65-101.

Macfarlane, Jean. Studies in Child Guidance. Monographs of the Society for Research in Child Development, 3 (1938).

—— The relation of environmental pressures to the development of the child's personality and habit patterning. *Journal of Pediatrics,* 15 (1939): 142-54.

Prescott, Daniel A. and others. Helping Teachers Understand Children. American Council on Education, 1945.

Rennie, Thomas A. C. and Luther E. Woodward. Mental Health in Modern Society. Commonwealth Fund. 1948.

Schachtel, Ernest G. On memory and childhood amnesia. *Psychiatry,* 10 (1947): 1-26.

Slavson, S. R. Play group therapy for young children. *The Nervous Child,* 7 (1948): 318-27.

Tipton, Gertrude. Mental hygiene principles adapted to a war nursery school. *The Nervous Child,* 4 (1944): 211-20.

Vanuxem, Mary. Notes and Comments: National Committee for Mental Hygiene undertakes kindergarten project. *Mental Hygiene,* 29 (1945).

Vigotsky, L. S. Thought and speech. *Psychiatry,* 2, No. 1 (1939): 29-51.

Washburn, Ruth W. Reeducation in a Nursery Group. Monograph 2, Vol. 2. Society for Research in Child Development, 1944.

White House Conference on Children and Youth at the Midcentury. Fact Finding Report on Children and Youth at the Midcentury. Children's Bureau, Federal Security Agency, 1950.

Chapters II and III: Dramatic Play

Andrews, E. The development of imagination in the preschool child. Studies in Character, Vol. 3, No. 4. University of Iowa, 1930.

Bach, G. R. Young children's play fantasies. Psychological Monographs, 59 (1945).

Despert, J. Louise. Technical approaches used in the study of emotional problems in children. Part 4, Collective Phantasy. *Psychiatric Quarterly,* 11 (1937) : 491-506.

Greenhill, M. Psychodramatic play therapy in disorders of childhood. Proceedings of the Twelfth Institute of the Child Research Clinic of the Woods School, 2 (1945) : 107-122.

Griffiths, Ruth. A Study of Imagination in Early Childhood and Its Function in Mental Development. Routledge, 1935.

Haas, Robert B., Psychodrama and Sociodrama in American Education. Beacon House, 1949.

Isaacs, Susan. Social Development in Young Children. Routledge, 1933.

—— Childhood and After: Some Essays and Clinical Studies. Routledge, 1948.

Jersild, A. T. Child Psychology. Prentice-Hall, 1940.

Lippitt, Rosemary. Psychodrama in the Home. Psychodrama Monograph, 22 (1947).

Lowenfeld, Margaret. A new approach to the problem of psychoneurosis in childhood. *British Journal of Medical Psychology,* 11 (1931) : 194-227.

Markey, F. V. Imagination. *Psychological Bulletin,* 32 (1935) : 212-36.

—— Imaginative behavior of preschool children. Child Development Monographs, No. 18. Bureau of Publications, Teachers College, 1935.

Moreno, J. L. and Florence B. Moreno. Spontaneity Theory of Child Development. Psychodrama Monographs, No. 8 (1944).

Shirley, Mary. Some Products of Child Psychology, in Fields of Psychology, pp. 75-106. Ed. by J. P. Guilford. Van Nostrand, 1940.

Shoobs, N. E. Psychodrama in the schools. *Sociometry,* 2 (1944) : 152-68.

—— The application of individual psychology through psychodramatics. *Individual Psychology Bulletin,* 5 (1946) : 3-21.

Spence, Ralph B. Psychodrama and education. *Sociatry,* 1 (1947) : 31-34.

Sullivan, L. A. Psychodrama in a child guidance clinic. *Sociometry,* 8 (1945) : 296-305.

White, R. W. Interpretation of Imaginative Productions, pp. 214-51, in Personality and the Behavior Disorders. Ed. by J. McV. Hunt. Ronald, 1945.

Chapter IV: In the Block Corner

Alschuler, R. H., and L. W. Hattwick. Painting and Personality: A Study of Young Children. Vol. I, Univ. of Chicago Press, 1947.

Bailey, Marjory W. A scale of block construction for children. *Child Development,* 4 (1933) : 121-39.

Brown, Jean. Block play and the growing child. *California Journal of Elementary Education,* 10 (1942) : 177-92.

Erikson, E. H. Studies in the interpretation of play. Genetic Psychology Monographs, 22 (1940) : 577-671.

Guanella, Frances M. Block building activities of young children. *Archives of Psychology,* 174 (1934).

Homburger, Erik. Configurations in play: clinical notes. *Psychoanalytic Quarterly,* 6 (1937) : 139-214.

Hulson, E. L., and H. L. Reich. Building blocks and children's play. *American Childhood,* 17 (1932) : 13 ff.

Johnson, Harriet. The Art of Block Building. Cooperative Schools Pamphlet, No. 1. John Day, 1933.

Layman, A. E. Block play—an essential. *Elementary School Journal,* 40 (1940) : 607-13.

Lowenfeld, Margaret. Play in Childhood. Gollancz, 1935.

Salisbury, E. C., and H. Ivey. Block building in a reading readiness program. *Childhood Education,* 16 (1940) : 221-25.

Chapter V: The Benefits of Water-Play

Gesell, Arnold, and Frances L. Ilg. Infant and Child in the Culture of Today. Harper, 1943.

Lake, A. Let them play with water. *Parents Magazine,* February, 1949: 28.

Shoemaker, Rowena. It's All in Play. Play Schools Assoc., in press.

Chapter VI: What Clay Can Do for the Child

Bender, L., and P. Schilder. Principles of form in the play of children. *Journal of Genetic Psychology,* 49 (1936): 254-61.

Bender, L. and A. Woltmann. The use of plastic material as a psychiatric approach to emotional problems in children. *American Journal of Orthopsychiatry,* 7 (1937): 283-300.

Despert, J. Louise. Technical approaches used in the study and treatment of emotional problems in children. *Psychiatric Quarterly,* 11 (1937).

Gesell, Arnold, and others. The First Five Years of Life. Harper, 1940.

Levy, David M. The use of play technique as experimental procedure. *American Journal of Orthopsychiatry,* 3 (1933).

Wheeler, Ida W. Playing with Clay. Macmillan, 1927.

Chapter VII: The Use of Graphic Materials

Alschuler, R. H., and L. W. Hattwick. Easel painting as an index of personality in preschool children. *American Journal of Orthopsychiatry,* 13 (1943): 616-25.

—— Painting and Personality: A Study of Young Children. University of Chicago Press, 1947.

Bender, Lauretta, and Jack Rapoport. Animal drawings of children. *American Journal of Orthopsychiatry,* 14 (1944): 521-27.

Bland, Jane Cooper. Understanding young children's art. *Parents Magazine,* October, 1944.

Brick, Maria. Mental hygiene value of children's art work. *American Journal of Orthopsychiatry,* 14 (1944): 136-46.

Despert, J. Louise. Emotional problems in children, technical approaches used in their study and treatment. Part 3, Drawing. State Hospitals Press, 1938.

Elkisch, Paula. Children's drawings in a projective technique. Psychological Monographs, 58 (1945): 1-31.

Goodenough, Florence L., and Dale B. Harris. Studies in the psychology of children's drawings. II. 1928-1949. *Psychological Bulletin,* 47 (1950): 369-433.

Liss, Edward. The graphic arts. *American Journal of Orthopsychiatry,* 8 (1938): 95-99.

McIntosh, Janette R., and R. W. Pickford. Some clinical and artistic aspects of a child's drawings. *British Journal of Psychology* (Medical Section), 19 (1941-43): 342-62.

Mosse, Eric P. Painting analysis in the treatment of neurosis. *Psychoanalytic Review,* 27 (1940): 68-82.

Oakley, C. A. The interpretation of children's drawings. *British Journal of Psychology,* 21 (1931): 256-70.

Schmidl-Waehner, Trude. Formal criteria for the analysis of children's drawings. *American Journal of Orthopsychiatry,* 12 (1942): 95-104.

Waehner, Trude. Interpretations of spontaneous drawings and paintings. Genetic Psychology Monographs, 33 (1946): 1-70.

Wolff, Werner. Projective methods for personality analysis of expressive behavior in pre-school children. Character and Personality, 4 (1942): 309-30.

Chapter VIII: The Finger-Paint Experience

Arlow, Jacob A., and Asja Kadis. Fingerpainting in the psychotherapy of children. American Journal of Orthopsychiatry, 16 (1946): 134-46.

Lerner, Eugene and Lois Barclay Murphy. Methods for the study of personality in young children, 6, Serial 30, No. 4. Monograph of the Society for Research in Child Development.

Napoli, Peter J. Finger-painting and personality diagnosis. Genetic Psychology Monograph, 1946: 129-231.

—— Interpretive Aspects of Fingerpainting, *Journal of Psychology,* 23 (1947): 93-132.

Shaw, Ruth F. Finger Painting. Little, Brown, 1934.

Shaw, Ruth F., and Jeanette Lyle. Encouraging Fantasy Expression in Children. Bulletin Menninger Clinic, 1 (1937): 78-86.

Spring, W. J. Words and Masses. *Psychoanalytic Quarterly,* 4 (1935): 244-58.

Wolff, Werner. The Personality of the Preschool Child: The Child's Search for His Self. Grune & Stratton, 1946.

Chapter IX: Music and Movement

Altshuler, Ira M. The past, present and future of musical therapy. *Educational Music Magazine,* 24 (1945): 116-17.

Altshuler, Ira M. The organism-as-a-whole and music therapy. *Sociometry,* 8 (1945): 227-32.

Bender, Lauretta, and Franziska Boas. Creative dance in therapy. *American Journal of Orthopsychiatry,* 11 (1941): 225-44.

Buttolph, Edna. Music for young children. *Childhood Education,* May, 1946: 443-45.

Coriat, I. H. Some Aspects of a Psychoanalytic Interpretation of Music. *Psychoanalytic Review,* 32 (1945): 408-18.

Lowenfeld, Margaret. Play in Childhood. Gollancz, 1935.

Sheehy, E. D. There's Music in Children. Henry Holt, 1946.

INDEX

handling of, 271
mixing, 252, 266
relation to anal interests and toilet training, 276
substitute for direct investigation and manipulation of body products, 232
use of, 248-50
Paper, 218
child's work affected by space limits of, 258-60
need of adequate supply, 266
use in painting, 255
Passivity needs, 125-32
Patterns of play in preschool centers and kindergartens, 27-40
Permissiveness
in water-play, 177, 180-84
of blocks, 142, 149
of clay, 213-17
Phonograph, 300, 330, 331
Piano, 300, 330
Play activity
child's use of, 8
patterns of, 27
study of potentials of, 3
See also specific type, e.g., Dramatic play
Play materials
child's relation to, 346-49
study of potentialities of, 3
Poorly adjusted child
dramatic play for, 51-53
use of blocks, 100
Poster paints, 218, 251
Power
expressed in use of clay, 203
fantasy of, 59-62, 107-9
need for, as expressed in dramatic play, 51
sense of achievement and control through blocks, 107-9
sense of, in water-play, 159
Product-process phase
in painting, 224
in use of clay, 197, 229

Protection, need for, 51
Psychic equilibrium, 17
Psychodrama, techniques of, 73
Psychotherapy
potential of music and movement to, 298
use of finger-painting in, 270
Puppets, use of, 10

Rappaport, Jack, cited, 231
Rattles, 330
Reality value of play experiences, 19
Recording observations
by observers, 340
by teachers, 345-50
daily series of notations useful in, 62
methods of, 14
of children at play, 3
suggestions for, 341-45
Records, play (protocol): *see* under specific behavior, e.g., Aggressive behavior; or specific role, e.g., Animal role; or specific play activity, e.g., Dramatic play
Relaxation
in cozy places made with blocks, 125-32
through finger-painting, 272
through painting, 227, 245
through water-play, 167-69
Resentment, water-play as outlet for, 165
Rhythmic activities, 334
Rhythmical body movements connected with painting, 226
Rhythm instruments, 330, 331
Rhythms, 304, 331
in preschool situation, 300
release of emotions through, 299
Role of authority, 90, 137
Role of cultural factors
in determining play activities of children, 25